CW01667171

VOICES

BEGINNER

EMILY BRYSON AND GARY PATHARE

Concorde International

NATIONAL GEOGRAPHIC LEARNING

Australia • Brazil • Canada • Mexico • Singapore • United Kingdom • United States

NATIONAL GEOGRAPHIC
LEARNING

National Geographic Learning,
a Cengage Company

Voices Beginner Student's Book, **1st Edition**
Emily Bryson and Gary Pathare

Publisher: Rachael Gibbon
Commissioning Editor: Kayleigh Buller
Associate Development Editor: Don Clyde Bhasy
Director of Global Marketing: Ian Martin
Product Marketing Manager: Caitlin Thomas
Heads of Regional Marketing:
Charlotte Ellis (Europe, Middle East and Africa)
Irina Pereyra (Latin America)
Justin Kaley (Asia)
Joy MacFarland (US and Canada)
Production Manager: Daisy Sosa
Media Researcher: Leila Hishmeh
Art Director: Brenda Carmichael
Operations Support: Hayley Chwazik-Gee
Manufacturing Manager: Eyvett Davis
Composition: Composure
Audio Producer: New York Audio
Contributing writer: Patrick Wallace (Endmatter)
Advisors: Bruna Caltabiano, Dale Coulter,
Catherine McLellan and Mike Sayer

© 2022 Cengage Learning, Inc.

ALL RIGHTS RESERVED. No part of this work covered by the copyright herein may be reproduced or distributed in any form or by any means, except as permitted by U.S. copyright law, without the prior written permission of the copyright owner.

"National Geographic", "National Geographic Society" and the Yellow Border Design are registered trademarks of the National Geographic Society
® Marcas Registradas

For permission to use material from this text or product,
submit all requests online at **cengage.com/permissions**
Further permissions questions can be emailed to
permissionrequest@cengage.com

Student's Book with Online Practice and Student's eBook:
ISBN: 978-0-357-45864-8

Student's Book:
ISBN: 978-0-357-44295-1

National Geographic Learning
Cheriton House, North Way,
Andover, Hampshire, SP10 5BE
United Kingdom

Locate your local office at **international.cengage.com/region**

Visit National Geographic Learning online at **ELTNGL.com**
Visit our corporate website at **www.cengage.com**

Printed in Greece by Bakis SA
Print Number: 01 Print Year: 2021

FSC
www.fsc.org
MIX
Paper from
responsible sources
FSC® C169932

Contents

1 Hello! 10

2 My home 22

3 My stuff 34

4 Habits 46

5 Inside or outside? 58

6 Food around the world 70

7 Family and friends 82

8 Things we can do 94

9 Travel 106

10 Staying healthy 118

11 People from the past 130

12 My story 142

Scope and sequence

		GRAMMAR	VOCABULARY	PRONUNCIATION
1 Hello! Pages 10–21		present simple *be* (singular); *yes/no* questions with *be* (singular)	countries and cities; nationalities; numbers (0–10)	stressing syllables; stressing important words
2 My home Pages 22–33		present simple *be* (plural); questions with *be* (plural); *who, what, where*	rooms in a house; places in town	saying contractions of *be*; understanding intonation in questions
3 My stuff Pages 34–45		*this, that, these, those*; possessive adjectives and *'s*	travel items; colours	saying /ð/; saying *your* and *their*
4 Habits Pages 46–57		present simple; present simple questions; adverbs of frequency	numbers (11–100); days of the week	saying /ʌ/; saying /ju:/
5 Inside or outside? Pages 58–69		*like, love* and *don't like* + *-ing* form; prepositions of time	common activities; months and seasons	saying /ŋ/; understanding connected speech: *would you*
6 Food around the world Pages 70–81		countable and uncountable nouns; *how much* and *how many*	food; places for groceries	understanding *of*; understanding the *h* sound

READING	LISTENING	WRITING	COMMUNICATION SKILL	CRITICAL THINKING	USEFUL LANGUAGE
an article about where people are from; scanning for names and places	conversations between people exchanging numbers; listening to long numbers	an online profile; using capital letters	introducing yourself	your information	talking about numbers; hellos and goodbyes; jobs
an article about tiny houses; understanding new words	an interview with explorers about their hometowns; getting ready to listen	an email about interesting tourist sites; writing a friendly email	asking where things are	email subject lines	talking about where things are; writing friendly emails
an article about things people take on trips; understanding commas and the word *and*	an interview with explorers about colours; listening for important words	a social media post about a special item; checking your writing	asking questions to understand	giving reasons	asking questions to understand; describing special things
an article about a long trip to work; scanning for useful information	an interview with explorers about their workdays; listening for tone	an email about a work meeting; writing work emails	making plans	using the correct tone	making plans; writing work emails
tips about fun things to do at home; getting ready to read	descriptions of the seasons in three different countries; knowing what to listen for	a bucket list; writing lists	inviting people to do things	ordering information	inviting people; activity verbs
an article about spicy food; skimming a text	an interview with explorers about groceries; writing notes	a restaurant review; writing main ideas	ordering food	understanding how the author feels	talking about uncountable nouns; ordering food; good, bad and OK feedback

Scope and sequence

		GRAMMAR	VOCABULARY	PRONUNCIATION
7 Family and friends *Pages 82–93*		present simple questions (*yes/ no*); present simple questions (open questions); adjectives	family members; appearance and personality	saying short and long vowel sounds; saying words with *gr*
8 Things we can do *Pages 94–105*		*can* and *can't; and, or, but, because*	common abilities; adjectives for animals	stressing *can't*; saying the letter *g*
9 Travel *Pages 106–117*		*there is* and *there are*; object pronouns	different ways to travel; the weather	saying /w/ and /v/; saying /θ/
10 Staying healthy *Pages 118–129*		present continuous; present continuous vs present simple	body parts; exercise and training	understanding word groups; understanding intonation in directions
11 People from the past *Pages 130–141*		past simple *be*; questions with *was / were*	life events; past time expressions	understanding *was* and *were*; responding to good and bad news
12 My story *Pages 142–153*		past simple (regular verbs); past simple (irregular verbs); past simple questions	life stages; feelings	saying syllables with two vowel sounds; stressing words in questions

READING	LISTENING	WRITING	COMMUNICATION SKILL	CRITICAL THINKING	USEFUL LANGUAGE
an article and infographic about family size; understanding purpose	explorers describe people they know; listening to descriptions	a text message asking for help; explaining your reasons	showing appreciation	finding things in common	showing appreciation; describing people
an article about virtual reality; understanding pronouns	an explorer describes an interesting animal; listening for general information	a job application form; applying for a job	asking for help	knowing what skills are important	asking for and offering help; job application forms
an article about two amazing journeys; understanding words in brackets	two advertisements about two interesting places; listening to advertisements	a postcard; using exclamation marks	speaking on the phone	reasons for writing	making a phone booking; writing about travels
a poster about mental health; understanding headings	two explorers talk about how they exercise; listening for specific information	a survey report; writing a report	asking for and giving directions	understanding charts	time expressions; directions; describing change
an article about an actress with a second life; understanding time order	explorers talk about their favourite historical events; understanding small and large numbers	a historical person's profile; writing a person's profile	showing interest	explaining why someone is special	expressions for showing interest; talking about important people
an explorer's life story; understanding voices and audiences	an explorer shares a funny story; understanding funny stories	your life story; including interesting information	using English in the real world	guessing what the reader wants	phrases to explain a word; expressions to talk about the past

Reflect and review *Page 154*
Vocabulary reference *Page 160*
Grammar reference *Page 166*
Irregular verbs *Page 178*
Extra speaking tasks *Page 179*
Audioscripts *Page 182*

Meet the explorers

ABBEY ENGLEMAN

Lives: US
Job: I'm a marine biologist. I study the ocean and the plants and animals in the ocean. I'm also a photographer and a diver. I teach science too. I want people to care about the ocean and protect it.
What's your favourite place to visit? I love Marrakech, Morocco. The city is colourful and full of life.
Find Abbey: Unit 1; Unit 4; Unit 5

ALEXIS CHAPPUIS

Lives: Indonesia
Job: I'm a marine biologist, a diver and a photographer. I explore new parts of the ocean, and I photograph and study the different places ocean animals live. I learn about ocean life and I work to protect our oceans.
You live in Indonesia, but what's your hometown? I'm from a small town in France, far from the sea.
Find Alexis: Unit 6

AFROZ SHAH

Lives: Brunei
Job: I'm a geologist. I study things like rocks and mountains. Right now, I'm making new maps of places like India, Pakistan, Borneo and New Guinea. I'm also looking for places where earthquakes can happen.
What languages do you speak? English, Kashmiri, Hindi and Urdu
Find Afroz: Unit 12

ANUSHA SHANKAR

Lives: US
Job: I'm a biologist. I study animals. I'm also a researcher at the University of Alaska Fairbanks. Right now, I'm really interested in hummingbirds and the interesting ways they save energy.
Describe yourself in three words: Salsa dancing biologist!
Find Anusha: Unit 8

ALEC JACOBSON

Lives: Canada
Job: I'm a journalist, a photographer and an adventurer. I use words and photographs to tell stories about important problems in the world. I also tell the stories of people from different parts of the world.
What do you always take with you when you travel? A hat. I'm bald.
Find Alec: Unit 2; Unit 11

ELLIE DE CASTRO

Lives: Philippines
Job: I'm an archaeologist. I study human history – the things people did thousands of years ago. I also try to get children interested in history through my National Geographic Young Explorer project.
What languages do you speak? Filipino, English and German. I'm also learning Tuwali.
Find Ellie: Unit 3; Unit 7

ISAÍ MADRIZ

Lives: Chile
Job: I work as an entomologist – I study insects. I'm interested in the insects of Patagonia, especially the ones in the water. Many are disappearing, so I travel there to find them before they're gone forever.
What do you miss when you're travelling in Patagonia? My wife and my dogs … and hot showers!
Find Isaí: Unit 1

JEFF KERBY

Lives: Denmark
Job: I study the Earth and its climate – things like the weather and the Earth's temperature. I'm also a photojournalist. I take photographs and write articles. I want my stories to show people why we need to protect the Earth.
What's your favourite memory? Camping in Greenland for two weeks.
Find Jeff: Unit 2; Unit 5

MARIA FADIMAN

Lives: US
Job: I'm a conservationist. My job is protecting the environment. I'm also a professor at the Florida Atlantic University. I'm interested in the rainforests of Latin America. I think the way the people and plants there live together is amazing.
Where do you call 'home'? My heart is with the redwood trees in California.
Find Maria: Unit 6; Unit 12

JEFF MARLOW

Lives: US
Job: I'm a geobiologist – I study tiny creatures in extreme places, like deep in the ocean or near volcanoes. I also write science articles for magazines and newspapers. Sometimes, I make films.
What did you want to do when you were younger? I wanted to be an astronaut.
Find Jeff: Unit 4

NORA SHAWKI

Lives: Egypt
Job: I'm an archaeologist. I study people and places from the past. A lot of my work is digging and doing research. Right now, I'm working in the Nile Delta in Egypt. I want to protect this area and its history.
Where was your best meal? A local restaurant named 'Prince' does amazing Egyptian food.
Find Nora: Unit 10

JENNY ADLER

Lives: US
Job: I'm a photographer and a photojournalist. I'm also a diver. I take a lot of photos underwater. I want my photos and the stories I tell to teach people. I also want to inspire others – women especially – to be interested in science.
Where's the best place to visit? Anywhere that has the ocean!
Find Jenny: Unit 3; Unit 9

RUBÉN SALGADO ESCUDERO

Lives: Mexico
Job: I'm a National Geographic Explorer and a photographer. I'm lucky. My job is to travel the world and take photos of beautiful things. I want to photograph amazing moments and use my photos to inspire people from all over the world.
What do you do in your free time? I do yoga, and I cook. I also make music.
Find Rubén: Unit 10

LIA NAHOMI KAJIKI

Lives: Brazil
Job: I'm an ornithologist. I study birds. I'm also a PhD student at the University of Brasilia. I'm trying to learn more about one bird: the helmeted manakin. This beautiful bird lives only in Cerrado, Central Brazil.
Where is your favourite place to visit? Jericoacoara in Brazil.
Find Lia: Unit 7; Unit 11

Two Iñupiat people from Alaska greet each other.

1

Hello!

GOALS

- Scan for names and places
- Talk about yourself and other people
- Learn about countries, nationalities and numbers
- Listen to long numbers
- Introduce yourself
- Write your information on an employee pass

1 Work in pairs. Discuss the questions.

1 Look at the photo. How do you greet people?
2 What do you do?
3 What do you say?

WATCH

2 ▶ 1.1 Watch the video. Choose the correct options to complete the sentences.

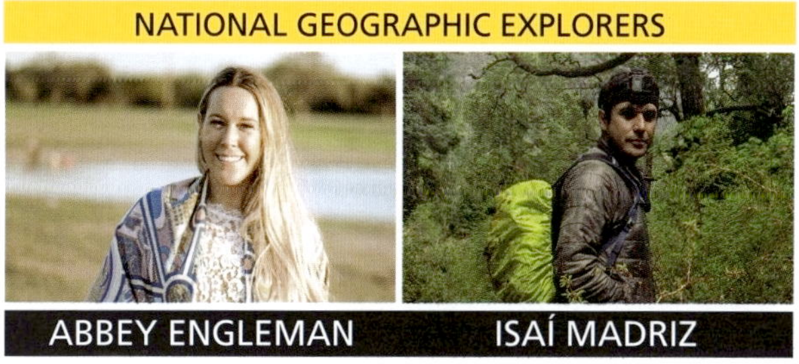

1 Explorer 1 is Abbey. She's from *the US / the UK*.
2 Explorer 2 is Isaí. He's from *Chile / Mexico*.

3 Make connections. Complete the sentences. Work in pairs. Say the sentences to your partner.

1 My name is ____________.
2 I am from ____________.

Hi! My name is Sara. I am from Spain.
Hello! My name is Hakan. I'm from Turkey.

1A Countries and cities

LESSON GOALS
- Learn about countries and cities
- Understand an article about where people are from
- Scan for names and places

VOCABULARY

1 Work in pairs. Look at the map on page 13. Where is your country?

2 1.1 Look at the flags. Write the countries. Then listen to check.

1  Ar__en__in__

2  Br__z__l

3  Ch__n__

4  Fr__n__e

5  G__r__an__

6  J__p__n

7  The U__it__d K__ng__om

8  The Uni__e__ St__t__s

Go to page 160 for the Vocabulary reference.

READING

3 Work in pairs. Ask and answer the questions.

1 What city are you from?
2 What country are you from?

I'm from Hanoi. Hanoi is in Vietnam.
I'm from Santiago. Santiago is in Chile.

NATIONAL GEOGRAPHIC EXPLORERS

4 Read the article about Abbey Engleman and Isaí Madriz. Are the sentences true (T) or false (F)?

1 Isaí is a scientist.
2 Kristina is from Berlin.
3 Abbey is a scientist.
4 Myrto is from the United States.

5 Look at the Reading skill box. Then scan the article. Circle the cities, countries and people's names.

READING SKILL
Scanning for names and places

Sentences begin with capital letters:
She's Sonia. She's from Bolivia.
Names, countries and cities have capital letters too:
Sarah *London* *United Kingdom*
To find names and places, look for capital letters.

6 Read the article. Complete the table.

Name	City	Country

PRONUNCIATION AND SPEAKING

7 1.2 Look at the Clear voice box. Listen and repeat.

CLEAR VOICE
Stressing syllables

Some words have different parts (syllables).
Words with more than one part have stress:
Ja-pan *Ger-ma-ny* *Bra-zil*
Ke-nya *Pe-ru* *Chi-na*
the U-ni-ted King-dom
the U-ni-ted States of A-me-ri-ca

8 1.3 Listen to the cities and countries. Underline the parts with stress.

1 Istanbul Turkey
2 Toronto Canada
3 Jakarta Indonesia

9 Work in pairs. Say the cities and the countries they are in.

Istanbul is in Turkey.

EXPLORE MORE!

Look at the countries in Exercise 2. What are some cities in these countries? Search online for 'cities in [country name]'.

Where are **you** from?

My name is Isaí Madriz. I'm a scientist. I'm from Guadalajara.

My wife is Kristina. She isn't from Guadalajara. She's from Palo Alto, a city in California.

Guadalajara is in Mexico.
California is in the United States.

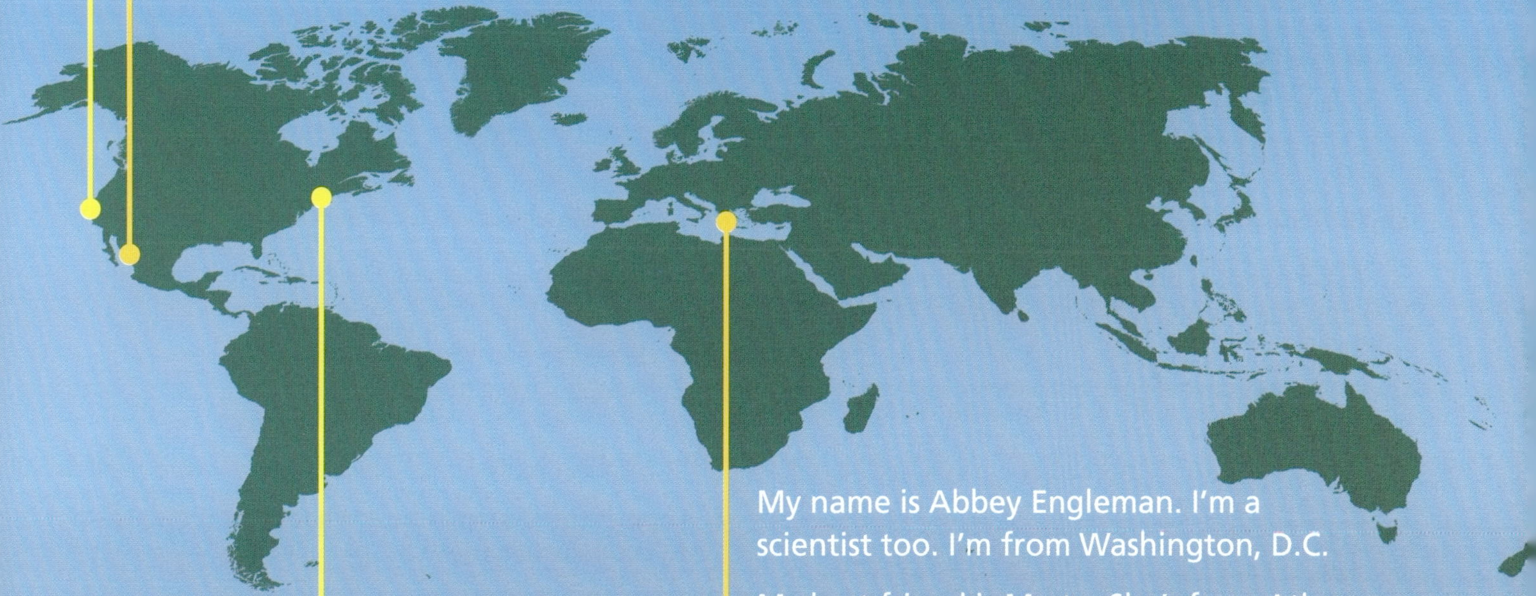

My name is Abbey Engleman. I'm a scientist too. I'm from Washington, D.C.

My best friend is Myrto. She's from Athens.

Washington, D.C. is in the United States.
Athens is in Greece.

1B She's American

LESSON GOALS
- Understand people talking about nationalities
- Use *be* with singular pronouns
- Talk about famous people around the world

VOCABULARY

1 Work in pairs. Answer the questions.

1 What country are you from?

2 What is your nationality?

I'm from Germany. I'm German.

2 Match the countries and nationalities.

1 Peru	a German
2 the UK	b Moroccan
3 Oman	c Turkish
4 Morocco	d Brazilian
5 Germany	e Vietnamese
6 Vietnam	f Peruvian
7 Turkey	g British
8 Brazil	h Omani

Go to page 160 for the Vocabulary reference.

LISTENING AND GRAMMAR

3 1.4 Work in pairs. Look at the photos. Do you know the people? Write the names. Listen and check.

Amanda Gorman Kylian Mbappé Kim Yuna

ice skater ______________

footballer ______________

writer ______________

4 1.4 Listen again. Complete the sentences.

American Korean French

1 Amanda Gorman is from the US. She's ______________.

2 Kylian Mbappé is from France. He's ______________.

3 Kim Yuna is from Korea. She's ______________.

5 Read the Grammar box. What are the three present simple forms of *be*?

> **GRAMMAR** Present simple *be* (singular positive)
>
> The verb *be* has three forms: *am*, *is* and *are*.
> Use *I* + *am*: ***I am** from France.*
> Use *you* + *are*: ***You are** Japanese.*
> Use *he/she/it* + *is*: ***It is** in the US.*
> Use these short forms:
> *I'm / you're / he's / she's / it's*

Go to page 166 for the Grammar reference.

6 Rewrite the sentences. Use short forms.

1 I am from France. *I'm from France.*

2 You are Japanese.

3 It is from the US.

4 She is American.

5 He is a footballer.

7 Complete the sentences. Use the correct form of *be*. Use short forms.

1 He______ from Italy.

2 She______ from the UK.

3 I______ Penelope. I______ from Greece.

4 Madrid is a city. It______ in Spain.

8 Look at the Grammar box. What word do we use to make *be* negative?

> **GRAMMAR** Present simple *be* (singular, negative)
>
> To make *be* negative, use *not*.
> ***I am not** from France.*
> ***You are not** American.*
> ***She/He/It** is not Japanese.*
> Use these short forms:
> *I'm not / You aren't / He isn't / She isn't / It isn't*

Go to page 166 for the Grammar reference.

Amanda Gorman

Kylian Mbappé

Kim Yuna

9 Rewrite the sentences. Use short forms.

1 I am not from France.
2 You are not American.
3 She is not Japanese.

10 Complete the sentences. Use the negative form of *be*.

1 I ______________ Australian. I'm from New Zealand.
2 He ______________ German. He's from France.
3 She ______________ a teacher. She's a student.
4 Vienna is in Austria. It ______________ in Germany.
5 Where are you? You ______________ in class.

SPEAKING

11 Work in groups. Look at the nationalities and choose three. Think of a famous person for each of the three nationalities.

American Australian Brazilian
British Egyptian Indian

12 Work in a new group. Tell your partners about your people in Exercise 11. Say their countries and nationalities.

Chris Hemsworth is from Australia. He's Australian.
Adele is from the UK. She's British.

EXPLORE MORE!

Do you like any singers, actors or sportspeople? Where are they from? What are their nationalities? Search online and find out.

1C What's your phone number?

LESSON GOALS

- Learn the words for 0–10
- Understand conversations about long numbers
- Ask *yes/no* questions with *be*

VOCABULARY

1 Work in pairs. What are the words for 0 to 10 in your language? Do you know the English words?

2 1.5 Write the numbers (0–10) next to the words. Listen to check.

zero	*0*	two	______
three	______	five	______
four	______	nine	______
eight	______	ten	______
six	______	seven	______
one	*1*		

3 How many things are in the pictures? Write the numbers in word form.

1  *three* books

2  ______ pens

3  ______ chairs

4  ______ tables

5  ______ teacher

Go to page 160 for the Vocabulary reference.

LISTENING

4 1.6 Listen to three conversations (a–c). What are they talking about? Write the letters.

______ an address

______ a phone number

______ a bank account number

5 1.6 Look at the Listening skill box. Listen again and write down the correct numbers.

LISTENING SKILL
Listening to long numbers

Some numbers are long:

My phone number is 02-111-3567-7924.

For long numbers, people say the numbers in groups:

My phone number is zero-two [pause] one-one-one [pause] …

You can say *zero* or *oh* for 0.

a ______________________________

b ______________________________

c ____________ West Street. Postcode: ____________

GRAMMAR

6 Read the Grammar box. Can you use short forms in positive answers?

GRAMMAR *Yes/no* questions with *be* (singular)

***Yes/no* questions**

I am → Am I — ***Am I** late?*

You are → Are you — ***Are you** Nigerian?*

He/She/It is → Is he / she / it — ***Is it** 9184-6683?*

Use a question mark (?), not a full stop (.).

Positive answers

Yes, you are. / Yes, I am. / Yes, it is.

Negative answers

No, I am not. / No, I'm not.

No, you are not. / No, you aren't.

No, it is not. / No, it isn't.

Go to page 166 for the Grammar reference.

7 Complete the questions. Use the correct form of *be*.

1 Good afternoon. ______ you John?
2 ______ she the new student from Japan?
3 What's your address? ______ it 624 Abel Drive?
4 Hey, Tom. ______ Nicole Dutch?
5 ______ I in the right class?

8 Look at the Useful language box. Complete the sentences.

Useful language Talking about numbers

My address is ...
My phone number is (66-456 ...)
Is it (65-446 ...)?
No. It's (66-456 ...) / Yes, it is.

1 A: What's your phone number, Michiko?
B: ______ phone number is 8345-2168.
2 A: My address ______ 2214 Smith Road.
B: ______ it 214 Smith Road?
A: No. ______ 2214 Smith Road.

SPEAKING

9 Work in pairs. Choose a number and say it. Your partner points at the number you say. Use the tips from the Listening Skill box.

1 0893456723
2 0993547682
3 783935492879
4 0894642098
5 783935492897
6 0894536732

10 Work in pairs. Take turns.

Student A: Choose a name. Answer Student B's questions.

Student B: Ask for Student A's phone number and address. Say the correct name.

Name:	Phone number:	Address:
Lucas	593-96-768-2985	209 Umari Street
Serena	1-202-555-0199	4371 Manford Lane
Lucia	252-61-959-5083	558 Dale Road
Hiroshi	66-2-081-2592	6701 Bank Street
Danny	60-3-2516-7948	339 Dutch Street
Celia	55-11-99306-5787	9040 Park View
Zahid	011-212-812-365-729	7219 Lake Avenue
Violet	996-803-61385	185 West Street

1D Introducing yourself

LESSON GOAL
- Learn how to introduce yourself
- Learn different greetings
- Practise introducing yourself to others

SPEAKING AND LISTENING

1 Work in pairs. What do you say when you meet someone new?

2 1.7 Listen to three conversations. Number the sentences in order. Listen again to check.

Conversation 1

a Hello. I'm Wei Ming. What's your name? 1

b Nice to meet you too Nader. ____

c Hi. I'm Nader. Nice to meet you, Wei Ming. ____

Conversation 2

d Yes, I am. It's nice to meet you! ____

e Yes, that's right. Are you Raul? ____

f Good morning. Are you Ahmed? ____

Conversation 3

g Hi. I'm Brian. I'm from the UK too! ____

h Good afternoon. I'm Colleen, from the UK. ____

i Nice to meet you, Brian. ____

MY VOICE

3 1.2 Watch the video about introducing yourself. Then match the words.

1 a greeting	a How are you?
2 a question	b It's nice to meet you.
3 something nice	c Good afternoon.

4 Look at the Communication skill box. Then work in pairs and greet your partner.

COMMUNICATION SKILL
Introducing yourself

When you meet someone new ...
Say a greeting:
Hi, I'm Colleen. I'm from the UK.
Ask a question:
How are you?
Answer questions:
I'm fine, thank you.
Use polite expressions:
It's nice to meet you.
Find common things:
I'm from the UK too!

5 When do people say the greetings? Tick (✓) the boxes. More than one box is possible.

Good morning	✓		
Good evening			
Good afternoon			
Good night			
Bye-bye			
Hi			

6 Look at the Useful language box. Then look at the expressions in the box. Which mean *hello*? Which mean *goodbye*?

Useful language Hellos and Goodbyes

Greetings
Hi. / Hello.
Good morning / afternoon / evening.

Questions and answers
What's your name?
How are you?
I'm fine, thank you.
I'm great.

Polite expressions
It's nice to meet you.
Nice to meet you too.

Saying goodbye
Goodbye. / Bye-bye. / Good night.

PRONUNCIATION

7 1.8 Look at the Clear voice box. Listen and repeat.

CLEAR VOICE
Stressing important words

People stress important words. They want you to hear them.
I'm Ellis. I'm from Japan.
Are you Dutch? I'm Dutch too.

8 1.9 Read the sentences. Underline the important words. Then listen. Which words have stress? Listen and repeat. Remember to stress the important words.

1 She's Su-Wei. She's Australian. She's from Sydney.
2 I'm Nirved. I'm from Sri Lanka. What's your name?
3 She's Anne. She's a friend from school. She's from Argentina too.

SPEAKING

9 Work in pairs. Read the sentences to your partner. Your partner responds. Use the Useful language to help you.

1 Hi. I'm Kirsty. What's your name?
2 Good afternoon. How are you?
3 Hi. It's nice to meet you. I'm Nala.

A: Hi. I'm Kirsty. What's your name?
B: Hello. I'm Layla. It's nice to meet you!

10 **OWN IT!** Work in groups. Introduce yourselves to each other. Use the Useful language to help you.

1 Say a greeting.
Hi.
2 Say your name.
I'm Lucas.
3 Ask and answer questions.
How are you?
4 Use polite expressions.
It's nice to meet you!
5 Find common things.
I'm Mexican too!

11 Look at the photos. Pretend you are in the situations. Introduce yourselves again.

A You're at a party. It's with friends from school.
B You're at a big work meeting. There are people from many countries.
C It's a wedding. Friends and family are there.

A: Hi. I'm Farhad. What's your name?
B: Hi Farhad. I'm Raymond. It's nice to meet you!

A: Good afternoon, Leticia. It's nice to meet you.
B: Good afternoon, Tom. Nice to meet you, too.

SITUATION A

SITUATION B

SITUATION C

1E My information

LESSON GOALS

- Learn to use capital letter
- Learn about common jobs
- Write your information on an employee pass

BELLA_4EVER

Name: Bella Dubois
Gender: female
Nationality: French
Country: France
City: Lyon
Job: student

Adriano.P_ELT

Name: Adriano Pereira
Gender: male
Nationality: Brazilian
Country: UAE
City: Abu Dhabi
Job: teacher

SPEAKING

1 Work in pairs. Look at Bella and Adriano's photos and information. Where can you find information like this?

READING FOR WRITING

2 Read Bella and Adriano's information again. Are the sentences true (T) or false (F)?

1 Bella is a teacher.
2 Bella is French.
3 Adriano is Brazilian.
4 Adriano lives in Brazil.

3 Look at the Writing skill box. Then read the paragraph. Circle the letters that should be capital letters. Use Martina's profile to help you.

WRITING SKILL
Using capital letters

In English, use capital letters:

- at the start of a sentence.
- for names of people.
- for countries, nationalities, cities, or towns.
- for the word *I*.

hi! i'm martina. i'm an actor and a writer. i'm american, but i live in portofino. portofino is a small town near genoa, italy. it's a beautiful town. i love it here!

MARTINA.R

Name: Martina Russo
Gender: female
Nationality: American
Country: Italy
Town: Portofino
Job: actor, writer

MEMBER PROFILE

Name:

Gender:

Country:

City:

Nationality:

Job:

4 Complete the profile above. Use these words.

female Imani Wallace Jamaica Jamaican Kingston pilot

5 Work in pairs. Look at the Useful language box. What other jobs do you know?

Useful language jobs

actor	pilot	teacher
doctor	scientist	writer

6 Look at the Critical thinking skill box. Work in pairs. Discus the questions.

CRITICAL THINKING SKILL
Your information

Where do you share your information? What do you share? Is it good to share your date of birth, your address or your phone number?

1 How many online profiles do you have?
2 Is the same information on all your profiles?
3 What information is not on your profiles?

WRITING TASK

7 **WRITE** You are in a new job. Write your information on the card below. Use your own information or imagine you're another person.

EMPLOYEE PASS

Name: ____________________

Nationality: ____________________

Country: ____________________

City: ____________________

Job: ____________________

8 **CHECK** Use the checklist.

☐ Your information is correct.
☐ Names and nationalities have capital letters
☐ Countries and cities have capital letters.

9 **REVIEW** Work in pairs. Read your partner's form. Do they do all the things in the checklist?

Go to page 154 for the Reflect and review.

EXPLORE MORE!

Find someone you know on social media. Look at their profile. What other information is on it?

Street artist Alex Lucas's house.

2

My home

GOALS

- Guess the meanings of words
- Talk about groups of people
- Learn about places at home and in town
- Get ready for listening tasks
- Ask people where things are
- Write a friendly email

1 **Work in pairs. Look at the photo. Would you live in a house like this? Why? / Why not?**

WATCH

2 ▶ 2.1 **Watch the video. Choose the correct options to complete the sentences.**

NATIONAL GEOGRAPHIC EXPLORERS

ALEC JACOBSON JEFF KERBY

1 Alec lives in *a house / an apartment*. It's *big / small*.
2 Jeff lives in *a house / an apartment*. The *garden / view* is nice.

3 **Make connections. Work in pairs. Where do you live? Tell your partner.**

I live in a flat. It's in the city. It's small.

I live in a house. It's in a small town. I love it!

2A Small houses

LESSON GOAL
- Learn about rooms
- Understand new words
- Understand an article about tiny houses

VOCABULARY

1 Work in pairs. Which room in your home is your favourite? Why?

2 2.1 Work in pairs. What are the names of the rooms? Write 1–5. Listen and check.

_____ kitchen _____ bathroom _____ bedroom
_____ dining room _____ living room

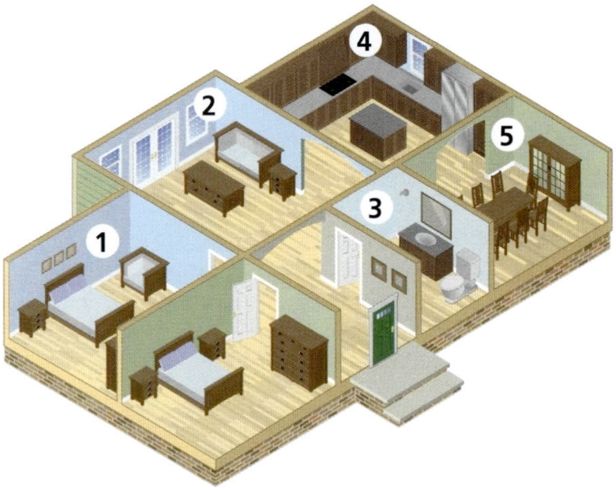

3 Work in pairs. Write the items and rooms.

bed dining table fridge shower softa toilet TV

Item	Room
bed	*bedroom*

Go to page 160 for the Vocabulary reference.

READING

4 Look at the photo. Is the house big or small? How many rooms do you think are in the house?

5 Work in pairs. Look at the Reading skill box. Then read the article. What do the **bold** words mean? Guess. Then use a dictionary.

READING SKILL
Understanding new words

For new words, guess the meaning:
- Use photos and pictures.
- Read the text again, slowly.

Use a dictionary if you can't guess the meaning.

6 Work in pairs. What are six things people like about tiny houses? Do you like tiny houses? Why? / Why not?

SPEAKING

7 Think about your home or a friend's home. Draw a floor plan, or use the example below. Label the rooms.

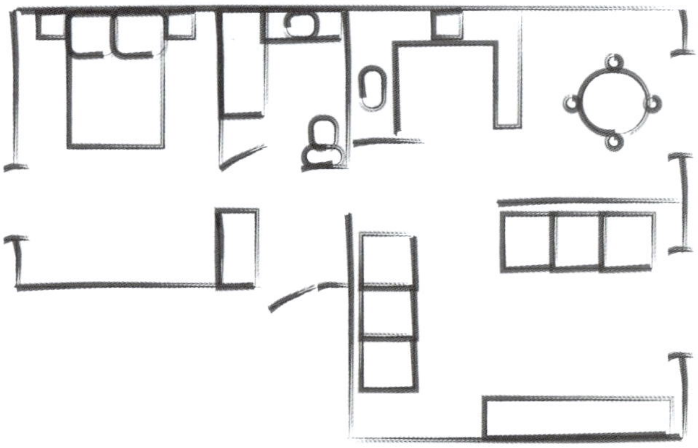

8 Work in pairs. Show your floor plan to your partner. Tell them about the house.

My friend's house is big. It has two bedrooms and a ...

EXPLORE MORE!

Do you want a house that's different? Search online for 'interesting houses'. Find photos of houses you like.

TINY HOUSES

Many people want big houses, but some people love small houses. Some small houses are really tiny – only ten square metres! Why do people like tiny houses? For some people, small houses are cute – they look nice. But here are other good things about small houses:

- Small houses are **cheap**.
- Small houses are **portable**.
- Small houses are easy to **clean**.
- Small houses use less **energy**.
- Small houses are good for the **environment**.

Jay Shafer **builds** tiny houses. He lives in a small house too. His house has four rooms: a kitchen, a living room, a bedroom and a bathroom. Jay loves small houses. He wants more people to live in them.

Jay Shafer with his family and his tiny house.

2B Working from home

LESSON GOALS

- Understand people talking about working from home
- Use *be* with plural pronouns
- Describe where things are

LISTENING AND GRAMMAR

1 Work in groups. Do you work or study at home? Where?

2 2.2 Listen to a phone conversation about working from home. Write ✓ or ✗.

	Felix	Ella	Josef
at home	☐	☐	☐
in the dining room	☐	☐	☐
in the living room	☐	☐	☐

3 Read the Grammar box. Then choose the correct option to complete sentences 1–2.

GRAMMAR BOX Present simple *be* (plural, positive and negative)

Use *we / you / they* + *are* to talk about more than one person or thing:

We are *in the dining room.*

You are *at home.*

They are *on the dining table.*

Use these short forms:

we are = we're

you are = you're

they are = they're

To make the sentence negative, add *not*:

We / You / They are not *in the dining room.*

Go to page 167 for the Grammar reference.

1 Use *we / you / they* to talk about one person and more than one person.

2 Use *we / you / they* to talk about people and things.

4 Complete the conversations. Use *we're*, *you're* or *they're*.

1 A: Where are Ella and Josef?
B: ___________ in the dining room.

2 C: Are you and Simone at school?
D: No, ___________ not.

3 E: Hi! Are Kumar and I late?
F: No, ___________ not.

4 G: Hi. ______________ Lisa and Tomas.
H: I'm Etta. Nice to meet you!

5 Read the Grammar box. Are short forms OK in both negative and positive answers?

GRAMMAR *Yes/no* questions with *be* (plural)

Questions:

Change the order of *we / you / they* and *are*:

Sentence: ***We / You / They are*** *at home.*

Question: ***Are we / you / they*** *at home?*

Positive answers:

Yes, we / you / they are.

(not *Yes, you're / we're / they're.*)

Negative answers:

No, you're / we're / they're not.

No, we / you / they aren't.

Go to page 167 for the Grammar reference.

6 Put the words in order to make questions.

1 they / are / in the library / ?

2 you / are / New Zealand / from / ?

3 the bags / under the table / are / ?

4 the / are / in / correct class / we / ?

7 Work in pairs. Ask and answer the questions in Exercise 6. Give positive and negative answers.

PRONUNCIATION

8 2.3 Look at the Clear voice box. Listen and repeat.

CLEAR VOICE

Saying contractions of *be*

When people speak, they usually use contractions, or short forms:

I am →	I'm	You are →	You're
He is →	He's	She is →	She's
It is →	It's		
We are →	We're	They are →	They're

9 2.4 Listen. Circle the word you hear.

1 *He's / She's* from Toronto.

2 *We're / They're* in the kitchen.

3 *I'm / It's* not in the dining room.

EXPLORE MORE!

Would you like to work from home? What jobs allow you to do that? Search online for 'jobs that let you work from home'.

SPEAKING

10 Work in pairs. Look at the photo. What are some of the things you see?

A laptop, a desk, a cup, scissors, a chair, ...

11 Work in pairs. Look at the four pictures below. Then say where the things in the photo are.

The laptop is on the table.

12 Work with a new partner. Look around you. Where are the people and things in your class? Ask and answer questions.

A: Where is my bag?

B: It's under the desk.

A: Where are Selma and Eugene?

2C My town

LESSON GOALS

- Learn about places in a town
- Understand people describing their hometowns
- Ask questions about people, things and places

VOCABULARY

1 Work in pairs. Where do you live? Is it a city, a town or a village?

2 2.5 Look at photos 1–10. Write the missing words. Listen to check.

bus restaurant school shopping train

1 park	6 museum
2 ___________	7 ___________ station
3 ___________ station	8 ___________
4 library	9 supermarket
5 ___________ centre	10 cinema

Go to page 160 for the Vocabulary reference.

LISTENING

NATIONAL GEOGRAPHIC EXPLORERS

3 2.6 Listen to Jeff Kerby and Alec Jacobson talking about their hometowns. Then look at the photo on page 29. Who is from that town: Jeff or Alec?

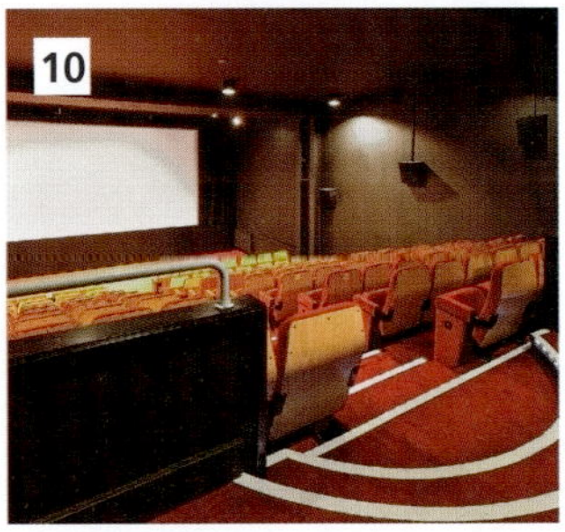

4 2.6 Look at the Listening skill box. Then listen again. Who talks about these things? Write J (Jeff) or A (Alec). Listen again to check.

LISTENING SKILL
Getting ready to listen

When doing listening exercises, try these tips:

Keep things quiet:

Don't talk. Ask your friends to be quiet too.
Turn off your phones and any music.

Relax:

Breathe and relax!

1 Sparta
2 Canada
3 Vermont
4 lakes
5 restaurants
6 a school
7 a library
8 a supermarket
9 a park
10 a forest

5 Read the Grammar box. Do you say *Who is your name?* or *What is your name?*

GRAMMAR *Who, what, where*

Some questions use question words. Different question words ask for different things.
Use *who* for people.
***Who** are you?*
Use *what* for things or names.
***What's** your name?*
***What's** in your hometown?*
Use *where* for places.
***Where's** Williston?*

Go to page 167 for the Grammar reference.

6 Match the questions and the answers.

1 What's in your bag?
2 What's your name?
3 Where's the supermarket?
4 Who's that person?

a It's next to the park.
b It's Anita Smith.
c It's a book about Brazil.
d He's my English teacher.

Houses next to a lake in Sparta, New Jersey, US.

SPEAKING

7 Work in groups of three. Complete the sentences. Write questions about where your partners live.

1 What's the name of your ___________?
2 Where's your favourite ___________?
3 Where's your ___________?

8 Ask your partners your questions in Exercise 7. Complete the table.

A: Where's your favourite park?
B: It's next to the museum.

Person A	Person B

EXPLORE MORE!

Which town do you like more: Sparta or Williston? Why? Search online for pictures and information about the two places.

2D Asking where things are

LESSON GOALS
- Ask where things are
- Listen to and give simple directions
- Understand intonation in questions

SPEAKING

1 Work in pairs. Look at the photo. What are they talking about?

2 Work in pairs. Discuss the question. How do you find places?
- I use a phone.
- I use a map.
- I look at street signs.
- I ask people.

MY VOICE

3 ▶ 2.2 Watch the video about asking where things are. Answer the questions.
1 What does *repeat* mean?
2 How do you *point* at something?

4 Look at the Communication skill box. Then number the sentences (a–g) in order.

COMMUNICATION SKILL
Asking where things are

Use these tips when you ask where things are:
1 Repeat answers as questions.
2 Ask more questions.
3 Check that you understand.
4 Point and ask.
5 Say 'thank you'.

a __1__ Excuse me. Where's the library?
b _____ Um ... Belle Avenue?
c _____ Oh. Is the bus station on my map?
d _____ It's in the shopping centre, on Belle Avenue.
e _____ Yes, it is. It's right ... here!
f _____ Yes. Over there. It's near the bus station.
g __7__ Great. Thanks so much!

5 Read the three questions. Match them with tips from the Communication skill box (1–5).
1 *Is the bus station on my map?* _____
2 *Um ... Belle Avenue?* _____
3 *Great. Thanks so much!* _____

6 Look at the Useful language box. Do you use *in* or *on* for street names?

Useful language Talking about where things are

Where's (the library)?
Is it (on Smith Street)?
It's over there.
It's near (the park)
It's in (the school)
It's on (Smith Street)

PRONUNCIATION

7 2.7 Look at the Clear voice box. Then listen to the questions. Notice how the voices go down, then up when repeating sentences as questions.

CLEAR VOICE

Understanding intonation in questions

When people repeat sentences as questions, their voices go down, then up. This 'up' sound tells people they are asking a question, not saying a sentence.

Next to the supermarket?
On Smith Street?
Near the bus station?
In the shopping centre?

SPEAKING

8 Work in pairs. Write the names of the four places in the four boxes on the map. You can write the place names in any box. Don't show your partner.

bus station cinema library school

9 Work in pairs. Ask questions. Find your partner's places.

Student A: Ask your partner *yes/no* questions. Then point to your map and guess where their places are.

Student B: Answer your partner's questions. Don't show your map to your partner.

A: Is it near the shopping centre?
B: No, it's not.

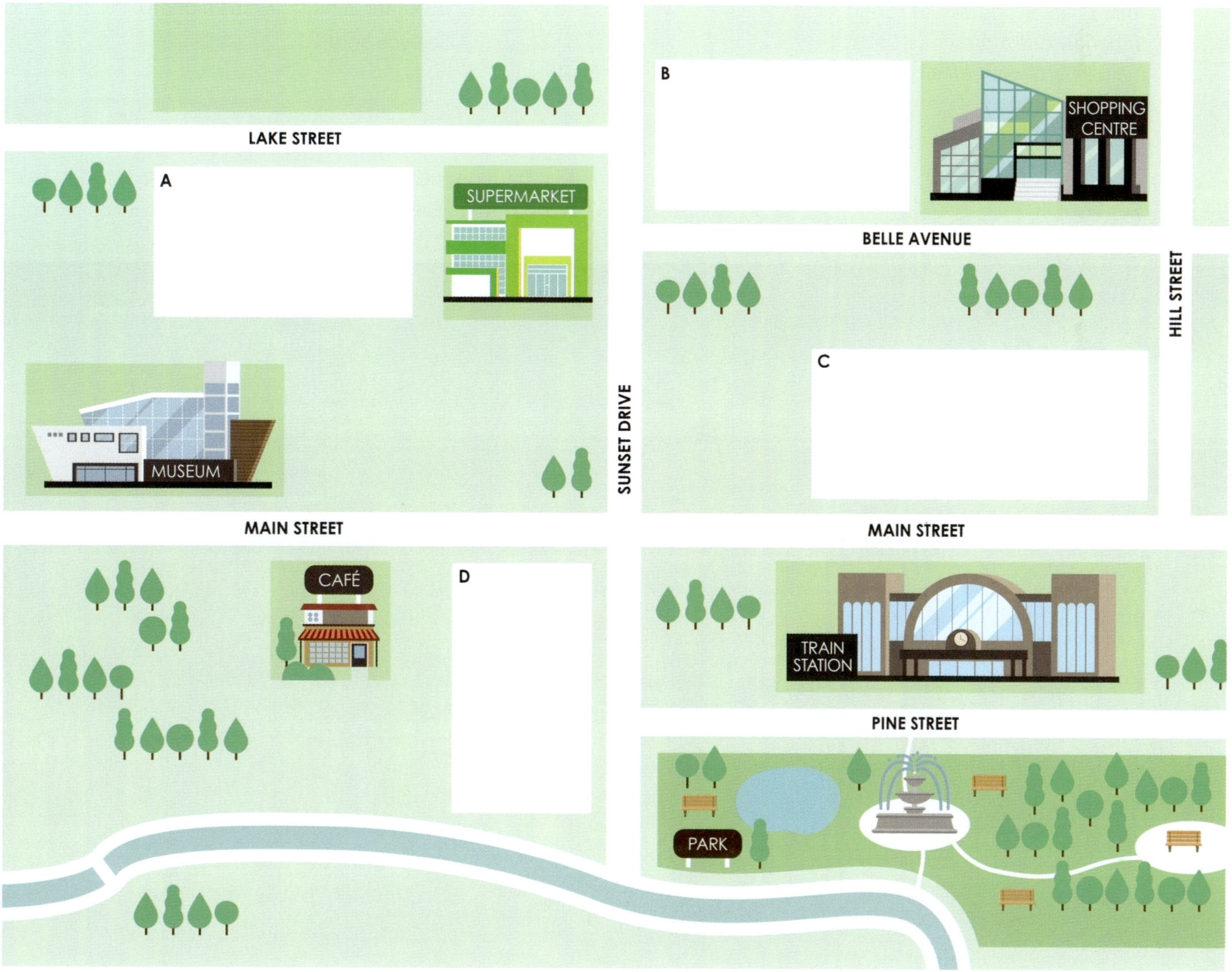

2E See you soon!

LESSON GOALS
- Learn how to write an email
- Learn common email expressions
- Write an email to a friend

SPEAKING

1 Work in pairs. A friend is visiting your town or city. Write down three good places to visit.

2 Discuss in groups. Are your places the same? Write down some other good places.

READING FOR WRITING

3 Read the email. Who is the email from? Who is the email to?

4 Match the parts of the email (1–7) with the descriptions below (a–g).

a friend's email address
b a friendly question
c main idea of your email
d sender's name
e sender's email address
f say hi or hello
g say goodbye

New Message

1 ____ From: gracepark4life@sendit.com
2 ____ To: minatruong@treemail.com
3 ____ Subject: Welcome to Hanoi
4 ____ Hi Mina
5 ____ How are you? I'm happy you're here in Hanoi! It's a great city with many nice places. The shopping centres are great and the museums are good. The restaurants are amazing too. My favourite place is Hoan Kiem Lake. It's beautiful at night. Here's a photo.
6 ____ See you soon!
7 ____ Grace

5 Work in pairs. Answer the questions.

1 Where does Grace live?
2 Does Mina live in the same place?

Hoan Kiem Lake in Hanoi, Vietnam.

6 Look at the Writing skill box. Then look at Grace's email. Why is she writing to Mina? What does she want to say?

WRITING SKILL
Writing a friendly email

To write a simple friendly email, think about what you want to say. Then:

- begin the email with a greeting
- ask the person how they are
- write a few sentences
- end the email in a friendly way

7 Look at the Useful language box. Which of the expressions are in Grace's email?

Useful language Writing friendly emails

To begin an email:
Hi / Hello (Mina),
How are you?
I'm great. / I'm well.

To finish an email:
Lots of love. / Write soon. / See you soon.

8 Complete the email below. Use expressions from the Useful language box.

[1] ______________ Lois

[2] ______________? [3] ______________. I'm in Prague. It's beautiful! The people are really nice. And the food is good! My hotel is next to a park. It's amazing. Wish you were here.

[4] ______________ !

Vicky

9 Look at the Critical thinking skill box. Then read Grace's email. Think of a different subject line for her email.

CRITICAL THINKING SKILL
Email subject lines

Good subject lines help readers understand emails better. They are short (just a few words). They say what the email is about, and why it is important.

WRITING TASK

10 **WRITE** A close friend is visiting your town. Write an email to your friend. Tell them about three of your interesting places in Exercises 1 and 2. Follow these steps:

1 Write your paragraph. Follow the steps in the Writing skill box.
2 Begin and end your email. Use the expressions in the Useful language box.
3 Write the main idea in the subject line.

New Message

From:

To:

Subject:

______________,

____

____

____

____

____

____

____

____

______________!

____

11 **CHECK** Use the checklist.

- ☐ My email describes three interesting places.
- ☐ It has friendly expressions and questions.
- ☐ The subject line describes the main idea.
- ☐ The spelling and punctuation are correct.

12 **REVIEW** Work in pairs. Read your partner's email. Do they do they things in the checklist? Write a short reply to the email.

Go to page 154 for the Reflect and review.

T0633
旭包鲜
力度伸
FedEx
aigo
Rowenta
云南白药
Beverly Hills Formula
COTTON LAND
HOMEBEAUTY
正骨扶药
马应龙麝香痔
Nutri-plus gel
ADVANCED
CHEN'S
Caltrate
NUTRILITE
D-Cal
迪巧
Meltykiss
Q蒂
德青源
阎润德
五谷道场
Côte d'Or
Fancy Feast

Photographer Hong Hao photographs 14 years of things from his life.

3

My stuff

GOALS

- Understand commas and the word *and*
- Learn how to talk about your things
- Describe things by their colours
- Listen for important words
- Ask questions to help you understand
- Write a social media post about a special item

1 Work in pairs. Discuss the questions.

1 Look at the photo. What things are in the photo?
2 What things in the photo have you got?

WATCH ▶

2 ▶ 3.1 Watch the video. Choose the correct option to complete the sentences.

NATIONAL GEOGRAPHIC EXPLORERS

ELLIE DE CASTRO

JENNY ADLER

1 Ellie's scarf is *black / red*.
2 Ellie uses her scarf when it's *cold / hot*.
3 Jenny's diving mask is *black / blue*.
4 Jenny's diving mask is *new / old*.

3 Make connections. What are your favourite things? Why? Tell a partner. Ask them to guess what it is. Change roles.

A: My favourite thing is small. It's on my desk now. It's black and red. It's from Korea.
B: Is it your phone?

3A My travel bag

LESSON GOALS

- Learn about things people travel with
- Understand a text about people's travel items
- Understand commas and the word *and*

VOCABULARY

1 Work in pairs. What do you carry to these places?

1 work or school
2 a park
3 a different town or city

2 3.1 Work in pairs. Look at the twelve photos. Match the words (1–12) with the photos (a–l). Then listen to check.

1 phone
2 book
3 bag
4 camera
5 toothbrush
6 water bottle
7 bank cards
8 keys
9 T-shirt
10 notepad
11 dress
12 passport

a

b

c

d

e

f

g

h

i

j

k

l

3 Work in pairs. Look at the photos in Exercise 2. Test your partner.

A: What's this?
B: It's a water bottle.

Go to page 161 for the Vocabulary reference.

READING

NATIONAL GEOGRAPHIC EXPLORERS

4 Read the text. Which things in Exercise 2 do Ellie de Castro and Jenny Adler talk about?

5 Read the text again. Answer the questions.

1 Ellie's travel bag is *big / small*.
2 Ellie travels with a *book / notepad* in her bag.
3 Jenny's travel bag is *big / small*.
4 Jenny has one or two *books / dresses* in her travel bag.

6 Look at the Reading skill box. Then look at the text. Underline commas and the word *and*.

READING SKILL
Understanding commas and the word *and*

Use *and* to talk about two things:
My water bottle ***and*** *my camera are in my bag.*

To talk about three or more things, use commas and the word *and*:
I always take my ***phone,*** *my bank cards* ***and*** *my passport.*

SPEAKING

7 Work in pairs. Turn to page 180. Look at the two photos. Imagine you are at these places. Choose three items from Exercise 2 to take with you to each place.

My phone is important. My water bottle too …

8 Work in groups. Look at the photos on page 180 again. Think of five things not in Exercise 2 to take with you. Use a dictionary to help you.

Five things? Maybe a football and an umbrella …

EXPLORE MORE!

What other items are good to have when you travel? Search online for 'useful travel items.' Choose three useful travel items not in this lesson.

The things I travel with

I travel a lot! When I travel, the most important things are my passport, my phone, my bank cards and money. I travel with a big bag. My water bottle and my camera are in it, and my notepad too. I also have clothes: lots of T-shirts, and of course, my favourite black scarf!

Ellie de Castro

Jenny Adler

When I travel, I always take my phone, my bank cards and my passport. I also take my camera – I love taking photos! I don't take many T-shirts or dresses – just a few. I carry a small bag. There's a water bottle in it and one or two books. I like to travel light – I don't like to carry many things.

3B Things people collect

LESSON GOALS

- Understand people talking about things they collect
- Talk about things near and far away
- Practise the /ð/ sound

This woman collects ukuleles.

LISTENING AND GRAMMAR

1 Work in groups. Look at the photo of the woman and her ukulele collection. Discuss the questions.

1 Do you collect anything?
2 What do you collect? Why?

2 3.2 Listen to four people. Match the people and the things they collect.

1 Alsana	a train tickets
2 Silvio	b coins
3 Peter	c mobile phones
4 Danica	d plastic bottles

3 3.2 Listen again. Complete the sentences.

1 Alsana's favourite coin is from *Peru / Thailand*.
2 Silvio's mobile phones are *old / new*.
3 Peter makes *tables / toys* from plastic bottles.
4 Danica's Russian train ticket is from *a friend / her father*.

4 Read the Grammar box. Tick (✓) the correct words.

GRAMMAR *This, that, these, those*

Use *this, that, these* and *those* when talking about things, people or animals.
Use *this* or *that* for one thing.
Use *these* or *those* for two or more things.
This *is a chair.* ***These*** *are my coins.*
this/these: the things are near
that/those: the things are far
This *one is from Russia.*
That *one in the box is really small.*

Go to page 168 for the Grammar reference.

	this	that	these	those
1 near	☐	☐	☐	☐
2 far	☐	☐	☐	☐
3 one	☐	☐	☐	☐
4 more than one	☐	☐	☐	☐

5 Look at the pictures. Complete the sentences. Write *This*, *That*, *These* or *Those*.

1 ____________ is a car.

2 ____________ is a wallet.

3 ____________ are keys.

4 ____________ are water bottles.

PRONUNCIATION

6 3.3 Look at the Clear voice box. Listen and repeat the words.

CLEAR VOICE

Saying /ð/

The *th* sound at the start of these words is voiced.

***th**is, **th**at, **th**ese, **th**ose, **th**ey, **th**e, **th**ere*

Some people use the *d* sound for these words. That's OK. Just use the sound that's easy for you.

7 Work in pairs. Read the conversations with your partner. Change roles.

A: Hey, Bob. What's that?
B: That's a cake.
A: That's not a cake ...
B: Yes, it is. Look!

C: Are those books?
D: These? No, they're not.
C: What are they?
D: They're bags.

SPEAKING

8 Work in pairs. Look at the paintings. What do you see? Ask and answer questions.

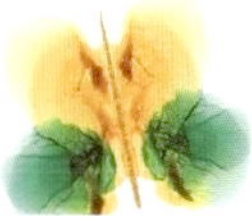

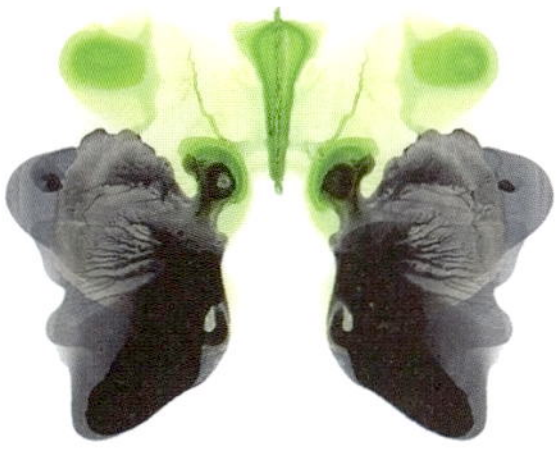

A: What's this?
B: Hmm. That's a fish, I think.
A: What are these?
B: Those are … dinosaurs!

EXPLORE MORE!

Some people and places like museums collect interesting items. Search online for 'interesting collections.' Which interesting collections do you like?

3C Colours of the world

LESSON GOALS
- Learn the words for different colours
- Understand people talking about colours
- Talk about things people own
- Say *your* and *their*

VOCABULARY

1 Work in pairs. Answer the questions.

1 What is your favourite colour?

2 What colours are your favourite things?

2 3.4 Work in pairs. Look at the pictures. Write the colours. Listen and check.

black blue green orange purple
pink red white yellow

1  ______

4  ______

7  ______

2  ______

5  ______

8  ______

3  ______

6  ______

9  ______

Go to page 161 for the Vocabulary reference.

LISTENING

NATIONAL GEOGRAPHIC EXPLORERS

3 3.5 Listen to Ellie de Castro and Jenny Adler talking about colours. Answer the questions.

1 What is Ellie's favourite colour?

2 What is Jenny's favourite colour?

3 What colour do people in the Philippines like?

4 3.5 Listen again. Which is the Philippines flag?

a  b  c 

5 3.5 Look at the Listening skill box. Then listen to Jenny and Ellie. What words in sentences 1–2 are loud and easy to hear?

LISTENING SKILL
Listening for important words

When people talk, they stress important words. Listen for them: important words are often loud and easy to hear.

1 The US flag is red, white and blue.

2 The Philippines flag is red, white, blue and yellow.

GRAMMAR

6 Read the Grammar box. Do possessive adjectives go before or after nouns?

GRAMMAR Possessive adjectives and *'s*

Possessive adjectives

Use *my, your, his, her, its, our, your* and *their* to show who something belongs to.

My things are pink. *Our favourite colour is red.*

's

Use *'s* after nouns or names.

Ruben's car is red. *Elsa's dress is green.*

Go to page 168 for the Grammar reference.

7 Match the pronouns (1–7) with the possessive adjectives (a–g).

1 I	a their
2 you	b our
3 he	c her
4 she	d its
5 it	e his
6 we	f your
7 they	g my

A colourful festival in the Philippines.

8 Complete the conversations. Use possessive adjectives.

1 Anh: Trang, what's your favourite colour?
Trang: Hmm. ______________ favourite colour is purple. Why?

2 Jia Hui: What are ______________ names?
Rizal: That's Osman, and that's Wei Ming.

3 Fiona: Lynn, where do you and Raul live?
Lynn: ______________ address is 101 Lake Street.

4 Josef: Is this Sofia's bag?
Adam: No. I think ______________ bag is blue, not yellow.

5 Sarah: What colour is the house?
Dana: The house is white, but ______________ doors are red.

9 Complete the sentences. Use the words in brackets and *'s*.

1 ______________ car is black. (Liz)
2 ______________ book is blue. (Omar)
3 This is ______________ toy. (my cat)
4 Is that the ______________ desk? (new student)

PRONUNCIATION

10 3.6 Look at the Clear voice box. Listen and repeat.

CLEAR VOICE
Saying *your* and *their*

The words *you're* and *your* sound the same:
You're *in class.* ***Your*** *friends are at home.*
The words *they're* and *their* also sound the same:
They're *from Brazil.* ***Their*** *homes are in Brazil.*

11 3.7 Listen and repeat the sentences.

1 Your book is not in the bag.
2 You're next to her house.
3 Are these their books?
4 They're in their living room.

SPEAKING

12 Work in groups. Ask and answer questions. What colour are the things in your class?

A: What colour is Sam's bag?
B: Her bag is pink.

EXPLORE MORE!

What festivals do people celebrate around the world? Which ones have a lot of different colours? Search online for 'colourful festivals.'

3D Asking questions to understand

LESSON GOALS
- Understand people who talk fast
- Ask for the meaning of difficult words
- Get people to say something again

SPEAKING

1 Look at the picture below. What is the problem?

a It's very noisy.
b The speaker is happy.
c The speaker talks too fast.

2 Work in pairs. What do you do when you ...

1 don't understand someone in your first language?
2 don't understand someone in English?

I say 'I don't know' when I don't understand someone.

I say 'Excuse me' when I don't understand someone.

MY VOICE

3 ▶ 3.2 Watch the video about asking questions to understand. What three problems does the video talk about?

a fast speakers
b quiet speakers
c noisy places
d difficult words

4 Look at the Communication skill box. Which of these things do you already do?

COMMUNICATION SKILL
Asking questions to understand

When you don't understand someone, don't worry. Try these tips.

1 Ask them to slow down.
2 Ask them to say it again.
3 Ask them to say what they mean.

5 Look at the Useful language box. Do you say words like *I'm sorry*, *excuse me* and *please* in your first language?

Useful language Asking questions to understand

a I'm sorry. I don't understand. What's a ... ?
b Excuse me. Can you repeat that?
c Can you slow down a little, please?

A: In my first language, we don't say 'please', but we say 'thank you' a lot.

B: In my first language, 'excuse me' and 'I'm sorry' are the same word.

6 Match the Useful language questions (a–c) to the three tips in the Communication skills box (1–3).

7 Read the three situations below. What is the best Useful language question for each of the situations?

SITUATION A

Anne asks for a 'tin of tomatoes' in a shop in the US. The shop assistant doesn't understand what a 'tin of tomatoes' is.

SITUATION B

Jodie asks Priscilla very quickly: 'Isthisyourfriend'sbluebag?'
Priscilla doesn't understand.

SITUATION C

Hector's house is very noisy. Lydia says something to Hector but he doesn't hear her.

SPEAKING

8 OWN IT! Work in pairs. Discuss the questions.

1 When don't you understand people in English?
2 Are your problems similar to those in Exercise 7?
3 What other questions do you ask to help you understand?

I don't understand people on the phone. They talk very fast.

9 Work in pairs. Ask and answer questions.

Student A: Ask the questions below. Use the Useful language questions to help you understand your partner's answers.

1 What's your phone number?
2 Is that your black laptop bag?
3 Where's the train station?

Student B: Answer the questions. Be difficult to understand: talk quickly or talk quietly.

A: It's 98562431.

B: Excuse me. Can you repeat that?

A: I'm sorry. It's 98562431.

10 Work in pairs. Try Exercise 9 again, but with your own questions. When you answer, be difficult to understand:

1 Talk quickly.
2 Talk quietly.
3 If you can, use difficult words.

A: What's your favourite place in our city?

B: My favourite place is the aquarium.

A: I'm sorry. I don't understand. What's an aquarium?

3E Special things

LESSON GOALS

- Talk about special things
- Learn how to check your writing
- Write a social media post

SPEAKING

1 Work in groups. Discuss the questions.

1 Have you got any special items?
2 Why are the items special to you?

READING FOR WRITING

2 Read the social media posts below. Why are the items special? Tick (✓) the reasons.

1 Osamu's guitar is ______.
a old c cheap
b new d expensive

2 Alara's dolls are ______.
a old c from Turkey
b beautiful d from the US

3 Rafael's father's tea cups are ______.
a expensive c from India
b cheap d old

3 Look at the Writing skill box. Then read sentences 1–4. Correct the mistakes in the sentences.

WRITING SKILL
Checking your writing

After you write, check your work.

- Check your spelling. Use a dictionary.

This is my new ~~fone~~ phone.

- Check for capital letters.

She's from ~~germany~~ Germany.

- Check for full stops.

It's my favourite ~~book it's amazing~~ book. It's amazing!

- Check for apostrophes.

~~Its~~ It's from my father.

1 This is my pianu.
2 is this omar's book?
3 Its not my guitar. Its Petes.
4 The house is white it's door is red

Osamu
3 hrs ago
This is my new guitar. It's a great guitar. And it's cheap! I love it. My friend Sakda and I play in our living room every day. Sakda's guitar is good, but it's very expensive.

Sakda Your guitar is amazing!

Alara
2 hrs ago
These are my dolls. They're old – about 40 years old. And they're beautiful. I love their eyes! They're from my country, Turkey. Now, they're with me in the US!

Li Ying They're really pretty!

Rafael
1 hr ago
These are my father's new tea cups. They're beautiful, and they're expensive - $120!

Alara They're lovely! Are they from your holiday in India?

Rafael Yes, they are!

4 Look at the Useful language box. Then look at the pictures below. Are the items old or new? Are they expensive or cheap?

Useful language Describing special things

This is my favourite … .
This is my new / old … .
It's very important / special to me.
It's from … .
It's very expensive / cheap.
It's amazing / great / beautiful.
I love it!

1

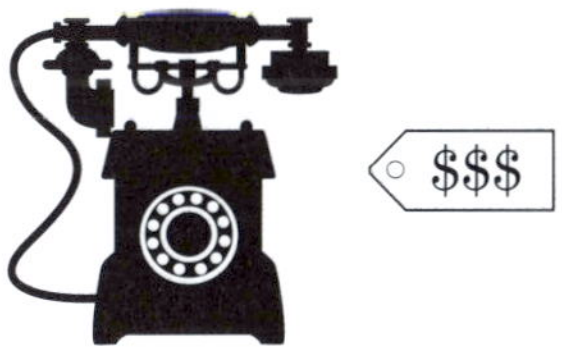

2

5 Complete the text. Circle the correct words.

This is my [1]*favourite / important* toy. Its name is Clifford. It's [2]*from / in* a shop in Uruguay. It's very [3]*old / new* – about 20 years old! But it's very [4]*special / great* to me. It's in all my travel photos. In this photo, we are on holiday in Iceland. It's a [5]*beautiful / favourite* photo!

6 Read Osamu's social media post about his guitar. Write a comment. Use the words and phrases in the Useful language box.

WRITING TASK

7 Look at the Critical thinking skill box. Think of an item that is special to you. Complete the mind map with reasons it is special.

CRITICAL THINKING SKILL
Giving reasons

Giving reasons helps readers understand why something is important. It makes writing interesting too.

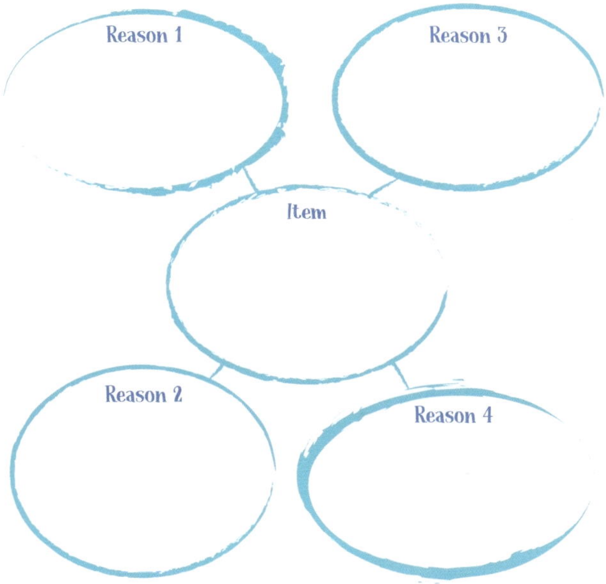

8 **WRITE** Write a social media post about your special item in Exercise 7. Use the three model posts on page 44 and your information in Exercise 7 to help you.

9 **CHECK** Use the checklist.

- ☐ My post says what the thing is.
- ☐ My post says why the thing is special.
- ☐ The spelling is correct.
- ☐ The punctuation is correct.

10 **REVIEW** Work in pairs. Read your partner's post. Do they do the things in the checklist? Reply with a comment.

Go to page 155 for the Reflect and review.

Breakfast before work in Istanbul, Turkey.

4

Habits

GOALS

- Scan an article for useful information
- Talk about people's habits
- Say the time and the days of the week
- Listen for tone
- Make plans
- Write a work email

1 Work in pairs. Discuss the questions.

1 Look at the photo. What meal are they having?

2 When do people usually have that meal?

WATCH

2 ▶ 4.1 Watch the video. Answer the questions.

NATIONAL GEOGRAPHIC EXPLORERS

ABBEY ENGLEMAN

JEFF MARLOW

1 What times of the day do Abbey and Jeff like?

2 What do they like to do?

3 Make connections. What's your favourite time of day? Why?

I like the morning. It's warm and it's quiet.

I like the afternoon. I enjoy being at work with my friends.

I like the evening. It's cool, and I can rest after work.

4A My commute

LESSON GOALS

- Learn the numbers 11–100
- Scan for useful information
- Understand an article about a long commute

VOCABULARY

1 Work in pairs. How many students are in your class? Write the number. Do you know how to say the number?

My class has sixteen students.

2 4.1 Write the numbers. Listen and repeat.

11 eleven	____ fourteen	____ seventeen
____ twelve	____ fifteen	____ eighteen
____ thirteen	*16* sixteen	____ nineteen

____ twenty	*65* sixty-five
____ twenty-one	____ seventy-six
32 thirty-two	____ eighty-seven
____ forty-three	____ ninety-eight
____ fifty-four	*100* one hundred

3 Work in pairs. Complete the sentences. Circle the correct answers.

1 A day is 24 *hours / minutes*.
2 A minute is 60 *hours / seconds*.
3 An hour is 60 *seconds / minutes*.

4 4.2 Match the times with the clocks. Listen and repeat.

1 

2 

3 

4 

a twelve thirty-seven
b eleven o'clock
c four twenty-five
d nine forty-eight

Go to page 161 for the Vocabulary reference.

READING

5 Work in pairs. How many minutes or hours is your trip to school or work?

My trip to school is 40 minutes long.

My trip to school is 1 hour and 10 minutes long.

6 Look at the Reading skill box. Then read the article quickly. Complete the timeline on page 49.

READING SKILL
Scanning for useful information

Scanning an article is a quick way to find useful information. Don't read the whole article. Look for useful words or numbers.

7 Read the article again. Answer the questions.

1 Andy travels ______________ kilometres to work.
2 His trip to work is ______________ hours long.
3 He waits ______________ minutes for the train.
4 He gets home at ______________.

PRONUNCIATION

8 4.3 Look at the Clear voice box. Listen and repeat.

CLEAR VOICE
Saying /ʌ/

You can make the /ʌ/ sound in words like *bus* with the letters *u* and *o*.

bus *but* *loves* *come*

9 4.4 Read the words. Then listen and circle the words with the /ʌ/ sound.

a some
b home
c fun
d put
e phone
f sun

SPEAKING

10 Draw a timeline for your trip to work or school. Think about the following:

- How long do you travel by bus, train or car?
- How long do you wait?
- How long do you walk?

11 Work in pairs. Share your timeline with your partner. Are your timelines the same?

I'm on the bus for 10 minutes.

I'm on the bus for 45 minutes!

A DAY IN THE LIFE OF A SUPER-COMMUTER

Andy Ross begins his long trip home.

ANDY ROSS: A SUPER-COMMUTER

How do you go to work or school every day? Many people walk, take the bus or train or drive. Some people do them all!

Andy Ross is a super-commuter. He travels a lot every day. Andy works in San Francisco, US. He lives about two hundred kilometres away.

In the morning, he travels four hours to work. In the evening, he travels four hours back home. That's eight hours in one day!

ANDY'S TRIP HOME

Andy finishes work at 4 p.m. He walks to the bus stop. At 4:10, he takes a bus. He reaches the train station at 4:20 and waits.

At 5 p.m., he gets on a train. He's on the train for two hours. He gets off at 7 p.m. and takes a bus.

At 7:50, he gets off the bus and walks to his car. At 7:55, he gets in his car and drives. He gets home at 8:05.

Andy's trip is very long but he doesn't want to look for a different job. For him, the long trip is OK because he loves his work.

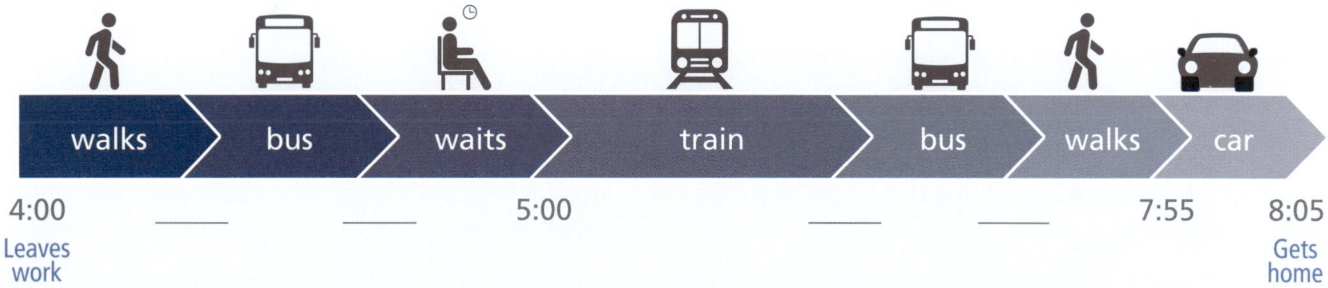

4B What time do you go to bed?

LESSON GOALS
- Understand an interview about sleep
- Talk about habits and true things
- Discuss sleeping habits

LISTENING AND GRAMMAR

1 Work in pairs. Discuss the questions and write your answers down.

1 What time do you go to bed at night?
2 What time do you wake up in the morning?

2 Work in groups. Look at your answers to Exercise 1. Who sleeps a little? Who sleeps a lot?

I sleep a lot. I go to bed at 10.30 p.m. and wake up at 7:30 a.m.

I don't sleep a lot. I go to bed at 12:30 a.m. and wake up at 7 a.m.

3 4.5 Listen to two people talking about sleep. Complete the table.

	Goes to bed	Wakes up	Hours of sleep
Josh	*1:30*	*10:30*	*9*
Yasmin			
Josh's parents			
Tom			

4 Read the Grammar box. Do you add *s* to verbs in negative sentences?

GRAMMAR Present simple

Use the present simple to talk about habits and true things.

I, you, we* and *they
Use the infinitive form of the verb.
*I **sleep** a lot.*

He, she* and *it
Use the infinitive form of the verb + *s* or *es*.
*She **works** at night.*
*He **goes** to bed at 10 a.m.*

Negative sentences:
Use *does not (doesn't)* / *do not (don't)* + infinitive form of the verb.
*He **doesn't sleep** at night.*
*They **don't sleep** a lot.*

Go to page 168 for the Grammar reference.

5 4.5 Circle the correct answers. Listen again to check.

1 I *sleep / sleeps* a lot – about 9 hours. I *go / goes* to bed at 1:30. And I *wake up / wakes up* at 10:30.
2 My parents *finish / finishes* work late. They *start / starts* work early. They don't *sleep / sleeps* a lot.
3 I *live / lives* with my brother, Tom. He *work / works* at night.

6 Read the sentences. Are they correct? Write ✓ or ✗.

1 They take the bus to school every day.
2 We goes to the museum on Sundays.
3 She plays basketball every day after school.
4 I reads a lot of books about science.
5 He watches a lot of films.

7 Circle the incorrect verbs in Exercise 6. Write the correct form of the verbs.

8 Complete the sentences. Write *don't* or *doesn't*.

1 They ______________ live in the US.
2 Salma ______________ like the colour purple.
3 He ______________ know the answer.
4 I ______________ work from home.

9 Make the sentences in Exercise 8 positive.

10 Read the Grammar box. In *yes/no* answers, do we repeat the infinitive form of the verb?

GRAMMAR Present simple questions and answers

***Yes/no* questions:**
Use *do* or *does* + the infinitive form of the verb.
***Do** they **sleep** a lot?*
***Does** she **sleep** a lot?*

***Yes/no* answers:**
***Yes**, they **do**. / **No**, they **don't**.*
***Yes**, she **does**. / **No**, she **doesn't**.*

***Wh-* and *How* questions:**
Use question word + *do* / *does* + infinitive verb:
***What does** he **work** as?*
***When do** they **wake** up?*

Go to page 169 for the Grammar reference.

11 Read the sentences. Circle the correct answers.

1 A: Do you *work / works* at night?
B: Yes, I *do / does*.

2 C: *Do / Does* she *take / takes* the bus?
D: No, she *don't / doesn't*.

3 E: When *do / does* the cat *sleep / sleeps*?
F: It *sleep / sleeps* all the time!

4 G: *Do / Does* they *eat / eats* at this restaurant?
H: No, they *don't / doesn't*.

5 I: What *do / does* we *do / does* now?
J: We *wait / waits* for the next train.

SPEAKING

12 Answer these questions about your sleep.

1 How many hours do you sleep?
2 Do you want to sleep more?
3 What do you do before you go to bed?

13 Work in groups. Ask and answer the questions in Exercise 12. Who wants to sleep more? Give them advice.

A: I sleep six hours a night. I want to sleep more.
B: What do you do before you go to bed?
A: I play video games.

EXPLORE MORE!

What are some ways to sleep better? Search online using the words 'how to sleep better'.

4C What do you usually do?

LESSON GOALS

- Learn the days of the week
- Understand people talking about their work days
- Talk about how often things happen
- Practise words with the /juː/ sound

VOCABULARY

1 Work in pairs. How many work or school days do you have in a week? How many days off do you have in a week?

2 4.6 Number the days of the week in order (1–7). Then listen to check.

_1_ Monday ____ Saturday ____ Friday
____ Thursday ____ Tuesday
____ Sunday ____ Wednesday

3 Work in pairs. Answer the questions.

1 Which days are weekdays?
2 Which days are the weekend?
3 What day is it today? What day is it tomorrow?

Go to page 161 for the Vocabulary reference.

LISTENING

NATIONAL GEOGRAPHIC EXPLORERS

4 4.7 Listen to Abbey Engleman and Jeff Marlow. Are they talking about their work days or their days off?

5 4.7 Listen again. Answer the questions.

1 Where does Abbey usually work?
2 Where does Abbey sometimes work?
3 Why does Abbey think her job is fun?
4 Where does Jeff work?
5 Does Jeff work five days a week?
6 When does Jeff usually read his emails?

Abbey Engleman at work on a boat.

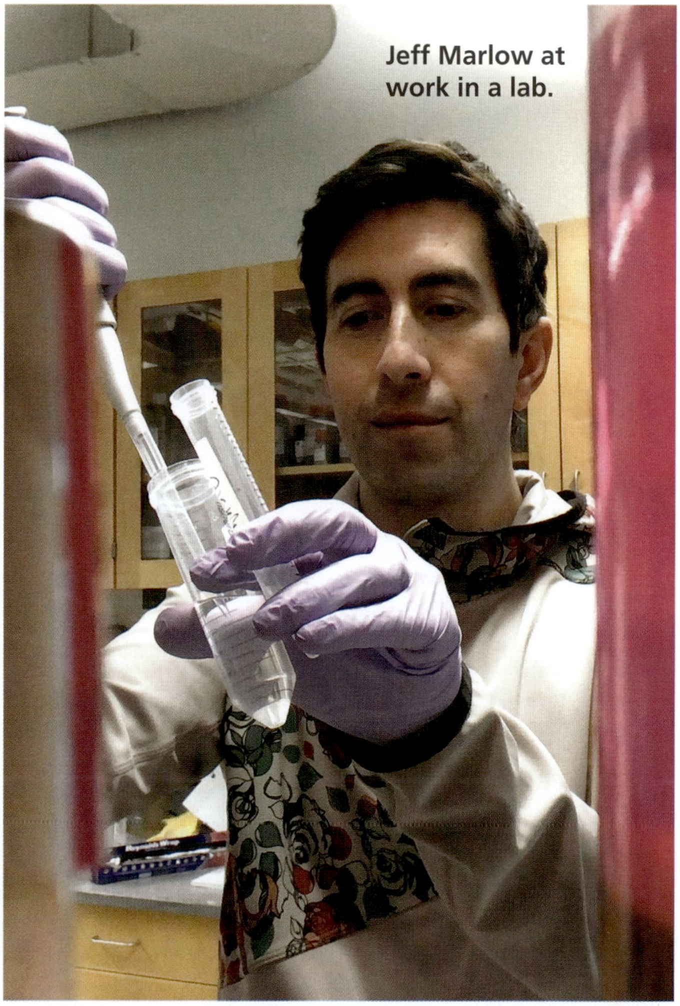
Jeff Marlow at work in a lab.

6 4.7 Look at the Listening skill box. Then listen again and answer questions 1–3.

LISTENING SKILL
Listening for tone

The tone of a person's voice tells us how they feel. Is their voice high or low? Does it sound happy or angry? Tone also tells us if something is interesting or important. Listen carefully for changes in tone.

1 How do Abbey and Jeff sound to you?
2 Do their tones change when they talk about different things?
3 Why do you think their tone changes?

Abbey sounds very happy to me.
Jeff sounds happy when he talks about his work in the lab.

GRAMMAR

7 Read the Grammar box. Then read the sentences below. Are they true (T) or false (F)?

GRAMMAR Adverbs of frequency

Adverbs of frequency say how often things happen:

never **sometimes** **usually** **always**

0% *100%*

*My job **is always** fun.*
*Is your job **always** fun?*
*I **never work** on Sundays.*
***Sometimes**, I **work** on a boat.*
*Where do you **usually work**?*

Don't start sentences with *always* or *never*.

~~Always / Never~~, I work on a boat. ✗
*I **always / never** work on a boat.* ✓

Go to page 169 for the Grammar reference.

1 Adverbs of frequency go before the words *is*, *are* or *am*.
2 Adverbs of frequency go before verbs like *work*.
3 When a sentence starts with an adverb of frequency, add a comma.

8 Complete the sentences. Circle the correct answers.

1 Lara reads a lot. She *never / always* has a book with her.
2 Where's Elaine? She isn't *always / usually* late.
3 Orhan is very nice. He *usually / never* says bad things about people.
4 Usually, I wake up early. But *sometimes / always*, I wake up late.

9 Number the sentences from a conversation in order.

a Hey Zoe, what do you usually do on Saturdays? *1*
b Well ... Yoga's a great way to relax. I never feel tired after a class.
c Would you like to go to a yoga class with me? It's at 3 p.m. on Saturday.
d 3 p.m.? I don't know ... I always feel tired on Saturdays.
e I usually study. Sometimes, I meet friends.

PRONUNCIATION

10 4.8 Look at the Clear voice box. Listen and repeat.

CLEAR VOICE
Saying /ju:/

The letter *u* can make different sounds. In *usually*, the *u* at the start sounds like *you*.
***U**sually* sounds like *you-sually*.
This sound is in other words too:

T**u**esday	comm**u**te	comp**u**ter
use	c**u**te	bea**u**tiful

SPEAKING

11 Work in groups. Do you usually do these things? Ask and answer the questions.

1 brush your teeth before bed
2 wake up before 8 a.m.
3 play computer games at night
4 have breakfast at home
5 take the bus to work or school
6 carry an umbrella
7 sleep more than seven hours

A: Do you usually wake up before 8 a.m.?
B: No, I don't. I never wake up before 8 a.m.

EXPLORE MORE!

What jobs do you think are interesting? Search online using the words 'interesting jobs'.

4D Making plans

LESSON GOALS
- Make plans with others
- Say if you're free or busy
- Talk about your plans for the weekend

SPEAKING

1 Work in pairs. Discuss the questions.

1 What do you usually do at the weekend?
2 Who do you do these things with?
3 Is it always easy to make plans? Why? / Why not?

I usually meet my friends.

MY VOICE ▶

2 ▶ 4.2 Answer the questions. Then watch the video about making plans to check your answers.

1 When making plans, give ______ and time.
   a an hour   b a day
2 If you are *free*, you have ______ to do.
   a nothing   b something
3 A *reason* explains ______.
   a when   b why

3 ▶ 4.2 Watch the video again. Answer the questions.

1 When does the woman suggest meeting?
2 Why doesn't the man want to meet this week?
3 Why does the man agree to meet?
4 When does the man suggest meeting?

4 Look at the Communication skill box. Then discuss in pairs. Do you need to follow the order in the box when you make plans?

COMMUNICATION SKILL
Making plans

When you make plans ...
- give a day and time.
- ask when they are free.
- say the reason you want to meet.

5 Read the conversation. Then number the tips below in the order (1–3) Tomas uses them.

______ Give a day and time.
______ Ask when the person is free.
______ Say the reason you want to meet.

L: Hey, Tomas.
T: Hey, Lukas. Do you want to play tennis with me? I want to practise! When are you free?
L: Hmm. Is Saturday afternoon OK?
T: Sorry, I can't. I usually help my parents at their shop on Saturdays. Is Sunday morning OK?
L: Yes, I think so. Let me see … Yes, I'm free.
T: Great. See you on Sunday!

6 Look at the Useful language box. Work in pairs. Answer the questions.

Useful language Making plans

Are you free on/at … ?
Do you want to (have lunch) on/at … ?
Can we meet on/at … ?
Yes, I'm free.
Sure. / OK.
That's great. / That's perfect.
Sorry, I can't. / Sorry, I'm busy.
When are you free?
Is (Sunday morning) OK?

Which expressions are for …

1 suggesting a day and time?
2 asking when someone is free?
3 agreeing to a plan?
4 not agreeing to a plan?

7 Complete the sentences. Use words from the Useful language box.

1 ______________ you want to have lunch tomorrow?
2 ______________ we meet on Wednesday?
3 ______________ you free today?
4 ______________ are you free?
5 ______________ tomorrow evening OK?
6 Tomorrow? Sorry, I ______________
7 Sorry, I'm ______________ on Friday.

8 Work in pairs. Ask and answer the five questions (1–5) in Exercise 7.

A: Can we meet on Wednesday?
B: Sorry, I can't. I always work late on Wednesdays.

SPEAKING

9 Make a list. Think about your weekends. Write down what you usually do, and when.

Things you do	Day	From	To
homework	*Saturday*	*9 a.m.*	*12 p.m.*

10 **OWN IT!** Work in groups. Make plans with your classmates. Use the ideas below, or your own ideas.

have lunch
visit a museum
go to the library
go for a coffee
cook a meal
watch a film
play a sport
go shopping
exercise
study for a test

Student A:

- Say hello to a group member.
- Suggest an activity you think they like.
- Check your table in Exercise 9.
- Suggest a time you are free.

Student B:

- Check your table in Exercise 9. Are you free?
- Agree on the time or suggest another time.
- Suggest a place to meet.

Repeat with the other people in your group.

A: Do you want to play tennis on Saturday morning?
B: Sorry, I'm busy. I usually do homework on Saturday mornings.

4E Thank you for your email

LESSON GOALS
- Talk about how people make plans
- Learn how to write work emails
- Write a work email to a manager

SPEAKING

1 Work in pairs. Look at the pictures and match the words.

1  *e*

2 

3 

4 

5 

a write a letter
b write an email
c talk face-to-face
d send a text message
e make a phone call

2 Work in pairs. Look at Exercise 1.

1 How do you usually make plans with friends?
2 How do people usually make plans at work?

I usually send text messages.
People at work usually send emails.

READING FOR WRITING

3 Read the two emails. Answer the questions.

1 When does Germaine want to meet?
2 Who isn't free on Tuesday?
3 Who isn't free on Friday? Why?
4 Who isn't free on Monday? Why?

4 Look at the Useful language box. Which expressions are only for replies?

Useful language Writing work emails

Hi / Dear (Melissa),
I hope all is well.
Thanks for your email.
It's good to hear from you.
Let me know.
I hope to hear from you soon.
Have a great day / evening / weekend!
Regards, / Best regards, / Many thanks,

New Message

From: Germaine L.
To: Melissa D.
Subject: Project meeting

Hi Melissa,

How are you? I hope all is well.

I'm in the Berlin office next week. I'd like to talk about the new project with you. When are you free? Is Tuesday OK?

Please ask Toby and Miguel to join too.

Hope to hear from you soon.

Best regards,

Germaine

Reply

From: Melissa D.
To: Germaine L.
Subject: Project meeting

Hi Germaine,

I'm great! It's good to hear from you.

Next week is OK, but I'm really busy on Tuesday. Is Wednesday or Thursday OK? Miguel usually doesn't work on Fridays. And Toby is usually busy with customers on Mondays. Any time after lunch is good.

Let me know. Have a great weekend!

Regards,

Melissa

5 Complete the emails. Use the expressions in the Useful language box.

Hi Sasha,

1____________________. Can we meet next week? I want to finish our report. I'm free all week, but not Thursday morning.

2____________________!

3____________________,

Linus

Hello Linus,

4____________________. Next week is good. Is Tuesday afternoon OK? Let's have lunch, and work on the report after lunch.

5____________________.

6____________________.,

Sasha

6 Look at the Writing skill box. What are some polite greetings?

WRITING SKILL
Writing work emails

In work emails, be friendly. But be professional too.

- Use polite greetings.
- Say why you are writing.
- End your email in a polite way.

Also, be clear:

- What is your email about?
- What information do you need?
- What do you want the other person to do?

7 Look at the Critical thinking skill box. Would you write the same way to the four people (1–4)?

CRITICAL THINKING SKILL
Using the correct tone

When you write a work email, ask:

- Who are you writing to?
- Do they know you?
- Are you friends with them?
- Are they senior to you?

1 the head of your company
2 people you have lunch with
3 your teammates
4 your manager

WRITING TASK

8 Your manager wants to plan a party for your team. Read the email and plan your reply. Make notes:

- Give a reason why Wednesday is not OK.
- List two days that are OK.
- List reasons why the other two days are not OK.

New Message

From: Sheila R.

Subject: Team party

Hi,

Great job on the presentation! Everyone's really happy. Let's have a small team party. Are you free on Wednesday? Please check with the team and let me know.

Best regards,

Sheila

9 **WRITE** Write a reply to your manager. Use your notes from Exercise 8 and the emails on page 56 as models.

10 **CHECK** Use the checklist. My email ...

- ☐ is friendly.
- ☐ is professional.
- ☐ uses expressions from the Useful language box.

11 **REVIEW** Work in pairs. Read your partner's email. Do they do the things in the checklist?

Go to page 155 for the Reflect and review.

EXPLORE MORE!

What other expressions do people use at the start of work emails? Search online for 'ways to start a work email'.

A person staying in a 'bubble dome' in Northern Ireland.

5

Inside or outside?

GOALS

- Get ready to read an article
- Talk about activities people like doing
- Talk about the months and seasons
- Know what information to listen for
- Invite people to do things
- Write a bucket list

1 Work in pairs. Discuss the questions.

1 Look at the photo. Is the person inside or outside?
2 What are some things you do inside?
3 What are some things you do outside?

WATCH

2 ▶ 5.1 Watch the video. Answer the questions.

NATIONAL GEOGRAPHIC EXPLORERS

JEFF KERBY ABBEY ENGLEMAN

1 Do Jeff and Abbey like being indoors or outdoors?
2 What are some things they like doing?

3 Make connections. Do you prefer being indoors or outdoors? Why?

I prefer being outdoors. I like trees and long walks.

I like indoor things like TV and books.

5A Indoor activities

LESSON GOALS

- Get ready to read an article
- Understand an article about indoor activities
- Learn activity collocations

READING

1 Look at the four photos on page 61. What are the people doing? Do you do these things?

2 Look at the Reading skill box. Then work in pairs. Answer the questions below.

READING SKILL
Getting ready to read

Before you read, look at the title, headings and pictures. Ask yourself:

- What is the topic?
- What do I know about the topic?
- What words do I know about the topic?

1 Look at the photos and the title of the article. What is the article is about?
2 Look at the four headings in the article (A–D). Think of two activities for each heading.
3 What words about the topics in the article do you not know in English? Look for the words in a dictionary or online.

I see people at home doing different things, and the title of the article is …

Running and swimming are types of exercises …

I know the word 'music', but I don't know what that thing in his hands is …

3 Read the article. Then match the four headings (A–D) with the photos.

4 Read the article again. Work in pairs and answer the questions.

1 Why do people sometimes prefer to stay indoors?
2 What are some ways to exercise at home?
3 How many musical instruments can you name in English?
4 What is *upcycling*? Do you have something old you can upcycle?
5 What are some activities you can do in an online party?

VOCABULARY

5 5.1 Match the words to make activities. Listen to check.

1 read — a to music
2 watch — b a book
3 listen — c online
4 chat — d TV

5 draw — e a song
6 sing — f a picture
7 play — g a friend
8 call — h video games

6 Match the activities in Exercise 5 to the pictures.

a 
e 
b 
f 
c 
g 
d 
h 

Go to page 162 for the Vocabulary reference.

SPEAKING

7 Work in pairs. Discuss the questions.

1 Are you at home a lot? When are you at home?
2 What do you do when you are at home?

I'm at home a lot. I don't go out much.

I like to read and watch TV when I'm at home.

8 Discuss in groups. Which activities in the article are fun or interesting? Which activities aren't fun or interesting? Why?

I think an online party is fun! Exercising at home isn't fun. I like exercising outdoors.

EXPLORE MORE!

What are some other fun things you can do inside? Search online for 'fun indoor activities'.

Fun things to do at home

Sometimes, the weather outside isn't good, or you're tired. You don't go out and you stay inside. Usually, you just watch TV, play video games or look at photos online. But what else can you do at home?

A Exercise

You don't need to go outside to exercise. Watch exercise videos on the internet, play exercise video games or join an online exercise class with your friends.

B Play music

It's nice to listen to music, but it's great to make your own music. Learn a musical instrument online, or write a song with friends or people from around the world.

C Make something

Draw a picture, bake a cake or make a hat. Or try upcycling. Do you have old tables and chairs at home? Find something old and make it look new and beautiful.

D Video call your friends

Alone at home? Video call your friends and have an online party! You can talk, dance, play games, have dinner and enjoy an evening together online.

5B I love swimming

LESSON GOALS
- Understand people talking about outdoor activities
- Use *like*, *love* or *don't like* with the *-ing* form of verbs
- Say the /ŋ/ sound at the end of words
- Talk about activities people like and don't like

LISTENING AND GRAMMAR

1 Match the emojis to the words.

1 like — a 

2 love — b 

3 don't like — c 

2 Work in pairs. What are some things you like, love and don't like? Think about:

- food
- books
- TV shows
- places
- films
- songs

3 Work in pairs. Match the photos below with the activities. Write 1–10 on the photos.

1 camping
2 climbing
3 cycling
4 doing yoga
5 horse-riding
6 playing basketball
7 playing football
8 playing tennis
9 running
10 swimming

NATIONAL GEOGRAPHIC EXPLORER

4 5.2 Listen to Jeff Kerby talking about activities he likes. Circle the activities in Exercise 3 he talks about.

5 5.2 Listen again. How does Jeff feel about the activities in Exercise 3 he talks about? Write L (like), DL (don't like) or LL (love).

6 Read the Grammar box. How do *like*, *love* and *don't like* change after *he*, *she* or *it*?

GRAMMAR *Like, love* and *don't like* + *-ing* form

Many activities use the *-ing* form:
camping / running

Making *-ing* forms:
Add *-ing*.
walk → *walk**ing***
Remove the e. Add *-ing*.
cycle → *cycl**ing***
Repeat the consonant. Add *-ing*.
swim → *swim**ming***

Using the *-ing* form:
Use the *-ing* form after *like*, *love* or *don't like*:
I love playing football. I don't like doing yoga.
Use *do* or *does* to ask questions:
Do you like playing football? Yes, I do.
Does he like doing yoga? No, he doesn't.

Go to page 170 for the Grammar reference.

7 Complete the sentences. Use the *-ing* form of the words in brackets.

1 I like ________________ (play) tennis with my friends.
2 He loves horse-________________ (ride) in the hills.
3 She doesn't like ________________ (climb).
4 Do you like ________________ (do) yoga?
5 Does she like ________________ (camp)?
6 Why do you love ________________ (cycle)?

Jeff likes camping and doing things outside.

8 Complete the sentences. Circle the correct answers.

1 I don't *like / likes* camping.
2 He *love / loves* playing volleyball.
3 Does she *like / likes* reading?
4 He *don't / doesn't* like doing homework.
5 *Do / Does* they like going to other countries?
6 We don't *like / likes* watching TV all day.

PRONUNCIATION AND SPEAKING

9 5.3 Look at the Clear voice box. Listen and repeat.

CLEAR VOICE
Saying /ŋ/

Verbs that end with *ing* have the /ŋ/ sound at the end.

camping	*hiking*	*swimming*
doing	*running*	*singing*

10 Work in groups. Ask and answer questions. Find out who likes, loves or doesn't like the activities. Write their names in the table.

A: Do you like camping?
B: Yes. I love it!

ACTIVITY	😊	😍	🙁
camping			
climbing			
cycling			
doing yoga			
horse-riding			
playing basketball			
playing football			
playing tennis			
running			
swimming			

EXPLORE MORE!
What are some popular outdoor activities people enjoy? Search online for 'popular outdoor activities'.

5C The seasons

LESSON GOALS

- Learn about the months and seasons
- Understand people talking about the seasons
- Talk about when things happen

VOCABULARY

1 5.4 Listen to and repeat the months.

January	May	September
February	June	October
March	July	November
April	August	December

2 Look at the picture. Does your country have hot, warm, cool or cold months?

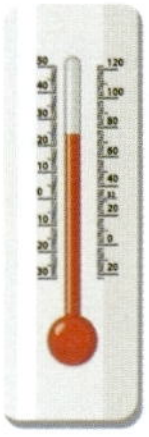

hot

warm

cool

cold

3 Look at the infographic on page 65. Answer the questions.

1 What are the four seasons?
2 When are the days long?
3 When are the nights long?

4 Work in pairs. Answer the questions.

1 Do all countries have four seasons?
2 When does winter start in Winterberg, Germany?
3 When does winter start in Santiago, Chile?

Go to page 162 for the Vocabulary reference.

LISTENING

5 5.5 Listen to three people talking about the seasons. Match the people with the places.

1 Alain	a Winterberg, Germany
2 Hannah	b Santiago, Chile
3 Isidora	c Libreville, Gabon

6 Look at the Listening skill box. Then read the questions in Exercise 7. What type of information does each question ask for?

LISTENING SKILL
Knowing what to listen for

Before you listen, look at the questions. Read the question words. What do they ask for? When you listen, pay attention to key words.

where: a place (listen for towns, cities, etc.)
when: a time (listen for a time, days, months, etc.)
who: a person (listen for the names of people)
why: a reason (listen for words like *because* or *so*)

7 5.5 Listen and answer the questions.

1 **Where** is it is hot all year? (*Libreville / Santiago*).
2 **When** does Alain like playing football? (*afternoon / evening*)
3 **Why** does Hannah like December? (*the sun / the snow*)
4 **Who** does Hannah make snowmen with? (*her sister / her brother*)
5 **When** does Isidora go dancing? (*morning / evening*)

GRAMMAR

8 Read the Grammar box. Do you say *on Sunday* or *in Sunday?*

GRAMMAR Prepositions of time

Use *at, in* or *on* to say when things happen.

At:
at the weekend
at 3 a.m.
at night

In:
in January / February / March …
in 2023 / in the year 2023
in the morning / afternoon / evening
in spring / summer / autumn / winter

On:
on Monday / Mondays …

Go to page 170 for the Grammar reference.

Summer starts in June.
Winter starts in December.

THE FOUR SEASONS

Summer starts in December.
Winter starts in June.

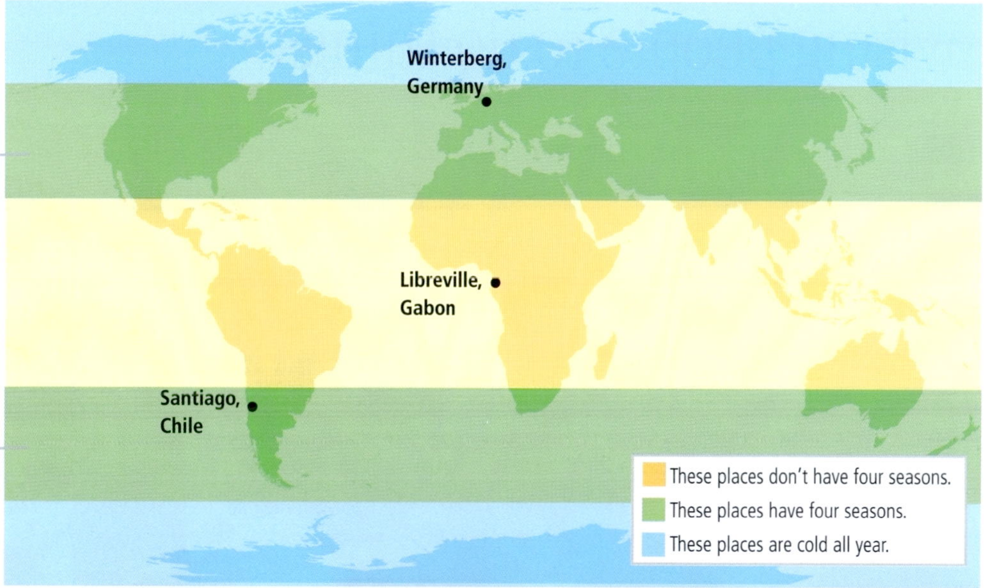

Spring: It's cool, then warm. Flowers grow.

Summer: It's hot. Days are long.

Autumn: It's warm, then cool. Leaves fall.

Winter: It's cold. Nights are long.

9 Complete the sentences with *at*, *in* or *on*.

1 I like snowboarding ______ the summer.
2 She has a dance class ______ the weekend.
3 He plays football ______ Saturdays.
4 The film starts ______ 7 p.m.
5 He usually does his homework ______ night.
6 He always goes skiing ______ June.
7 What do you do ______ Mondays?

10 Complete the text with *at*, *in* or *on*.

I love doing fun things [1]______ the summer. I usually go camping [2]______ the weekend. And [3]______ Wednesdays, I meet my friends. I finish work [4]______ 3 o'clock, and we try new things like horse-riding or rock climbing. I also exercise a lot. [5]______ the morning, I go cycling. And [6]______ night, I go running.

SPEAKING

11 Work in pairs. Turn to page 180. Think of a country with four seasons you would like to visit and complete the table. Use the internet to help you.

A: What country would you like to visit?

B: I want to go to Georgia. It's beautiful! Where would you like to visit?

12 Work in new pairs. Tell your new partner about your place in Exercise 11.

Georgia is a beautiful country. Winter starts in December. It ends in February. In winter, people love …

5D Inviting people to do things

LESSON GOALS

- Invite people to do things
- Decide on a time, place and activity
- Understand connected speech

SPEAKING

1 5.6 Listen to two people talking. Answer the questions.

1 Does Ling want to go to the cinema?
2 Does Ling want to have lunch?
3 What do they agree to do together?

2 Work in pairs. Discuss the questions.

1 What activities do you like doing with others?
2 Who do you do these activities with?
3 When do you say 'no' to invitations?

I like going to the cinema with others. I don't like watching films alone.

I like going to the cinema with my good friends.

I say no to invitations when I'm busy, or when I don't like the activity.

MY VOICE

3 5.2 Watch the video about inviting people to do things. Then work in pairs and discuss the questions.

1 Is it easy to invite good friends to do things with you? Why? / Why not?
2 Is it easy to invite people you don't know to do things with you? Why? / Why not?

4 Look at the Communication skill box. Then discuss in pairs. Which of the tips are easy to do in English? Which are not?

COMMUNICATION SKILL
Inviting people to do things

When you invite someone to do something for the first time, choose ...

- an activity you both like.
- a good place for both of you.
- a time you are both free.

5 Look at the Useful language box. Then complete the conversation below. Use words from the box.

Useful language Inviting people

Inviting people:
Do you want to … on Saturday?
Would you like to … tomorrow?

If your friend says *yes*:
Great! Is 3 p.m. OK?
Fantastic! Let's meet at the park.

If you can't agree on the time or place:
How about Sunday?
When is a good time for you?
How about the park?

After you agree on the time and place:
Perfect! See you then / there.

Josef: Would you [1]_________ to go for a run tonight?
Yuki: Sorry. I have plans.
Josef: Oh. Is tomorrow [2]_________?
Yuki: Sure. [3]_________ meet at the river, at 6 p.m.
Josef: Hmm. The river's really far.
Yuki: [4]_________ about the museum?
Josef: Perfect! See you [5]_________!

PRONUNCIATION

6 5.7 Look at the Clear voice box and listen to the examples. Notice how people join *would* and *you* when they talk quickly.

CLEAR VOICE
Understanding connected speech:
would you

Many English speakers join *would* and *you* when they talk quickly.
Would you /ˈwʊdʒuː/ *like to watch a movie?*
Some also change the /uː/ sound in the word *you*:
Which movie ***would you*** /ˈwʊdʒə/ *like to watch?*

SPEAKING

7 **OWN IT!** Write down five interesting activities you would like to do.

8 Work in groups. Invite others to do the activities in your list from Exercise 7 with you.
- Use the phrases in the Useful language box.
- Agree on a time and place.
- Write the activities in the timetable below.

A: Do you want to go hiking on Saturday at 4 p.m.?
B: Sorry, I'm busy. Is Sunday OK?

	Monday	Tuesday	Wednesday	Thursday	Friday	Saturday	Sunday
10 a.m.							
12 p.m.							
2 p.m.							
4 p.m.						*Running with Andrea in the park*	

5E I'd like to see the world

LESSON GOALS

- Learn how to write and order lists
- Talk about things you want to do
- Write a bucket list

SPEAKING

1 A bucket list is a list of things you want to do in your life. Work in pairs. Discuss the questions.

1 What new activities would you like to try?
2 What places would you like to visit?
3 What other things would you like to do?

READING FOR WRITING

NATIONAL GEOGRAPHIC EXPLORER

2 Read Abbey Engleman's bucket list. Match the bucket list items and the groups below. Write the numbers 1–10.

Places to visit: ______________________

Things to learn: ______________________

Things to do: ______________________

3 Work in pairs. Read the bucket list again. Answer the questions.

1 Which items would you like to try? Why?
2 Which items do you not want to try? Why?

I'd like to get a puppy. I don't want to learn to knit.

4 Look at the Writing skill box. List five things you want to do this week. Work in pairs. Check your partner's list.

WRITING SKILL
Writing lists

Lists are a great way to plan or remember things. To write a good list …

- begin each item with a verb
- use a new line for each item
- keep each line short

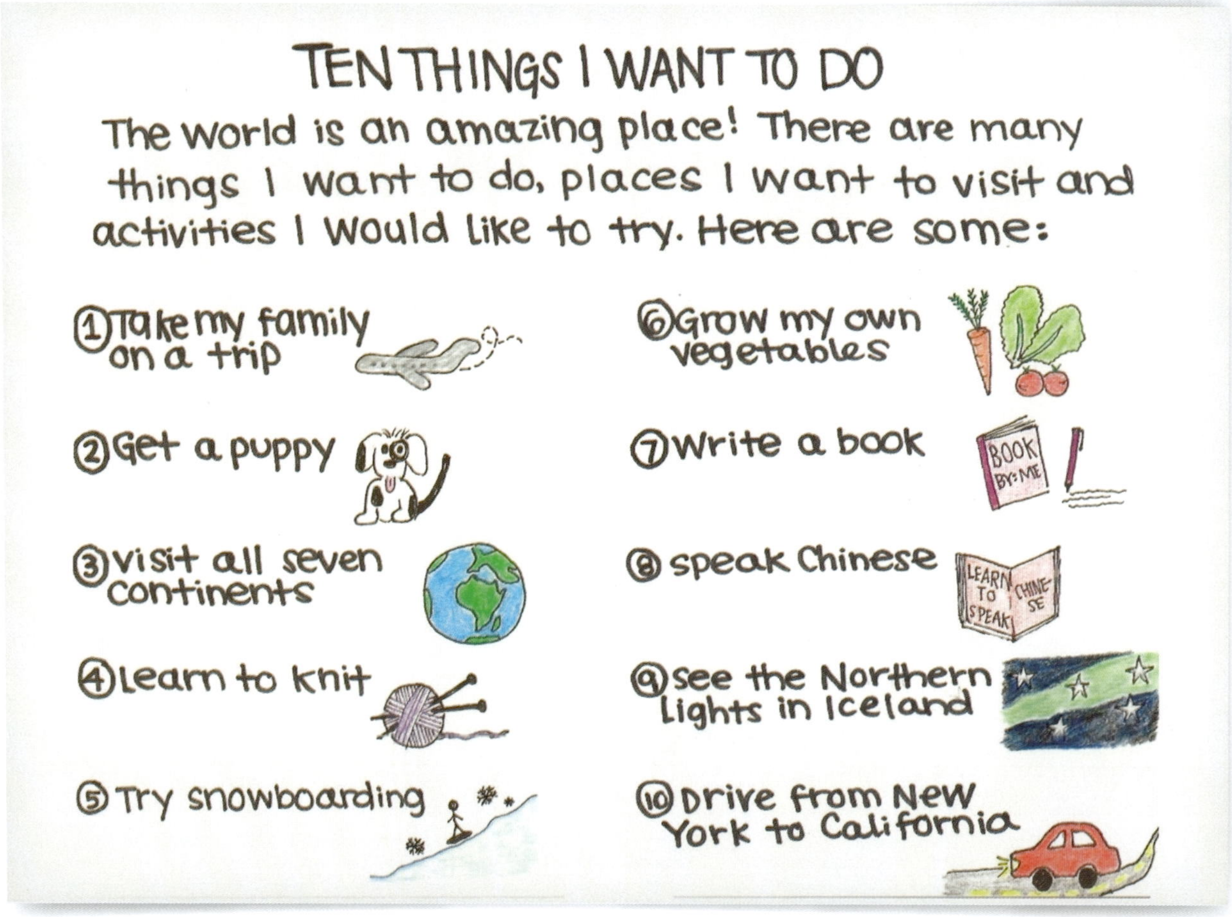
TEN THINGS I WANT TO DO

The world is an amazing place! There are many things I want to do, places I want to visit and activities I would like to try. Here are some:

1 Take my family on a trip
2 Get a puppy
3 Visit all seven continents
4 Learn to knit
5 Try snowboarding
6 Grow my own vegetables
7 Write a book
8 Speak Chinese
9 See the Northern Lights in Iceland
10 Drive from New York to California

Abbey Engleman loves travelling and would like to visit all seven continents.

5 Read the Useful language box. Work in pairs. Which verbs can you use for 1–4?

Useful language activity verbs

visit	help	try	learn
see	meet	drink	go
eat	buy	make	write

1 places   2 people   3 things   4 activities

6 Work in groups. Make phrases with six verbs from the Useful language box.

help people, visit my uncle, learn to drive ...

7 Look at the Critical thinking skill box. Then work in pairs. Choose a good option for each list below.

CRITICAL THINKING SKILL
Ordering information

We can order a list many ways. For example:
Option 1: by how important the items are
Option 2: alphabetically, from A–Z
Option 3: using numbers (e.g., dates/how many)

1 to-do list
2 list of important dates
3 vocabulary list
4 shopping list

8 Look at the items from your list in Exercise 4. How important is each item? Change the order of your list.

WRITING TASK

9 **WRITE** Write your own bucket list. Include ten bucket list items. Use Abbey's bucket list as a model.

10 **CHECK** Use the checklist. My list ...

- ☐ has ten things I want to do.
- ☐ begins each line with a verb.
- ☐ uses a new line for each item.
- ☐ is in a useful order.

11 **REVIEW** Work in pairs. Read your partner's bucket list. Do they do the things in the checklist? Do you want to try the things on their bucket list?

Lucia's bucket list is interesting! She wants to paint, dance and act ...

Go to page 156 for the Reflect and review.

EXPLORE MORE!

Search online. What are some popular bucket list items people around the world have? Are your bucket list items popular?

Tex-Mex food is popular in Texas and other parts of the US.

6

Food around the world

GOALS

- Skim a text for general information
- Talk about countable and uncountable things
- Learn about different food items and dishes
- Listen and write notes
- Order food at a restaurant
- Write a simple restaurant review

1 Work in pairs. Does the food in the photo look nice? Why? / Why not?

WATCH

2 ▶ 6.1 Watch the video. Which dish has the ingredients below? Circle V (veggie delight sandwich), R (ratatouille) or both.

NATIONAL GEOGRAPHIC EXPLORERS

MARIA FADIMAN   ALEXIS CHAPPUIS

1 bread	**V**	**R**
2 tomatoes	**V**	**R**
3 onions	**V**	**R**
4 olive oil	**V**	**R**

3 Make connections. Would you like to try the two dishes? Why? / Why not?

I think the veggie delight sandwich is nice. It has avocado.

6A Some like it hot

LESSON GOALS

- Learn about different foods
- Skim a text for general information
- Understand an article about spicy dishes

VOCABULARY

1 Work in pairs. Answer the questions.

1 Do you always have breakfast?
2 Do you usually have lunch at home?
3 What time do you have dinner?

2 6.1 Match the words and the photos. Listen and check.

bread	cheese	coffee	eggs
fish	fruit	meat	milk
noodles	rice	tea	vegetables

1  ____________

2  ____________

3  ____________

4  ____________

5  ____________

6  ____________

7  ____________

8  ____________

9  ____________

10  ____________

11  ____________

12  ____________

3 Work in pairs. Which foods and drinks in Exercise 2 do you:

1 have for breakfast?
2 have for lunch?
3 have for dinner?
4 never have
5 not like

Go to page 162 for the Vocabulary reference.

READING

4 Look at the Reading skill box. Skim the article. What is the article about?

READING SKILL
Skimming a text

Skimming is reading a text quickly to get the main idea. When you skim, don't read every word, but look for important words or information. Skimming helps you know if the information in a text is important or useful.

5 Work in groups. List all the ingredients in the article. Do you know what they are? Use the internet or a dictionary to find out.

6 Read the article. Answer the questions.

1 Where are the three dishes from?
2 Which dish do you eat with bread?
3 Which foods are in all three dishes?

7 Work in pairs. Discuss the questions.

1 Do you think the three dishes look or sound nice?
2 Would you like to try the dishes? Why? / Why not?

I'd like to try berbere curry. I really like curries.
I wouldn't like to try som tam. I think it's very hot!

SPEAKING

8 Work in pairs. Discuss these situations.

1 You go to live in a new country. Which three foods or drinks from your country would you take with you?
2 Three friends come to your house for dinner. What dish would you make them?
3 You take a friend out for a special dinner. Which restaurant would you go to? What country is the food from?

What would I take to another country? Rice, I think.
I always make pizza for my friends. It's easy and we all love it.
My favourite restaurant sells Thai food.

EXPLORE MORE!

What are some other famous spicy dishes from around the world? Search online for 'famous spicy dishes'.

Some like it **HOT**

Chilli. It's hot, and many people don't like it. But in some countries, people love chilli. And doctors say it's good for you! Here are some spicy dishes.

SALSA A LA HUANCAÍNA

The countries in South America have many spicy dishes. *Salsa a la huancaína* is a spicy sauce from Peru. It has hot yellow chillies, onions, salt, garlic, milk and cheese. Sometimes, it has eggs. In Peru, people usually eat it with potatoes.

BERBERE CURRY

Africa also has many spicy dishes. *Berbere* curry is from Ethiopia. It usually has chicken, red meat or fish. It also has onions, garlic, vegetables, salt and the Ethiopian *berbere* spice. The *berbere* spice is full of chilli. It's very hot! People usually eat *berbere* curry with bread.

SOM TAM

In Asia, many people love spicy food. *Som tam* is a spicy salad from Thailand. It's green papaya with salt, garlic, lime, fish sauce, peanuts, sugar and – of course – chillies! Thai people usually put a lot of chilli in their *som tam*.

6B Sweet things

LESSON GOALS
- Understand an article about sugar
- Talk about uncountable nouns
- Practise understanding the word *of*

READING AND GRAMMAR

1 Work in pairs. Look at the photos. Answer the questions.

chocolate

ice cream

cake

biscuits

1 When do you usually eat sweet things?
2 What sweet foods are popular in your country?

2 Read the article quickly. What words have these meanings?

1 tastes good ______________
2 good for your body ______________

3 Read the article. How many teaspoons of sugar are there in:

2 chocolate bars ______________
1 cup of ice cream ______________
3 slices of cake ______________
6 biscuits ______________

4 Work in pairs. Discuss the questions.

1 Do you like eating sweet things?
2 What are some ways to eat less sugar?
3 Is it easy to eat less sugar? Why? / Why not?

Sugar How much is too much?

Sugar is delicious, but too much sugar is not healthy. Doctors tell us to eat less sugar: no more than 6 teaspoons a day for women, or 9 teaspoons for men. But how much sugar is in our food?

Chocolate

A chocolate bar (50 grams) has about 5 teaspoons of sugar.

Ice cream

Half a cup of ice cream (75 grams) has about 4 teaspoons of sugar.

Cake

A slice of cake (70 grams) has about 5 teaspoons of sugar.

Biscuits

You eat 1 teaspoon of sugar when you eat a biscuit.

That's a lot of sugar! But don't worry: it's OK to enjoy a little sugar sometimes. Just think about how much you eat every day.

1 biscuit has about 1 teaspoon of sugar.

5 Read the Grammar box. Do you use *is* or *are* with uncountable nouns?

GRAMMAR Countable and uncountable nouns

Many nouns are countable:
one biscuit / two biscuits
Some nouns are uncountable:
sugar / rice / bread / milk
Uncountable nouns are like singular nouns:
***Sugar is** delicious, but ...*
To use numbers with uncountable nouns, you need other words:
*A slice of cake has **5 teaspoons of sugar**.*

Go to page 171 for the Grammar reference.

6 Work in pairs. Are the words countable or uncountable?

1 teaspoon
2 cake
3 fruit
4 egg
5 sugar
6 biscuit
7 cheese
8 milk

7 Look at the Useful language box. Then complete the sentences.

Useful language talking about uncountable nouns

a little (rice)
some (sugar)
a lot of (bread)

1 He puts ______________ salt in his food. It's not healthy.
2 I don't like spicy food. I only use ______________ chilli when I cook.
3 Please get me ______________ milk from the shop.

8 Work in pairs. Are the sentences correct? Write ✓ or ✗.

1 This dish has a lot of oil in it.
2 Do I cook one rice or two?
3 These three dishes are delicious.
4 Would you like a salt in your food?
5 I usually eat three breads in the morning.

PRONUNCIATION

9 6.2 Look at the Clear voice box. Listen to the examples. Notice how people often say the word *of*.

CLEAR VOICE
Understanding *of*

English speakers often say the word *of* quickly. They say it with the *schwa* sound, /ə/.
*a lot **of** /əv/ salt*   *a teaspoon **of** /əv/ sugar*
Sometimes, they also don't say the /v/ sound of the letter *f*.
*a cup **of** /ə/ ice cream*   *a slice **of** /ə/ cake*

SPEAKING

10 Work in pairs. Think of an easy dish. List the ingredients. Use the internet to help you.

Banana split ingredients:
- ice cream
- banana
- peanuts
- cream
- biscuits

11 Discuss your dish with another pair. Tell them the ingredients. Do they like it? Think of other ingredients to add to each other's dishes.
Our dish is a banana split ice cream. It has ice cream, some peanuts and a banana.

EXPLORE MORE!
What sweet foods do people eat around the world? Find three you would like to try. Search online for 'desserts around the world'.

6C Shops and markets

LESSON GOALS

- Learn about where to buy groceries
- Understand people talking about grocery shopping
- Use *how much* or *how many* to ask questions

VOCABULARY

1 6.3 Work in pairs. Look at the three photos below. Listen and repeat. Then discuss the questions.

1 Which of these places do you or your family like going to?
2 What do you usually buy from these places?

I like the supermarket. It's far, but everything is cheap.

I like the corner shop near my house. It's small, but it has everything I need.

Go to page 162 for the Vocabulary reference

LISTENING

NATIONAL GEOGRAPHIC EXPLORERS

2 6.4 Look at the Listening skill box. Then listen to Maria Fadiman and Alexis Chappuis talking about where they buy things. Complete the notes.

LISTENING SKILL
Writing notes

Sometimes, it helps to write notes as you listen. That way, you don't have to remember everything you hear. Write down the main points. Also, note down other important words and details.

Maria:

- Sometimes buys food at a supermarket.
- Usually buys food at a farmer's market:
- The food is fresh and clean.
- It's [1]______________ and it tastes amazing.
- Buys bread, pasta and nuts from the [2]______________.
- Buys vegetables and fruit from the [3]______________.
    - Loves [4]______________.
    - eats one or two a day.

Alexis:

- Buys groceries at a local market:
    - The food is not from a different [5]______________.
- Alexis is a vegetarian:
    - Doesn't eat [6]______________.
    - But he eats [7]______________.
- Buys eggs, vegetables, fruit and bread.
- Loves French [8]______________.
    - Lives in Indonesia, so he doesn't buy a lot.

3 6.4 Answer the questions. Use the notes on page 76. Then listen again and check your answers.

1 Where does Maria buy bread from?
2 Where does she buy fruit from?
3 How many apples does she eat in a day?

4 Does Alexis eat meat?
5 Does Alexis eat eggs?
6 Why does Alexis not buy a lot of French bread?

GRAMMAR

4 Read the Grammar box. Then complete the sentences. Use *How much* or *How many*.

GRAMMAR *How much* and *how many*

Use *how many* with countable nouns.
How many apples *do you eat in a day?*
I eat ***one apple*** *a day.*
Use *how much* with uncountable nouns.
How much bread *do you buy?*
I don't buy ***a lot of bread.***

Go to page 171 for the Grammar reference.

1 ______________ salt is in this dish?
2 ______________ tomatoes do you want?
3 ______________ pepper would you like?
4 ______________ eggs do you eat in the morning?
5 ______________ chicken do you want me to buy?

5 Read the questions. Circle the correct words.

1 How many *apple / apples* do you want?
2 How much *garlic / garlics* do you use?
3 How much *oil / oils* does she need?
4 How many *biscuits / biscuit* do you want?
5 How many *teaspoon / teaspoons* of sugar are there?

PRONUNCIATION

6 6.5 Look at the Clear voice box. Listen to the examples. Notice the different ways people say words with *h*.

CLEAR VOICE
Understanding the *h* sound

We make the *h* sound by breathing out:
h*ow much* ***h****ow many*
h*e* ***h****er* ***h****im*
Sometimes, people don't say the *h* sound:
(h)ow much *(h)ow many*
(h)e *(h)er* *(h)im*

SPEAKING

7 You invite a friend for lunch. What dish do you make? Make a shopping list.

- Write three countable food items.
- Write three uncountable food items.

8 Work in pairs.

Student A: Ask your partner to help you buy things in your shopping list. Answer your friend's questions.
Student B: Help your partner. Ask your partner how much or many of each item they want. Write a list of things to buy for your partner.

A: I want some apples from the supermarket.
B: Sure. How many apples do you want?
A: I'd like three apples, please. And some milk too.
B: How much milk do you want?
A: Hmm ….

6D Ordering food

LESSON GOALS
- Learn how to order food at a restaurant
- Learn expressions to use with a waiter
- Practise ordering food for you and a friend

SPEAKING

1 Work in pairs. Discuss the questions.

1 Do you like to eat at cafés and restaurants?
2 What are your favourite cafés and restaurants?
3 What do you usually order?

Sometimes, I go to the Mexican restaurant near my house. The tacos are great, and the enchiladas are amazing!

MY VOICE ▶

2 ▶ 6.2 Watch the video about ordering food. Answer the questions.

1 What should you not do when trying to get a waiter's attention?
2 What are some polite ways to call a waiter?
3 What is a polite expression you can use to order a dish from a waiter?

3 Look at the Communication skill box. Complete the conversation. Use words from the box.

COMMUNICATION SKILL
Ordering food

When you order food at a restaurant:
- begin with a greeting
  Hello. / Hi. / Good evening. / How are you?
- use polite words and phrases
  I'd like the … please. Thank you!

If you need to get someone's attention:
- raise your hand
- say *Excuse me*

Customer: [1] ______________ me …
Waiter: Hi. How can I help you?
Customer: [2] ______________. How are you? Can I have the chicken noodles, [3] ______________?
Waiter: Of course. Would you like anything to drink?
Customer: Just some water, [4] ______________.

4 Look at the Useful language box. Then work in pairs. Ask and answer the four questions from a waiter at a restaurant. Take turns.

Useful language Ordering food

Waiters:
How can I help you?
Are you ready to order?
Would you like ... ?
Is that all?

Customers:
Excuse me.
I'd like …
Yes, please.
No thanks. / No, thank you.
That's all, thanks.

1 Good afternoon. How can I help you?
Hello. I'd like a black coffee, please.
2 Good evening! Are you ready to order?
3 Would you like to try today's special?
4 Is that all?

SPEAKING

5 Look at the menu above. Choose three dishes.

Dish 1 ______________________________

Dish 2 ______________________________

Dish 3 ______________________________

6 Work in groups of three or four. One of you is a waiter. The rest are customers. Take turns.

Customers: Order your three dishes from the waiter. Follow the tips in the Communication skill box. Ask about one dish you don't know.

Waiter: You're busy. The customers must get your attention. Ask the customers what they'd like and ask them follow-up questions.

A: Excuse me. Excuse me!
B: Ah, good evening! Would you like to order?
A: Hello. Yes, please. Can I have a cheeseburger?
B: Yes, of course. Would you like anything else?
A: Yes. I'd like fresh fruit and …

EXPLORE MORE!

Menus often have different sections. What are *appetisers, main courses* and *desserts*? Search online for these words.

6E Restaurant reviews

LESSON GOALS
- Learn how to begin paragraphs
- Use positive and negative adjectives
- Write a simple restaurant review

SPEAKING

1 Work in pairs. Look at the review below. Why do people sometimes read restaurant reviews?

I don't read restaurant reviews, but my brother does. He wants to know if the food is good.

2 When you eat out, what is important to you? Write V (very important), I (important) or N (not very important).

price: is it expensive?

taste: is it delicious?

location: is it in a nice place?

service: are the waiters fast and friendly?

READING FOR WRITING

3 Read the review quickly. How does the author feel?

1 She *likes / doesn't like* the food.
2 She *likes / doesn't like* the restaurant.

4 Read the review again. Work in pairs. Answer the questions.

1 What ingredients are in the chilli?
2 Does the writer think the food is expensive?
3 Does the writer like the location?
4 What does the writer think about the service?

HOME ABOUT RESTAURANTS CONTACT

HUP CHOY'S RESTAURANT: Chicken rice

★★★★☆ 28 April | Singapore | #review

Melissa P.
food reviewer
★★★★☆

Chicken rice is a popular dish in Asia, but Hup Choy's chicken rice is really popular. Here's what I think.

Taste It tastes great! The rice is really good. The chicken is delicious too. The chilli is interesting. It has garlic, salt and sugar.

Price The price is OK. It's $8 a plate. That's a lot for chicken rice, but the food is good and the meals are big.

Location The location is good. It's far from the city centre, but it's in a nice park.

Service The service is OK. The people there are nice. But service is slow. There are a lot of customers.

Many restaurants sell chicken rice, but Hup Choy's Restaurant is special. It's a great restaurant, and their chicken rice is amazing. Try it!

Details

DISHES
chicken rice
chicken noodles
chicken soup

SIDES
tofu, vegetables

FEATURES
wheelchair access
takes reservations
parking available

OPEN FROM
11 a.m. to 9 p.m.

5 Look at the Writing skill box. What is the main idea for each paragraph in the review?

WRITING SKILL

Writing main ideas

Begin each paragraph with a main idea. Then explain your main idea.
Main idea: *It tastes great!*
Explain: *The rice is really good …*
This makes it easy for readers to see what's important.

6 Look at the Useful language box. Work in groups. Think of some things you feel are good, bad and OK.

Useful language Good, bad and OK feedback

good	**OK**	**bad**
great	alright	poor
delicious	average	terrible
amazing	fine	horrible
excellent	not bad	awful

7 Complete the restaurant review below. Use words from the Useful language box.

ALFREDO'S ITALIAN CAFÉ ★★★☆☆

There's a new Italian restaurant in town. But is it good?

Taste:

Their pasta tastes 1_______________. The sauce is 2_______________. I only taste salt.

Price:

The price is 3_______________. It's not expensive, but it's also not cheap.

Location:

The location is 4_______________. It's near the beach. I like it.

Service:

The service is 5_______________. The people are really nice.

Alfredo's sells 6_______________ pasta, but the location is 7_______________. The service is 8_______________ too. Go there for drinks, not food!

8 Look at the Critical thinking skill box. Then look for 4 to 5 adjectives in the review on page 80. Are the adjectives positive or negative?

CRITICAL THINKING

Understanding how the author feels

Adjectives – like *good*, *bad* or *OK* – say a lot. Are they positive or negative? Adjectives help us understand how the author feels.

WRITING TASK

9 Think of a restaurant you know, or imagine a restaurant. Then think of a dish. Write notes about taste, price, location and service.

Tere's Tapas

Dish: *patatas bravas*

Taste: *Good. Spicy.*

Price: *Expensive.*

Location: *OK. It's in a park.*

Service: *Fast and friendly.*

10 **WRITE** Write a short restaurant review. Use your notes in Exercise 9 and the review on page 80 as a model.

- Write an introduction: one or two sentences about the food and the restaurant.
- Write your review: begin each paragraph with a main idea.
- End with a conclusion: say how you feel about the food and the restaurant.
- Add a star rating.

11 **CHECK** Use the checklist. My review …

☐ begins with an introduction.
☐ begins each paragraph with a main idea.
☐ explains the main idea in each paragraph.
☐ ends with a conclusion.
☐ includes a star rating.

12 **REVIEW** Work in pairs. Read your partner's review. Do they do the things in the checklist? Is how they feel clear? Do you want to go to their restaurant?

Go to page 156 for the Reflect and review.

A family camping together at Lake Dukan, Iraq.

7

Family and friends

GOALS

- Understand the purpose of a text
- Ask questions with the present simple
- Talk about people in your family
- Listen to descriptions of people
- Show appreciation
- Write a text message asking for help

1 Work in pairs. Discuss the questions.

1 Look at the photo. How many family members can you see?
2 Is this family big or small?

WATCH

2 ▶ 7.1 Watch the video. Are the sentences true (T) of false (F)?

NATIONAL GEOGRAPHIC EXPLORERS

ELLIE DE CASTRO

LIA NAHOMI KAJIKI

1 Ellie lives with her mum and dad.
2 Ellie's sister has three children.
3 Lia has two sisters.
4 Lia and her sisters live in the same city.

3 Make connections. Work in pairs. Which family is more like yours? Why?

My family is like Ellie's family. I don't have a sister, but I have one brother. He has two children too.

7A My family

LESSON GOALS
- Talk about people in your family
- Understand the writer's purpose
- Understand an article about families around the world

VOCABULARY

1 Work in pairs. Answer the questions.
1 Do you have a big or small family?
2 How many people live in your house?

2 7.1 Listen to and repeat the family words. Then write F (female) or M (male) for each word.

1 son	daughter
2 mother	father
3 grandfather	grandmother
4 brother	sister
5 wife	husband

3 Look at the family tree. Circle the correct answers.
1 Lana and Tim are Mitra's *parents / children*.
2 Sam is Mel's *father / mother*.
3 Joy is Mitra's *daughter / son*.
4 Julian is Joy's *brother / sister*.
5 Mel is Mitra's *wife / husband*.
6 Pete is Jared's *grandmother / grandfather*.

Go to page 163 for the Vocabulary reference.

READING

4 Look at the Reading skill box. Then read the article quickly. What is the purpose of the article? Circle the answer below (a or b).

READING SKILL
Understanding purpose

Writers write articles for different reasons. The reason is the purpose. For example:
1 to describe something (e.g., a magazine article describing a city)
2 to teach people how to do something (e.g., a book explaining how to cook Thai food)
3 to give an opinion (e.g., an article about why someone likes their big family)

a to describe families around the world
b to show us that big families are better

5 Read the article. Complete each sentence with one word from the article.
1 In parts of Africa, the Middle East and Asia, families are often ______________.
2 In Europe and the US, families are often ______________.
3 In places with big families, children often look after their ______________ when they get old.
4 In places with big families, grandparents often look after their ______________.

6 Work in pairs. Look at the graph and discuss.
1 Which countries have more than three family members living together?
2 Which country is your family like?

SPEAKING

7 Work in pairs. Turn to page 179. Read the information and draw a family tree.
A: Who's Michael's sister?
B: His sister is …

8 Work in pairs. Draw your family tree. Explain it to your partner.
This is my family. I have one brother and …

A family from Belo Horizonte, Brazil.

FAMILIES AROUND THE WORLD

How big is your family? Are other families in your country like your family? What about families in other countries?

In some parts of Africa, the Middle East and Asia, families are often big: many family members live together in one home. In Europe, the US and other parts of Asia, families are often small: only a few family members live together.

Why are these places different? One reason is the number of children. But this is not the biggest reason. In places with small families, parents and children live together, but not grandparents. In places with big families, children, parents and grandparents all live together. Children often help look after their parents when they get old, and grandparents help look after their grandchildren.

NUMBER OF FAMILY MEMBERS PER HOME

EXPLORE MORE!

How big are families in your country? Search online for 'family size + [your country]'. Is your family big or small for your country?

7B Happy families

LESSON GOALS

- Understand an interview about happy families
- Ask different types of questions
- Practise long and short vowel sounds

LISTENING AND GRAMMAR

1 Work in pairs. Look at the infographic. Tick (✔) the three things you think are the most important for a happy family.

2 7.2 Listen to a family expert. Tick (✔) the three things she says are important below. Are your answers in Exercise 1 the same?

Happy families ...

a eat together	e play games together
b have fun together	f celebrate special events
c help each other	g talk to each other
d travel together	h know their family history

3 Read the Grammar box. Do you use *wh-* question words like *what* or *where* in yes/no questions?

GRAMMAR Present simple questions (yes/no questions)

Questions with *be:*

***Is** your family small?*	***Yes**, it **is**. / **No**, it **isn't**.*

Questions with *do / does*:

***Do** you **eat** at home?*	***Yes**, I **do**. / **No**, I **don't***
***Does** she **talk** a lot?*	***Yes**, she **does**. / **No**, she **doesn't**.*

Go to page 171 for the Grammar reference.

4 Complete the yes/no questions with *are, is, do* or *does*.

1 ______________ he have a grandmother?
2 ______________ your grandfather's name Tomas?
3 ______________ your sisters at university?
4 ______________ they have a big family?
5 ______________ your parents at the party?

5 Read the Grammar box. Which question word asks for a reason?

GRAMMAR Present simple questions (open questions)

Open questions can have many answers. To ask open questions, use question word + *be / do / does* + subject

What'*s number two?*
Who *are their grandparents?*
When *do you eat together?*
Where *are they from?*
Why *is it important?*
How *do I do that?*

Go to page 172 for the Grammar reference.

6 Complete the questions with question words.

1 ___*Where*___ do you study?
I study in New York.
2 ______________ do you like summer?
Because it's hot!
3 ______________ is the next class?
It's at 2:15.
4 ______________'s your friend's name?
Her name's Badria.
5 ______________ do you play tennis with?
I play with my brother Dimitri.
6 ______________ do you spell your name?
It's Z-E-H-R-A.

7 Put the words in order to make present simple questions.

1 they / are / friends / your / ?
2 football / your / does / like / sister / ?
3 science teacher / your / is / who / ?
4 your / what / father's / is / name / ?
5 do / how / get / you / school / to / ?

PRONUNCIATION

8 7.3 Look at the Clear voice box. Listen and repeat.

CLEAR VOICE
Saying short and long vowel sounds

There are five vowels in the English alphabet:
a, e, i, o, u
In English, vowels can have different sounds. Here are some words with short and long vowel sounds.

Short vowel sounds	Long vowel sounds
family	*name*
red	*these*
sister	*wife*
hot	*home*
husband	*usually*

9 7.4 Write long vowel (L) or short vowel (S) for each word. Listen, check and repeat.

1 hand	same
2 evening	bed
3 fish	life
4 long	phone
5 excuse	run

SPEAKING

10 Look at the infographic again. Plan an activity for your family or friends. Think about the following and make notes.

1 Who would you like to invite?
2 Where is a good place for it?
3 What are the details of your plan?

11 Work in pairs. Ask and answer questions about your activities in Exercise 10. Use *wh-* questions and *how*. Do you like your partner's activity? Why? / Why not?

A: My activity is a big family meal.
B: Good idea. Who's the cook?
A: Everyone!

7C She's tall and she's funny

LESSON GOALS

- Talk about appearance and personality
- Understand people describing their best friends
- Use adjectives to describe people and things

VOCABULARY

1 Work in pairs. Look at the photos. How are the two people different?

A: Their hair colours are different.

B: She looks tall. He doesn't look tall.

A: Yeah. He's short.

2 7.5 Listen to what the people look like. Circle the correct answers.

1 Jessica is *tall* / *short*.
2 Her hair is *long* / *short* and *blonde* / *dark*.
3 Antonio is *tall* / *short*.
4 His hair is *long* / *short* and *blonde* / *dark*.

3 7.6 Match the words and sentences. Listen to check.

clever funny interesting nice quiet

1 Antonio often makes me laugh.
2 Jessica does very well at school.
3 Antonio is kind and easy to talk to.
4 Jessica has a lot of ideas. She's never boring.
5 Sometimes, Antonio doesn't talk much.

Go to page 163 for the Vocabulary reference.

LISTENING

NATIONAL GEOGRAPHIC EXPLORERS

4 7.7 Listen to Ellie de Castro and Lia Nahomi Kajiki. What words do they use to describe their best friends, Mittsu and Miriam?

	Mittsu	Miriam
hair		
eyes		
height		
personality		

Ellie de Castro (left) and her best friend Mittsu.

Lia Nahomi Kajiki (right) and her sister Miriam.

5 Work in groups. Look at the Listening skill box. Then describe a person in your group to your partners. Don't say who it is. Your partners guess the person.

LISTENING SKILL
Listening to descriptions

When you hear a description of a person, imagine what they look like.

1 Pay attention to words that describe them.
2 Think about what they look like. Do they look like someone you know?

6 Read the Grammar box. Do adjectives have plural forms?

GRAMMAR *Adjectives*

Adjectives describe nouns.
You can use adjectives after *be*.
She ***is clever***. *Her eyes* ***are blue***.
You can also use adjectives before a noun.
She is a ***clever person***. *She has* ***blue eyes***.

Go to page 172 for the Grammar reference.

7 Correct one mistake in each sentence.

1 Her eyes is blue.
2 My father tall.
3 I like people friendly.
4 Are they tall or shorts?

8 Rewrite the sentences.

1 She has brown hair.
Her *hair is brown* ______.
2 Maya's dress is beautiful.
Maya has ______.
3 They live in a very big house.
Their ______.
4 My teachers are really nice.
I have ______.

SPEAKING

9 Work in pairs. Look at the photo.
Student A: Describe one person. Don't say who it is.
- What do they look like?
- What do you think their personality is like?

Student B: Listen and guess. Which person is it?
She has a blue shirt. I think she's very friendly!

10 Work in pairs. Choose a person you both know. Think of different ways to describe them.
A: Well, Rami is Egyptian. He's about twenty or twenty-one …
B: Yes, and he has blue eyes. I like him because …

EXPLORE MORE!
What eye colours are common in your country? What eye colours are common around the world? Search online using the words 'common eye colours in [country]'.

7D Showing appreciation

LESSON GOALS

- Learn how to show appreciation
- Say words with the *gr* sound
- Practise showing appreciation

People clapping for a band in Barcelona, Spain

SPEAKING AND LISTENING.

1 Work in pairs. Discuss the questions.

1 How do you feel when people help you?

2 What do you say when people help you?

2 7.8 Listen to two conversations between people at work. Do you think Cindy is friendly? What about Pei Ling? Why?

MY VOICE

3 7.2 Watch the video. What is *showing appreciation*?

a asking someone how they did something

b telling someone you're happy with their work

c telling someone their work is OK

4 Look at the Communication skill box. Which tip do you think is the most important?

COMMUNICATION SKILL
Showing appreciation

When people you work with do a great job, show appreciation.

1 Tell them 'great work'.

2 Explain why you are happy.

3 Say 'thank you'.

5 Work in pairs. Do you always have to follow all three tips in the Communication skill box? Think about these situations. What do you do?

1 Someone holds a door open for you.

2 A family member cooks you an amazing meal.

3 A friend plans the perfect holiday for you.

6 Look at the Useful language box. Work in pairs. Which expressions explain why you're happy with someone's work?

Useful language Showing appreciation

Great work!
Good job!
This is great.
It's perfect.
Everyone loves it.
They're really happy.
It looks amazing.
Thank you very much.

7 Work in pairs. Complete the conversation with expressions from the Useful language box.

Tish: Hey, Jonah. I have your photographs. Great [1]_______________!

Jonah: Oh, wow. Really?

Tish: Yes, of course. They look [2]_______________.

Jonah: Thanks, Tish. I'm glad you like them.

Tish: It's not just me. Everyone [3]_______________ them! We're all really [4]_______________.

Jonah: That's great. I'm so glad to hear that.

Tish: They're [5]_______________. Thank you [6]_______________!

8 Work in pairs. Practise the conversation in Exercise 7.

PRONUNCIATION

9 7.9 Look at the Clear voice box. Listen and repeat.

CLEAR VOICE
Saying words with *gr*

Words with *gr* can be difficult to say.
***Gr**eat work!*
Some words begin with *gr*:
***gr**een*
***gr**am*
***gr**andmother*
Some words have *gr* in the middle:
*a**gr**ee*
*hun**gr**y*
*photo**gr**aph*

SPEAKING

10 **OWN IT!** Work in pairs. Act out situations A–C.
Student A: Choose one situation. Help Student B, or do something nice for them.
Student B: Show your appreciation to Student A. Follow the tips in the Communication skill box and use the expressions in the Useful language box.
A: Hey, are you hungry? Here's some food ...
B: Oh, wow. Thank you very much. It looks great!

11 Work in groups of four. Watch another pair act out a situation. Give feedback. Did they do a good job?
Wow! Great job, you two! That was amazing!

A: You are at your office. Your partner is very busy. You give them an important report they need for a meeting tomorrow.

B: You're back from a holiday. You have a present for your friend. It's something your friend really wants. You give it to them.

C: You're working on a school project with your friend. You're both hungry. You go to a café, and come back with some delicious sandwiches.

EXPLORE MORE!
What are some other ways to show appreciation? Search online for 'good ways to show appreciation'.

7E My friend is in town

LESSON GOALS
- Use reasons to explain things
- Learn new ways to describe people
- Write a message asking a friend for help

SPEAKING

1 Work in pairs. Discuss the questions.

1 Do you and your friends have similar personalities?
2 Do your friends enjoy the things you enjoy?
3 Do you like spending time with people who aren't like you? Why? / Why not?

READING FOR WRITING

2 Read the text messages. Then look at the people in the photo above. Which one is Hiroto?

3 Look at the Writing skill box. Answer the questions.

WRITING SKILL
Explaining your reasons

When you want someone to help you, it helps to explain ...
- what you want them to do.
- why they are right for the job.
- why they will enjoy it.

1 What does Niko want Emre to do?
2 Why is Emre the right person for this?
3 Do you think Emre will enjoy helping Niko?

Niko

Hi Emre. Are you free on Saturday? My good friend Hiroto is in Istanbul. It's his first time here. I can't be there with him, so I need someone to show him the city. I think you're perfect! Hiroto is really friendly and interesting, like you. And you both love music. Here's a photo. He's on the right – the tall guy in the yellow T-shirt, with the guitar.

Emre

Hey Niko. No problem! I'm free. What does he want to do? Does he want to see the Grand Bazaar? Or Topkapi Palace?

Niko

Thanks very much, Emre! Yes, he wants to see both those places. He also wants to meet other musicians. He's really excited – he knows you play the guitar! He plays the drums, and the piano too. Do you know any musicians in Istanbul?

4 Look at the Useful language box. What words can you use to make adjectives stronger?

Useful language Describing people

Appearance
She's (tall).
He has (brown eyes / short hair).

Personality
He's really (nice).
She's very (interesting).

Other information
He's old / young / (nineteen) years old.
She's from (Portugal).
He's a (university student).
She looks like (your friend Maya).

5 Complete the description with words from the Useful language box.

My brother's name is Leon. He's [1]________ Germany, like me. He's twenty years [2]________. He [3]________ long hair and grey eyes. He looks [4]________ my father. He's a [5]________ student. He's [6]________ clever.

6 Look at the Critical thinking skill box. Then read about the two people. What do they have in common? What's different? Complete the Venn diagram on the right.

CRITICAL THINKING SKILL
Finding things in common

You're with someone new, and you need something to talk about. Find out what you have in common. Do you both like books, sports or music? Or are you from the same country or city? It's easier to talk to people when you have things in common with them.

Hussam is Emirati. He isn't tall. He has brown hair and brown eyes. He's 24 years old. He likes sports, reading and watching films. He loves food. He's friendly and very funny.

Malik is also 24 years old. He's French. He has black hair and grey eyes. He's tall. He's friendly and he's very clever. He likes books, films, music and art.

7 Work in pairs. Look at your Venn diagrams. Are Malik and Hussam similar or different?

WRITING TASK

8 Make notes. A family member is in town. You're busy. You want your friend to show your family member your town. Think of the following:

1 What is your family member's personality like?
2 What does your family member look like?
3 What do your friend and family member have in common?
4 Why will your friend enjoy helping you?

9 **WRITE** Write a text message to your friend. Ask for help. Use your notes in Exercise 8 to help you, and Niko's text message as a model.

10 **CHECK** Use the checklist. My text message …

- [ ] says what I need help with.
- [ ] describes my friend clearly.
- [ ] lists a few things in common.
- [ ] says why my friend will enjoy it.

11 **REVIEW** Work in pairs. Read your partner's text message. Do they do the things in the checklist? Write a short reply to your partner's text message.

Go to page 157 for the Reflect and review.

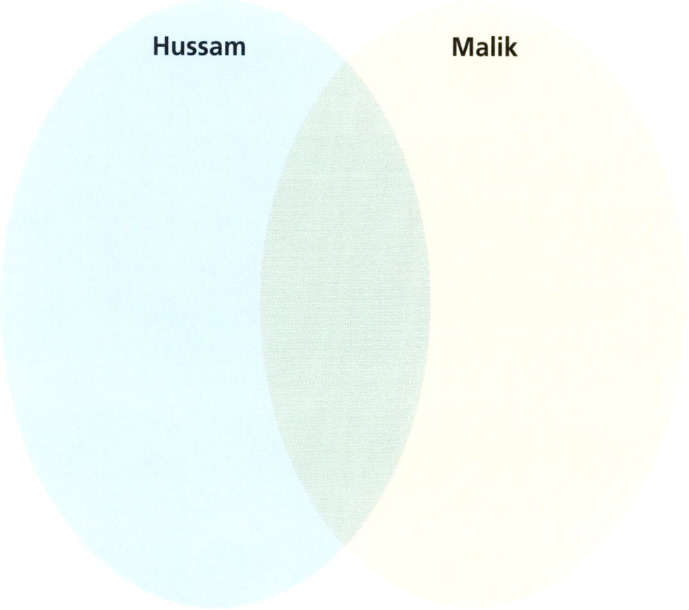

Mike Coots is a surfer and an underwater photographer.

8

Things we can do

GOALS

- Understand pronouns
- Talk about things people can do
- Learn common adjectives
- Listen for general information
- Ask others for help
- Write a job application

1 Work in pairs. Discuss the questions.

1 Look at the photo. What can the person do?
2 Can you do what the person is doing?
3 Would you like to learn how to do it? Why? / Why not?

WATCH

2 ▶ 8.1 Watch the video. Tick (✓) the things Anusha says she can do.

NATIONAL GEOGRAPHIC EXPLORER

ANUSHA SHANKAR

a speak Spanish
b sing
c paint
d fly a plane
e salsa dance
f play an instrument
g make bread
h ride a horse

3 Make connections. What things in Exercise 2 can you do? What other interesting things can you do? Tell a partner.

I can speak Japanese, Korean and French.

I can drive.

8A Yes, you can!

LESSON GOALS
- Talk about activities and abilities
- Understand an article about virtual reality
- Understand pronouns

VOCABULARY

1 Work in pairs. What are some things you would like to learn?

I would like to learn how to drive.

I want to learn how to paint.

2 8.1 Work in pairs. Match the verbs (1–8) to the nouns (a–h). Listen and check.

1 drive	a a picture
2 ride	b a car
3 paint	c a mountain
4 climb	d a bike
5 bake	e a meal
6 play	f a musical instrument
7 cook	g a language
8 speak	h a cake

3 Work in pairs. Discuss the activities in Exercise 2.

1 Which do you know how to do?
2 Which do you not do? Why?

I know how to drive a car, ride a bike and ...

I don't bake. I don't know how.

Go to page 163 for the Vocabulary reference.

READING

4 Work in pairs. Look at the photographs and read the article quickly. Discuss the questions.

1 What do you see in the photos?
2 Do you think virtual reality (VR) is fun? Why? / Why not?

5 Find the bold words below in the article. What do they mean? Match the parts to complete the sentences.

1 An **app** is something you ...
2 **Astronauts** are people who ...
3 If you do something **in real life**, you don't ...

a do it online or in VR.
b travel to and work in space (e.g. the moon).
c use on your computer or smartphone.

6 Read the text again. What can you do with VR? Tick (✓) the activities in the article.

a fly a plane	g drive a racing car
b play video games	h play football
c climb a mountain	i go for a run
d chat to friends	j listen to music
e watch a film	k ride a bike
f learn things	l visit a museum

7 Look at the Reading skill box. Then look for the pronouns *they* and *it* in the article. What do the two pronouns refer to?

READING SKILL
Understanding pronouns

Usually, writers don't like using the same noun again and again. Pronouns help writers talk about things without repeating the noun many times. For example, these two sentences mean the same thing:

Young people love VR. ***Young people*** *use* ***VR*** *to play video games.*

Young people love VR. ***They*** *use* ***it*** *to play video games.*

They = Young people, and *it* = VR.

1 The word *they* refers to ______________.
2 The word *it* refers to ______________.

SPEAKING

8 Work in pairs. Design your own VR game or app. Answer the questions.

What can you do?
Where can you go?
What can you see?
What can't you do?

9 Work in groups. Discuss your VR ideas. Which ideas do you like?

With my VR app, you can swim in the ocean and ...

With my VR app, you can go to space and ...

EXPLORE MORE!

How can VR help in people's jobs? Search for 'jobs that use VR'.

A person wearing a virtual reality headset.

VIRTUAL REALITY

Can you fly a plane or drive a racing car? Yes, you can – with virtual reality (VR)! All you need is a headset, and you're ready to go!

Use VR to ride a bike in a different city, climb a really tall mountain or visit an art museum in a different country – and you don't even need to leave your living room.

Today, VR is very popular. The headsets aren't cheap, but there are lots of games and apps, and **they**'re great fun.

People usually use VR to play video games, travel to new places or try new things. But VR is great for teaching too. Pilots use **it** to learn to fly. Driving schools use it to teach their students. And NASA uses it to train astronauts.

VR is fun, but it's also very useful. It's a great way for us to try all the things we can't do in real life.

8B They can do amazing things!

LESSON GOALS

- Understand people talking about amazing abilities
- Use *can* and *can't* for ability
- Say *can* and *can't*

Courtney Dauwalter is a famous ultra-runner from the US.

SPEAKING

1 Work in pairs. Discuss the questions.

1 Do you know anyone who is very good at something?
2 What are you very good at?
3 What would you like to be very good at?

Jin Young Ko is really good at golf.

I'm very good at playing …

2 Look at the photo and the caption. What is the person very good at?

LISTENING AND GRAMMAR

3 8.2 Listen. Match the people (1–4) to what they can do (a–d).

1 Naofumi Ogasawara
2 Rebecca Sharrock
3 Krishnan Kumar
4 Courtney Dauwalter

a can do difficult maths without a calculator.
b can stand on his head for three hours.
c can remember every day of her life.
d can run very long distances.

4 Discuss in pairs. Would you like any of their abilities? Why? / Why not?

5 Read the Grammar box. Complete the two statements below with *can* or *can't*.

GRAMMAR *Can* and *can't*

Abilities are things people are good at or know how to do. Use *can* or *can't* to talk about abilities.
*He **can** stand on his head for three hours.*
*She **can't** forget the things she sees.*
***Can** you remember your first birthday?*
*Yes, I **can**. / No, I **can't**.*

Go to page 172 for the Grammar reference.

1 Use ______________ to talk about something you're good at or know how to do.
2 Use ______________ to talk about something you're not good at or don't know how to do.

6 Look at the pictures. Write *can* or *can't*.

1 She ______________ drive.

2 He ______________ cook.

3 She ______________ snowboard.

4 He ______________ play the guitar.

7 Complete the sentences with *can* or *can't*.

1 I don't want to go to the swimming pool. I ______________ swim.
2 I'm very bad at yoga. I ______________ touch my toes.
3 He ______________ play the guitar but not the piano.
4 She ______________ cook amazing dishes. Her food is delicious!
5 He says he ______________ dance, but he ______________. He's a great dancer.

8 Put the words in the correct order to make questions. Then work in pairs. Ask and answer the questions.

1 you / speak / English / can / ?
2 you / can / sing / ?
3 play / can / you / tennis / ?
4 can / friend / best / your / paint / ?
5 speak / your / can / teacher / French / ?

PRONUNCIATION AND SPEAKING

9 8.3 Look at the Clear voice box. Listen and repeat.

CLEAR VOICE
Stressing *can't*

People usually say *can* quickly. It's not stressed.
*I **can** swim. I **can** drive.*
People usually stress the word *can't*.
*I **can't** snowboard. I **can't** play the guitar.*

10 8.4 Listen to the sentences. Write *can* or *can't*. Then listen again and repeat.

1 I ______________ swim two kilometres.
2 She ______________ stand on her head.
3 They ______________ drive.

11 Work in pairs. What are some things your partner can and can't do? Write ten questions.
Can you touch your toes?

12 Work in pairs. Ask and answer your questions in Exercise 11.

EXPLORE MORE!

Look for videos or more information about the people in Exercise 3. Search online for their names and the things they can do. For example, 'Krishnan Kumar + headstand'.

8C They're small, but they're fast

LESSON GOALS
- Learn adjectives to describe animals
- Understand a talk about hummingbirds
- Join ideas using conjunctions

VOCABULARY

1 Work in pairs. What are your favourite animals? What do you like about them?

2 8.5 Listen and repeat the words. Then work in pairs. Look at the photos and choose three adjectives for each animal.

beautiful	fast	heavy	large
light	slow	small	strong

3 Work in small groups. What other animals can you describe with the adjectives in Exercise 2?

Cats are small and fast.

Cows are large.

Bears are strong!

Go to page 163 for the Vocabulary reference.

LISTENING

NATIONAL GEOGRAPHIC EXPLORER

4 8.6 Look at the Listening skill box. Then listen to Anusha Shankar talking about hummingbirds. Answer the questions.

LISTENING SKILL
Listening for general information

When listening, it's important to hear the main points, or general information. Don't only listen to the small details. Listen for the big ideas too. Write down these big ideas while you listen.

1 Where do hummingbirds live?
2 Are they light or heavy?
3 Are they fast or slow?
4 What can hummingbirds do that other birds can't?
5 Where do they get their food?

5 Work in pairs. Tell your partner some general information about hummingbirds. Use your answers in Exercise 4 to help you.

6 8.6 Listen again. Answer the questions.

1 How big are small hummingbirds?
2 How heavy are large hummingbirds?
3 How fast can hummingbirds fly?

GRAMMAR

7 Read the Grammar box. Which word gives a reason?

GRAMMAR *And, or, but, because*

Use *because* to give reasons:
Everyone loves hummingbirds ***because*** *they're beautiful.*
Use *and* to give extra information:
There are 330 types of hummingbirds, ***and*** *they are many different colours.*
Use *but* to join ideas that are different:
Hummingbirds are tiny, ***but*** *they're really fast.*
Use *or* to join different choices:
They can fly backwards ***or*** *stay in the same place when they fly.*

Go to page 173 for the Grammar reference.

8 Complete the statements and question with *and, or, but* or *because.*

1 I think trees, flowers, birds ______ animals are very interesting.
2 The bear is small, ______ it's very strong.
3 Is that your phone ______ is it Andrew's?
4 I like Jessie ______ she's clever and funny.

PRONUNCIATION

9 8.7 Look at the Clear voice box. Listen and repeat. Which *g* sounds like the letter *j* in words like *jump* or *job*?

CLEAR VOICE
Saying the letter *g*

The letter *g* sounds different in different words.

/g/ *bi**g**, do**g**, **g**arden*
/dʒ/ *lar**ge**, messa**ge**, pa**ge***
/ŋ/ *hummi**ng**bird, si**ng**, interesti**ng***

SPEAKING

10 Complete the table. Think of four adjectives. Write two nouns for each adjective.

Adjectives	Word 1	Word 2
beautiful	*birds*	*cheetahs*

11 Work in pairs. Talk about the things in your table. Use *and, or, but* and *because*.
I like birds because they are beautiful.
Cheetahs are beautiful, and they're really fast too.

EXPLORE MORE!
Look for videos of hummingbirds flying, eating or singing. Search for 'hummingbirds + video'.

8D Asking for help

LESSON GOALS

- Learn how to ask people for help
- Respond to people asking for help
- Practise asking for and offering help

SPEAKING

1 Work in pairs. Answer the questions.

1 Why do people sometimes ask others for help?
2 Why do people sometimes not ask for help?
3 What do you do or say when someone helps you?

People ask for help because they are busy, or because they can't do something.

Sometimes, they don't ask for help because ...

When someone helps me, I say ...

MY VOICE ▶

2 ▶ 8.2 Work in pairs. Answer the questions. Then watch the video to check your answers.

1 When do people say *please*?
2 When do people say *thank you*?

3 ▶ 8.2 Watch again. Work in pairs and answer the questions.

1 Why do some people not ask for help?
2 What's another way of asking 'Can you help me?'
3 Why do people say 'Excuse me' when asking for help?

4 Work in pairs. Look at the Communication skill box. Then read situations A–D below. Who would you ask for help in each situation? Why?

COMMUNICATION SKILL
Asking for help

When something is difficult, it's good to ask for help. Help can make a difficult job easy to do. When asking for help, remember to ...

- ask the right person.
- be nice.
- say thank you.

Your phone or computer is broken.

You need help with your English homework.

5 Look at the Useful language box. Then answer the questions below.

Useful language Asking for and offering help

Excuse me.
Can you help me (please)?
Can you give me a hand (please)?
No problem. / Sure. / Of course.
How can I help?
Sorry. I can't / don't know how.
Why don't you ask (Pete)?
Can I help you with that?
Do you need a hand?

Which phrase or phrases do you use when ...

1 you need help.
2 you can help someone.
3 you can't help someone.
4 you think someone else can help.
5 you see someone who needs help.

6 Complete the conversation. Use expressions from the Useful language box.

Alex: Hi Jo. Can you give me a [1]____________ please?
Jo: Sure. How can I [2]____________?
Alex: My bike is broken. Can you help me fix it?
Jo: Oh, I'm sorry. I don't know [3]____________. [4]____________ don't you ask Silvia?
Alex: Thanks, Jo. Silvia, can you [5]____________ me?
Silvia: Of [6]____________. I'm good with bikes.

SPEAKING

7 **OWN IT!** Make notes. List some things you want help with.

8 Work in groups. Look at your problems in Exercise 7. Ask your partners for help.

A: Can you help me? My band needs a singer.
B: Sorry, I can't. I'm terrible at music! Why don't you ask Caleb?

C

You don't know what to wear to a party.

D

You feel a bit sad. You need a friend to talk to.

8E I can do that job!

LESSON GOALS
- Learn what to say in a job application
- Understand what skills are important for a job
- Write a simple job application

SPEAKING

1 Work in pairs. Answer the questions.

1 What jobs do you think are interesting? Why?
2 What skills do you need for these jobs?

READING FOR WRITING

2 Work in pairs. Read the advertisement.

1 What kind of advertisement is it?
2 Who posted the advertisement?

3 Read the two job applications on page 105. Tick (✓) the things they can do.

	Jun Ming	Eliza
Can they drive?		
Can they cook?		
Can they clean?		
Can they talk to guests?		
Can they work in a team?		
Can they write good emails?		
Are they good with computers?		
Can they speak different languages?		

4 Discuss in pairs. Look at your tables in Exercise 3.

1 Are Jun Ming and Eliza similar or different?
2 What jobs do you think are right for them? Why?

5 Look at the Writing skill box. Do Jun Ming and Eliza follow these tips?

WRITING SKILL
Applying for a job

When you apply for jobs, follow these tips:
1 Say why you want the job.
2 Say what you can do.
3 Don't say what you can't do.
4 Say what you are like as a person.

6 Look at the Useful language box. Which expressions do Jun Ming and Eliza use?

Useful language Job application forms

Say why you want the job:
I want to work for you because …
I would like to work at the train station because …

Say what you can do:
I can (drive and cook)
I am good at (talking to people)
I like / love (making people happy)

Say what you are like:
I am (friendly)
I always (do a good job)

Riverside Hotel: Job application form

Name	Tan Jun Ming	Address	675 Mandalay Street, 764896
Email	Junming99@h.mail.com	Phone	+61 7863 9021

Education:

IT Certificate (UWS College)

Experience:

-

Extra information:

I want to work at the Riverside Hotel because it is a great place to meet people from around the world. I am very friendly, and I love talking to people. I also enjoy helping others, answering phone calls and writing emails. I am great with computers, and I can speak three languages: Mandarin, English and Spanish.

Riverside Hotel: Job application form

Name	Eliza Portman	Address	43 Palace Avenue, 651284
Email	liz.p@m.mail.com	Phone	+61 9223 4618

Education:

Diploma (Stamford West High)

Experience:

Cook
Captain of Stamford West Football Team

Extra information:

Right now, I am a cook at a small café. I want to work at your hotel because the food is amazing! I usually cook pasta and pizza, but I can cook many Asian dishes too. I can also clean, drive and do many other things. I am always on time, and I always work hard. I want to work in a big team and learn more about hotel work.

7 Look at the Critical thinking skill box. Then look at the jobs and skills in the Riverside Hotel job advertisement. What skills do you need for each job?

CRITICAL THINKING SKILL
Knowing what skills are important

Skills are things you are good at. Every job needs different skills. When you apply for a job, list skills you have that are important for that job. Don't list skills that aren't important.

WRITING TASK

8 Think of a job you would like to apply for. Make notes.

1 Why do you want the job?
2 What skills are important for that job?
3 What are you good at?

9 **WRITE** Apply for the job. Use Jun Ming and Eliza's applications as models and the Useful language expressions to help you.

Name:
Education:
Experience:
Extra information:

10 **CHECK** Use the checklist. My application …

- ☐ says why I want the job.
- ☐ says what I can do.
- ☐ says what I'm like.
- ☐ lists only important skills.

11 **REVIEW** Read your partner's job application. Does it do the things in the checklist?

Go to page 157 for the Reflect and review.

Montaña de Siete Colores, Peru.

9

Travel

GOALS

- Understand words in brackets
- Use *there is* and *there are*
- Talk about transport and the weather
- Listen to advertisements
- Speak on the phone
- Write a postcard

1 Work in pairs. Discuss the questions.

1 Look at the photo. Where is this place?
2 What do you see in the photo?
3 Would you like to visit this place?

WATCH

2 ▶ 9.1 Watch the video. Answer the questions.

NATIONAL GEOGRAPHIC EXPLORER

JENNY ADLER

1 What does Jenny take photos of?
2 Where does she like travelling to?
3 Why does she like it there?

3 Make connections. What place do you visit often? What can you find there?

I often go to Oman. My brother lives there. It has a lot of beautiful beaches!

9A Amazing journeys

LESSON GOALS
- Talk about different ways to travel
- Understand an article about interesting journeys
- Understand words in brackets

VOCABULARY

1 Work in pairs. Why do you think people travel? Read the reasons below. Write very important (V), important (I) or not very important (N).

1 see new places
2 meet interesting people
3 relax
4 buy things
5 learn about the world
6 have fun

2 9.1 Work in pairs. Answer the questions. Then listen to check.
Which can you:

1 ride
2 drive
3 take
4 sail
5 fly
6 travel by

3 Discuss in pairs. How do you like to travel? What are some good and bad things about each way to travel?

I like travelling by plane. It's expensive, but it's fast.

I like riding a bike. It's slow, but you can stop and see many things.

Go to page 164 for the Vocabulary reference.

READING

4 Read the article. Which ways to travel does it mention?

5 Read about the two train journeys again. Write the letters (a–h) in the Venn diagram.

a one country
b many countries
c one day long
d many days long
e see animals
f see mountains
g beds on the train
h food on the train

6 Work in pairs. Which journey sounds more interesting to you? Why?

7 Look at the Reading skill box. Then look for the words in brackets in the article. Do they give meaning or extra information?

READING SKILL
Understanding words in brackets

Writers use brackets (…) to explain what something means or to give extra information.

Meaning:
You can see giraffes (animals with very long necks).

Extra information:
There are snacks (sandwiches and cakes).

SPEAKING

8 Work in pairs. How do you travel to these places from your home?

a park | the next city | the mountains
a supermarket | the beach | the shopping centre

I walk to the park. It's very near.

I ride my bike to the beach.

9 Work in pairs. Think about a journey you would like to do.

1 Is it a short or a long journey?
2 Where does it start and end?
3 How would you travel?

I really want to travel from Hanoi to Ho Chi Minh City by motorbike.

EXPLORE MORE!
Find out about other long and exciting journeys. Search online using the words 'exciting journeys'.

The Shongololo Express

The Shongololo Express train travels through South Africa, Eswatini, Namibia, Zimbabwe and Mozambique. The journey is long [2](it takes about 12 to 15 days), but it's amazing. You can see many things from your window: lakes, rivers, mountains, villages and many beautiful animals. Some people see lions, elephants and giraffes. There's great food on the train, and there are comfortable beds to sleep on at night.

The journey of your life!

The destination [1](the place you're going to) isn't the only reason to travel. Sometimes, it's about the journey, or how you get there. Here are two amazing journeys you can take.

The Ticlio Pass

Ticlio is a mountain pass [3](a road through the mountains) in Peru. It's up in the Andes mountains, 90 kilometres from Lima. It's nearly 5000 metres high. By car, the journey is short [4](it takes about three hours) but beautiful. There's also a train from Lima. There are only two trains a month, but the view is amazing. The ride is 12 hours long, and there are no beds. You can get snacks on the train or you can buy food at the town of Matucana.

9B There are beaches with black sand

LESSON GOALS
- Understand someone talking about their favourite holiday spot
- Talk about things you can find in a place
- Talk about famous tourist attractions

A holiday photo by Jenny Adler.

SPEAKING

1 Work in pairs. Answer the questions.

1 Do tourists visit your town?
2 What places do they visit?

2 Work in groups. Look at the infographic below. Discuss the questions.

1 Do you know these famous tourist attractions?
2 Which ones would you like to visit the most?

LISTENING AND GRAMMAR

NATIONAL GEOGRAPHIC EXPLORER

3 9.2 Listen to Jenny Adler. Where's her favourite place to go for a holiday?

4 9.2 Listen again. Tick (✓) the things Jenny says you can see or find there.

a beaches
b old buildings
c large animals
d hot pools
e northern lights
f shopping centres
g restaurants
h friendly people

WHERE DO TOURISTS GO?

VISITORS PER YEAR	
30 million	Niagara Falls (Canada/US)
15 million	The Egyptian pyramids
8 million	The Sydney Opera house
7 million	The Eiffel Tower (France)
3 million	Angkor Wat (Cambodia)

5 Read the Grammar box. Do you use *some* and *any* for singular or plural nouns?

GRAMMAR *There is* and *there are*

Positive sentences:
Use *There* + *is* / *are*.
There's *a hot pool.*
You can also use numbers, or words like *some* or *many*.
There are *(two / some / many) beaches.*

Negative sentences:
Use *There* + *isn't* + *a*.
There isn't a *big moon.*
Use *There* + *aren't* + *any*.
There aren't any *clouds.*

Questions:
Use *Is* + *there* + *a*.
Is there a *museum?*
Yes, there is. / No, there isn't.
Use *Are* + *there* + *any*.
Are there any *restaurants?*
Yes, there are. / No, there aren't.

Go to page 173 for the Grammar reference.

6 Complete the sentences. Circle the answers.

1 There *is / are* a shower in the bathroom.
2 There *is / are* fifteen people in my class.
3 There *isn't / aren't* any tomatoes in this dish.
4 There *isn't / aren't* a TV in his house.
5 *Is / Are* there a computer in your room?
6 *Is / Are* there any trains to your town?

7 Complete the conversation. Write *is, are, isn't* or *aren't*.

A: Hey Miko. 1_______________ there fun things to do in your town?
B: Yes, there 2_______________. There 3_______________ a museum, and there 4_______________ an art gallery.
A: 5_______________ there any mountains?
B: No, there 6_______________, but there 7_______________ a hill.
A: 8_______________ there a nice park?
B: Yes. There 9_______________ two beautiful parks.
A: Nice. And is there a cinema?
B: No, there 10_______________. I watch movies at home.

Kuang Si Waterfall, Laos.

8 Complete the information about Laos using *a*, *any* or *some*.

Are there 1_______________ interesting things in Laos? Of course there are! Laos is an amazing country. There are many beautiful waterfalls. Kuang Si Waterfall is my favourite. And there are 2_______________ big mountains too. There aren't 3_______________ beaches in Laos, but there are 4_______________ hot springs (natural pools of hot water). My favourite place is Luang Prabang. It's a small town, but it's really pretty. There's 5_______________ restaurant there I really like.

SPEAKING

9 Work in pairs. Turn to page 180. Choose a place. Don't tell your partner.
Student A: Ask questions with *Is there* and *Are there*. Guess your partner's place.
Student B: Answer your partner's questions.

A: Are there any mountains?
B: Yes, there are.

10 Work in pairs. Talk about a place you want to visit. Ask and answer questions using *Is there* and *Are there*. Use the words in Exercise 4 to help you.

A: I'd like to visit Morocco.
B: Why do you want to visit Morocco?
A: It's beautiful. There are many amazing markets.
B: Are there any … ?

EXPLORE MORE!
Learn about popular tourist places around the world. Search for '[country] + tourist attractions'.

9C The weather is perfect!

LESSON GOALS
- Learn weather words
- Understand two travel advertisements
- Use object pronouns

VOCABULARY

1 Work in pairs. Answer the questions.
1 Do you sometimes check the weather? How?
2 What are some reasons people have for checking the weather?
3 Do you like wet weather or dry weather more? Why?

2 [9.3] Match the words to the pictures. Listen and check.

1  a wind

2  b snow

3  c rain

4  d sun

3 Work in pairs. Do you use these items in the sun, wind, rain or snow?

1 
umbrella

3 
hat

2 
jacket

4 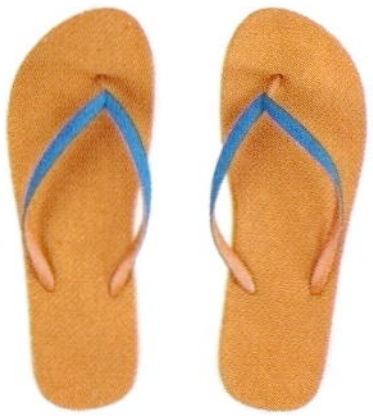
flip flops

Go to page 164 for the Vocabulary reference.

LISTENING

4 [9.4] Listen to two advertisements. Where is the weather warm? Where is the weather cold?

5 9.4 Look at the Listening skill box. Then listen again. Complete the sentences (1–8) with the verbs you hear.

LISTENING SKILL
Listening to advertisements

Advertisements often make suggestions or ask you to take action. These suggestions often begin with verbs. For example:

Visit Finland in December.

Listen for these verbs to understand the message.

enjoy forget go learn relax swim visit worry

Jamaica:

1 ____________ at our wonderful hotel.
2 ____________ to cook Jamaican dishes.
3 ____________ some reggae music.
4 Don't ____________ your dancing shoes.

Finland:

5 ____________ Finland in December.
6 ____________ on a dog sled adventure.
7 Don't ____________ about the weather.
8 ____________ in a cold lake.

6 Work in pairs. Which holiday sounds more interesting? Why?

GRAMMAR

7 Read the Grammar box. Write the object pronouns.

GRAMMAR Object pronouns

Object pronouns are for people or things that actions happen to.

me *you* *him*
her *it* *us* *them*

Object pronouns usually come after a verb.

*Everyone **loves it**!*
*Get to **know them**.*

Go to page 174 for the Grammar reference.

1 I *me* 2 you ______ 3 he ______
4 she ______ 5 it ______ 6 we ______
7 they ______

8 Work in pairs. Answer the questions.
1 Which object pronouns are for people?
2 Which object pronouns are for things?
3 Which are for more than one person or thing?

9 Write the sentences. Change the nouns to object pronouns.
1 Give **this wallet** to **your sister**.
2 Help **Larry** find **Mel and Stella**.
3 Send **the email** to **Miguel and me** now.
4 Tell **Sofia** to show **the report** to **Jen and me**.

PRONUNCIATION

10 9.5 Look at the Clear voice box. Listen and repeat.

CLEAR VOICE
Saying /w/ and /v/

The /w/ and /v/ sounds are similar, but they are not the same.

water *vegetable*

Practise saying /w/ and /v/ to make your English clear.

weather *wind* *always*
very *video* *heavy*

11 9.6 Listen and repeat the sentences.
1 The **wind** is **very** strong today.
2 The rain is **always heavy** in June.

SPEAKING

12 Look at the words below. Think of one thing for each word and write it down.
1 weather *rain*
2 a band ____________
3 a place ____________
4 an activity ____________
5 a type of food ____________

13 Work in pairs. Ask and answer questions about your things in Exercise 12.

A: Do you like the rain?
B: Yes, I do. I love it!
A: Why do you love it?
B: I like to lie in bed and read ...

EXPLORE MORE!

What is the weather like around the world? Which places have a lot of sun, snow, wind and rain? Search for 'places with a lot of [weather word]'.

9D Speaking on the phone

LESSON GOALS
- Learn how to speak on the phone
- Make a phone booking
- Say /θ/ in ordinal numbers and dates

SPEAKING

1 Work in pairs. Answer the questions.

1 Do you like speaking on the phone? Why? / Why not?
2 How often do you speak on the phone?
3 Who do you usually speak to on the phone?

A: I like speaking on the phone. It's quick.

B: I don't like speaking on the phone. I can't see the person.

MY VOICE

2 ▶ 9.2 Work in pairs. Watch the video. Answer the questions.

1 What greetings can you use on the phone?
2 Do you always need to say who you are?
3 How can you *sound* friendly on the phone?

3 Look at the Communication skill box. Answer the questions.

COMMUNICATION SKILL
Speaking on the phone

When you call someone you don't know, try these tips:

1 Say hello.
2 Ask if it's the right person.
3 Say the reason for your call.
4 Speak in a clear voice.
5 Be friendly.

1 Is it easy to do these things in English?
2 Which tips are easy? Which are difficult?

I think tips 4 and 5 are difficult to do in English ...

4 Look at the Useful language box. Which phrases can you use when you call:

1 a restaurant
2 a travel company
3 a hotel
4 anyone

Useful language Making a phone booking

Saying hello
Hello? Can I speak to ... ?
Hi. Is this ... ?
This is (Dan).

Making a booking
Can I book a (room for 23rd November)?
I'd like to book a (tour tomorrow at 4 p.m.).
Do you have a table for (five people at 6 p.m.)?

Answers
I'm sorry, we're fully booked.
Yes, of course. For how many people?
Yes, sure. For what date, please?

Saying dates
thirty-first of March / second of June

5 We use ordinal numbers to say dates. Look at the calendar and write the missing words. Then practise saying the dates in pairs.

PRONUNCIATION

6 9.7 Listen and repeat the words slowly.

CLEAR VOICE
Saying /θ/

Many ordinal numbers have the /θ/ sound. This can be difficult to say.

four**th**	fif**th**	six**th**	seven**th**
eigh**th**	nin**th**	ten**th**	eleven**th**
twelf**th**	thirteen**th**	twentie**th**	thirtie**th**

SPEAKING

7 Work in pairs. Call your partner. Book a hotel room, a tour or a table at a restaurant. Use the Useful language expressions.

8 **OWN IT!** Work in pairs.
Student A: You're planning a holiday. Your partner works for the Riverside Hotel. Call your partner and book a room for three nights. Use the calendar below and choose the best dates for you.
Student B: You work at the Riverside Hotel. Use the calendar on page 181 and help your partner book a room.
A: Hello. Riverside Hotel. How can I help you?
B: Hi. I'd like to book a room for ...

August

Monday	Tuesday	Wednesday	Thursday	Friday	Saturday	Sunday
1st first	2nd second	3rd third	4th fourth	5th fifth	6th sixth	7th seventh
8th eighth	9th ninth	10th tenth	11th eleventh	12th twelfth	13th thirteenth	14th ________
15th fifteenth	16th sixteenth	17th ________	18th ________	19th ________	20th twentieth	21st twenty-first
22nd ________	23rd ________	24th twenty-fourth	25th ________	26th ________	27th ________	28th ________
29th ________	30th thirtieth	31st thirty-first	1st	2nd	3rd	4th

9E I love it here!

LESSON GOALS
- Learn how to use exclamation marks
- Learn expressions for writing about travel
- Write a postcard

Hi Mum and Dad!

It's your son, Yujiro! I'm in Ilhabela, Brazil. It's a beautiful island near São Paulo. I love it! The weather here is perfect. The sun is always out, and the wind is strong. It's a great place for sailing!

There are two lovely beaches, and there's a waterfall in the south. It's beautiful! There's also a big forest. I go hiking there every morning. Brazilian food is amazing. My hotel is famous for its food!

I really miss you. Text me or email me.

Lots of Love,

Yujiro

870-7866, Oita Ken
Oitashi
778-9 Oaza
Japan

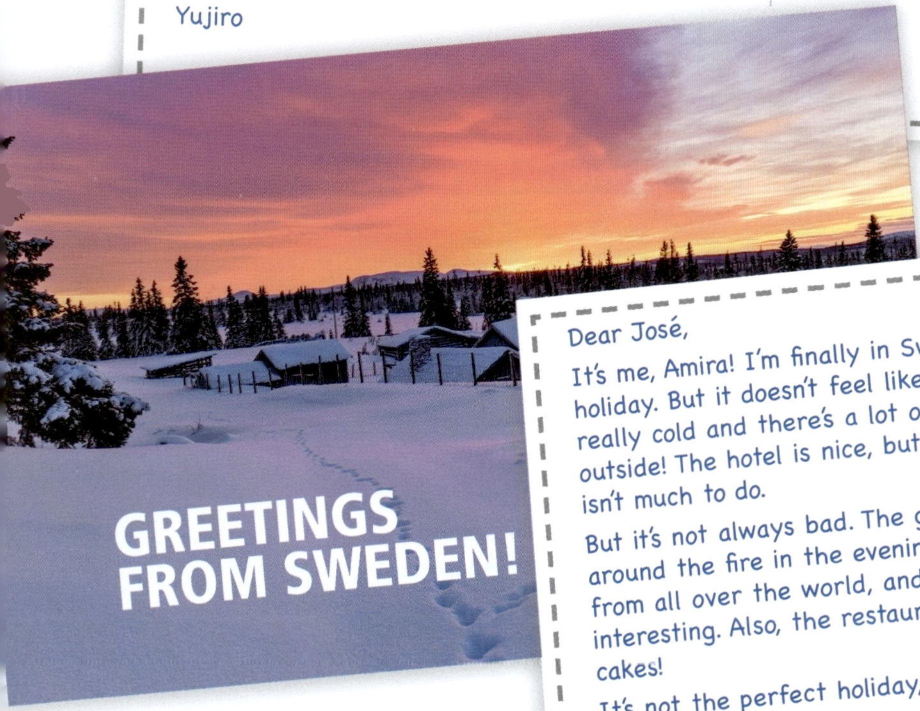

Dear José,

It's me, Amira! I'm finally in Sweden for my holiday. But it doesn't feel like a holiday. It's really cold and there's a lot of snow. I can't go outside! The hotel is nice, but it's small and there isn't much to do.

But it's not always bad. The guests like to sit around the fire in the evening and talk. They're from all over the world, and they're very interesting. Also, the restaurant makes delicious cakes!

It's not the perfect holiday, but I'm alright. I hope you are too!

Your best friend,

Amira.

Blvd Venezuela
No 1256, San Salvador
El Salvador

SPEAKING

1 Work in pairs. Look at the postcards. Answer the questions.

1 Do you sometimes get or send postcards?
2 Why do people send postcards? Are postcards better than text messages or emails?

READING FOR WRITING

2 Read the postcards. Where are Yujiro and Amira? Who are they writing to?

3 Read the postcards again. Write Y (Yujiro), A (Amira) or B (both). Are they both having a good time?

1 The weather is great.
2 There isn't much to do.
3 There are many things to see.
4 The food is good.

4 Look at the Writing skill box. Circle all the exclamation marks in the postcards. Why do Yujiro and Amira use them?

WRITING SKILL
Using exclamation marks

Exclamation marks (!) can mean different things. Use them at the end of sentences to show ...

- you feel happy.
- you feel angry.
- you are surprised.
- something is important.

5 Look at the Useful language box. Can you find examples of the expressions in the two postcards?

Useful language Writing about travels

I'm on holiday in (Mombasa).
It's beautiful / amazing / great / lovely!
I love it here!
The weather is great / perfect / terrible.
There's a (beautiful beach).
There are (excellent cafés).
There are so many things to do.
It's a great place to (read a book).

6 Complete the text. Use words from the Useful language box.

The town of Arslanbob in Kyrgyzstan is beautiful. I [1]______________ it here. The [2]______________ is great. It's cool all day. And there are many mountains and waterfalls. There are so many [3]______________ to do. It's a great [4]______________ to go hiking and camping, and to relax too.

7 Rewrite the sentences in the Useful language box. Make them about a popular tourist site you know in your country or in another country.

I am on holiday in Miami. It's beautiful! There are amazing beaches, and many ...

8 Look at the Critical thinking skill box. Why are Yujiro and Amira sending their postcards?

CRITICAL THINKING SKILL
Reasons for writing

When you write, think about why you're writing. For example, people send postcards because they want to ...

- say they miss someone.
- say they are OK.
- tell people where they are.
- share their travel plans.

WRITING TASK

9 Imagine you're on holiday. Think of someone to send a postcard to. Write notes.

1 Where are you? What's it like there?
2 What is the main reason for your postcard?
3 What else do you want to say in your postcard?

10 **WRITE** Write a postcard. Use your notes and the Useful language expressions to help you.

11 **CHECK** Use the checklist. My postcard ...

☐ says where I am.
☐ describes the place I'm in.
☐ shows the reason I'm writing.

12 **REVIEW** Work in pairs. Read your partner's postcard. Does it do everything in the checklist? Would you like to visit the place in their postcard?

Go to page 158 for the Reflect and review.

Many people believe that bathing in the warm sands of Japan's Ibusuki Beach is good for the mind and body.

10

Staying healthy

GOALS

- Understand headings and parts of an article
- Describe things that are happening now
- Name different parts of the body
- Listen for specific information
- Ask for and give directions
- Write a simple report

1 Work in pairs. Discuss the questions.

1 Look at the photo. What are the people doing?
2 Why do you think they are doing it?
3 Would you like to try it?

WATCH

2 ▶ 10.1 Watch the video. Answer the questions.

NATIONAL GEOGRAPHIC EXPLORERS

RUBÉN SALGADO ESCUDERO

NORA SHAWKI

1 How do Rubén and Nora stay healthy?
2 Which tip do you think is the most important?

3 Make connections. Work in pairs. Answer the questions.

1 Why is good health important?
2 How do you try to stay healthy?

Good health means I can do more things.
I usually exercise and eat good food.

10A A healthy mind

LESSON GOALS
- Name different body parts
- Understand headings in an article
- Understand an article about having a healthy mind

VOCABULARY

1 10.1 Look at the photo of the face. Label the parts. Listen and check.

ear eye hair mouth nose

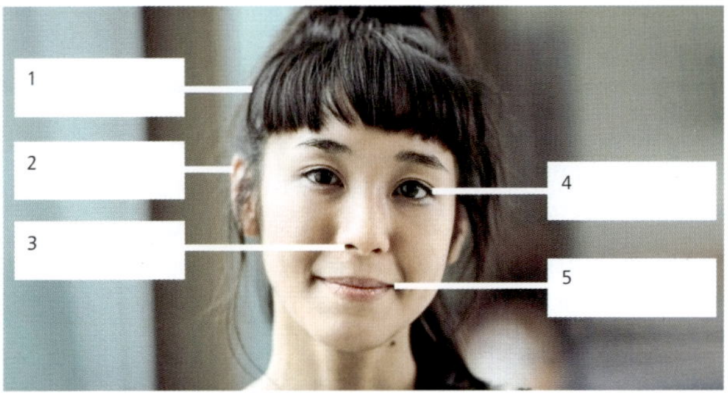

2 10.2 Look at the photo. Label the body parts. Listen and check.

arm foot hand head leg

3 Work in pairs. Close your books. Point to a part of your face or body. Your partner names it.

Go to page 164 for the Vocabulary reference.

READING

4 Work in pairs. Look at the picture and title on page 121. Answer the questions.

1 Which do you think is more important: a healthy mind or a healthy body? Why?
2 What do you think are some ways to have a healthy mind?

5 Look at the Reading skill box. Then read the article quickly. Write the missing headings.

Be creative Eat healthy food Rest

READING SKILL
Understanding headings

Some articles have sections, or parts. Headings make these parts easy to see and understand. Each section has a main idea. Headings describe that main idea.

6 Read the article. Answer the questions.

1 When you *take a break*, you ...
 a finish your work. b rest for a short time.
2 *Stress* is something people usually feel when they are ...
 a very busy. b very happy.
3 A *balanced diet* is one with ...
 a a little of everything. b a lot of one thing.
4 How can you *exercise your brain*?
 a learn things b run more
5 How can you *spend time* with a friend?
 a send them an email b meet them for lunch

SPEAKING

7 Write notes. Look at each tip in the article. Think of one or two things you can do for each.

I can take more breaks when I study.

I can go for a walk after lunch.

8 Work in pairs. Tell your partner your ideas. Which do you think you can do?

I can take more breaks and go for more walks.

How to have a healthy mind

Many people exercise and look after their bodies. But a healthy mind is important too. Here are six ways to keep your mind healthy.

1 ____________________

When your mind is tired, your whole body feels tired too. Take breaks and get enough sleep. Go on a holiday if you can.

2 Exercise

Exercise is good for your mind too. It helps with stress, and it helps you sleep better. Try to exercise a little every day.

3 ____________________

There isn't one special 'brain food'. Eat a balanced diet. Is the food you're eating good for the body? Then it's also good for the mind.

4 Learn new things

Exercise your brain. Learn new things in your free time. Read a book or listen to an interesting podcast.

5 ____________________

Give your mind something fun to do. Write a song, paint a picture or make videos. There are many ways to be creative!

6 Make friends

We all need people who care about us. Make new friends and spend time with old ones. Talk about your lives. It's good for the mind.

EXPLORE MORE!

What other things can you do to keep your mind healthy? Go online and look for tips. Search for 'secrets to a healthy mind'.

10B I'm buying running shoes

LESSON GOALS

- Understand conversations about sports equipment
- Describe things that are happening now
- Group words together when speaking

LISTENING AND GRAMMAR

1 Work in pairs. Discuss the questions.

1 What do you wear when you exercise?
2 What other sports or exercise equipment do you use?

A: I wear running shoes.
B: I wear a T-shirt.
A: I have a yoga mat.
B: I have a bicycle.

2 10.3 Listen to three interviews at a sports shop. What are the people buying? Number the pictures below 1–3.

3 10.3 Listen again. Complete the sentences.

boots heavy light long shirt tennis

Conversation 1:
1 He's training for a _______________ run.
2 He's looking for _______________ running shoes.

Conversation 2:
3 She's learning how to play _______________.
4 She's using a _______________ racquet.

Conversation 3:
5 He's not buying football _______________.
6 He's getting a football _______________.

a tennis racquet

b running shoes

c football shirt

4 Read the Grammar box. Look at the *-ing* verb. What is the infinitive form of the verb?

GRAMMAR Present continuous

Use the present continuous to talk about things happening now.

Positive sentences:

Subject + *am / is / are* + *-ing verb*

I'm buying *a new tennis racquet.*

Negative sentences:

subject + *am / is / are* + *not* + *-ing* verb

I'm not buying *football boots.*

Questions:

am / is / are + subject + *-ing* verb

Are you buying *these football boots?*

What ***are you buying*** *today?*

Go to page 174 for the Grammar reference.

5 Complete the sentences. Use the correct form of the verbs.

1 She's ______________ (swim) in the pool.
2 Where are you ______________ (go)?
3 Cass isn't ______________ (buy) shoes.
4 Is he ______________ (play) golf with his friends?
5 They aren't ______________ (make) any noise.
6 Who are they ______________ (talk) to?
7 Is she ______________ (look) for me?
8 What phone are you ______________ (use)?

6 Correct the mistake in each sentence.

1 She are shopping.
2 What is the girls doing?
3 I playing the piano right now.
4 My family watching a film on TV.
5 They not are going to the cinema.
6 I'm writeing a postcard to my mum.
7 Is Ashok and Lara studying at the library?
8 Where she is walking to?

7 Work in pairs. Look around the classroom or outside. Say what people are doing.

The teacher is answering a question.

Ollie and Jean are laughing!

PRONUNCIATION

8 10.4 Look at the Clear voice box and listen to the examples. Notice the word groups and words with stress. Listen again and repeat.

CLEAR VOICE

Understanding word groups

When people speak, it sounds like the words are in groups. They stress the last word in each group.

I'm ***taking***	*the* ***bus***	*to* ***school***.
She's ***walking***	*in the* ***park***	*with her* ***friend***.

9 10.5 Listen to the three sentences. Notice how the words are in groups. Underline the words with stress.

1 We're watching	a movie	at the cinema.
2 They're meeting	their teacher	after class.
3 I'm listening	to music	with my friends.

SPEAKING

10 Work in pairs. Identify people at a fitness centre.
Student A: Turn to page 179.
Student B: Turn to page 181.

EXPLORE MORE!

Running shoes are often expensive! Want to save money? Search for 'how to make my running shoes last longer'.

10C Exercise

LESSON GOALS

- Talk about exercise and training
- Understand people talking about how they exercise
- Use present simple and present continuous together

VOCABULARY

1 Work in pairs. Answer the questions.

1 How do you or your friends **exercise**?
2 Are there any sports you want to **learn**?
3 What are some things that people **practise**?
4 How do sportspeople **prepare** for competitions?

I like running. My friends swim.

I want to learn golf and table tennis.

My friend practises the piano every day.

They run a lot and go to the gym.

2 10.6 Read the sentences. Circle the correct answers. Listen and check.

1 He swims every day. He's *exercising / preparing* for a big race.
2 She's *learning / preparing* how to play tennis. She goes for lessons every week.
3 He's *practising / exercising* more because he wants to be healthy.
4 They have to keep *learning / practising* if they want to get good at it.

Go to page 164 for the Vocabulary reference.

LISTENING

NATIONAL GEOGRAPHIC EXPLORERS

3 10.7 Listen to Rubén Salgado Escudero and Nora Shawki talking about exercise. Then read sentences 1–4. Are they true (T) or false (F)?

1 Rubén and Nora are talking about sports.
2 Rubén can't exercise when he travels.
3 Nora studies animals.
4 Nora's work is like exercise.

4 10.7 Look at the Listening skill box. Then read questions 1–4 below. Listen again and answer the questions.

LISTENING SKILL
Listening for specific information

When you listen, first, write down the main points. Next, listen again and write down specific information. Read the questions first so you know what to listen for.

1 Where does Rubén often exercise when he travels?
2 How long are the exercise sessions on Rubén's app?
3 How does Nora exercise when she's not at work?
4 How does Nora 'exercise' when she's at work?

GRAMMAR

5 Read the Grammar box. Which tense shows that an action is new and different?

GRAMMAR Present continuous vs present simple

You can use the present simple and the present continuous together to show that something new is happening.

Use the present simple to talk about habits, or things you usually do:

*Usually, **I can't exercise** when I travel.*

Use the present continuous to talk about something you are doing that's new or different:

*Right now, **I'm using an app** to help me.*

Go to page 175 for the Grammar reference.

6 Complete the sentences. Use the correct form of the verbs.

1 They always ______________ (take) the bus to school.
2 Right now, I'm ______________ (learn) how to do yoga.
3 She ______________ (not study) often, but right now, she's ______________ (prepare) for a test.
4 John usually ______________ (watch) TV at night. Tonight, he's ______________ (read) a book.
5 We don't usually ______________ (go) very far, but we're ______________ (cycle) sixty kilometres today.

7 Look at the Useful language box. Answer the questions.

Useful language Time expressions

right now
at the moment
today
tonight
this week / month / year
every day / week / month / year
every morning / afternoon / night

1 What month is this month?
2 What year is this year?
3 What does every year mean?

8 Complete the sentences. Use words from the Useful language box.

1 I'm having fun at the ______________.
2 My sister has dinner ______________ evening at 7:30 p.m.
3 I'm doing my homework ______________ now.
4 I'm not exercising ______________ month.
5 I usually go to the gym ______________ week. ______________ week, I'm exercising at home.

SPEAKING

9 Work in pairs. Complete the table. What habits are you trying to change? Write what you usually do and what you are doing now.

A: I eat a lot of fast food ...

B: I always wake up late ...

Usually ...
I wake up late

Now ...
I'm waking up at 7 a.m.

Why?
I want to exercise in the morning.

10 Work in pairs. Discuss your activities.

Usually, I wake up late, but this week I'm waking up at 7 a.m. every morning.

Why are you waking up early?

EXPLORE MORE!

How often do we need to exercise? Go online and find out. Search using the words 'How much exercise do I need'.

10D Asking for and giving directions

LESSON GOALS

- Ask for and give directions
- Use intonation when giving directions
- Practise giving directions with a map

Street signs in Sicily, Italy.

SPEAKING

1 Work in pairs. Discuss the questions.

1 Do you write with your left hand or right hand?
2 Look to your left and right. What do you see?

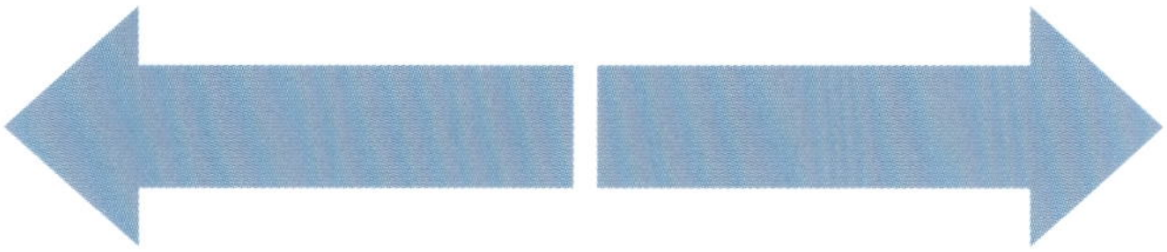

left right

2 Look straight ahead. What do you see?

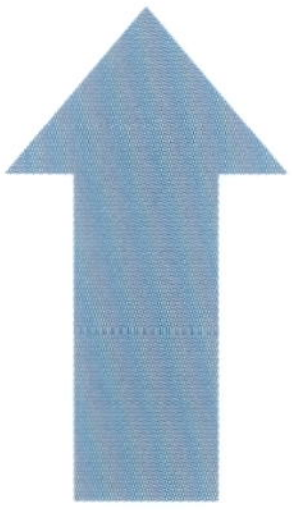

straight

MY VOICE

3 ▶ 10.2 Watch the video. Answer the questions.

1 What question can you ask to get directions?
2 What can people do to make their directions easy to understand?

4 Look at the Communication skill box. Is it easier to ask for or give directions? Why?

COMMUNICATION SKILL
Asking for and giving directions

Asking for directions:

First, ask how to get there.

- Ask where it is.
- Ask which way to go.

Then, listen carefully to the directions.

- Make a simple map in your mind.
- Ask questions if you don't understand.

Giving directions:

- Point and show.
- Say what they can see.

5 Look at the Useful language box. Then complete the conversation using words from the box.

Useful language Directions

Asking for directions
Excuse me
Do you know where the (library) is?
Which way is the (cinema)?
How do I get there?
How do I get to the (park)?

Giving directions
go straight
turn right / left at the …
it's on / near …

A: [1]_______________ me?
B: Yes, how can I help you?
A: How do I [2]_______________ to the cinema?
B: It's easy. Go [3]_______________, then [4]_______________ left at the supermarket.
A: Oh, is it [5]_______________ the big shopping centre?
B: Yes, it is. It's [6]_______________ Denver Avenue. You can't miss it.
A: That's really helpful. Thank you!

PRONUNCIATION AND SPEAKING

6 10.8 Look at the Clear voice box and listen to the directions. Notice the rising and falling intonation in the directions.

CLEAR VOICE
Understanding intonation in directions

When giving directions, speakers often have to list many steps.

For example:

Go straight, turn left at the cinema, …

turn right near the library and left again at the museum.

The arrows show intonation. An 'up' arrow means the speaker's voice goes up. A 'down' arrow means the speaker's voice goes down. Notice how the voice goes up for each step, but not the last one. The falling intonation tells listeners it's the final step.

7 10.9 Listen to the directions and repeat the sentences. Try to match the speakers' intonation.

1 Turn left at the school, go straight for fifty metres and turn right at the Thai restaurant.
2 Walk that way, turn left when you see the café, go straight and turn right at Pine Street.

8 **OWN IT!** Work in pairs. Look at the map. Tell your partner how to go from:

1 the university to the shopping centre
2 the park to the library
3 the museum to the cinema

9 Work in pairs. Ask for and give directions.
Student A: Think of a place near your school. Ask your partner how to get there.
Student B: Give your partner directions. Use a map if you need help.

10E More people are exercising.

LESSON GOALS
- Learn about the parts of a report
- Learn words to describe change
- Write a simple report

A ski slope in Vancouver, Canada.

SPEAKING

1 Work in pairs. Look at the survey form below. Answer the questions.

1 Do you sometimes answer surveys? What are some surveys you remember doing?

2 How do you think surveys help people?

WINTER EXERCISE SURVEY

1 Every winter, I usually exercise ...
- ☐ once a week or less
- ☐ twice a week
- ☐ 3 times a week or more

2 This winter, I'm exercising ...
- ☐ once a week or less
- ☐ twice a week
- ☐ 3 times a week or more

READING FOR WRITING

2 Read the survey report. Then complete the sentences.

1 Usually, ______________ per cent of people exercise two times a week or more.

2 This winter, ______________ per cent of people are exercising two times a week or more.

WINTER EXERCISE REPORT

The people of our town usually exercise a lot in winter. But this winter, people are exercising less.

	Usually		This winter	
once a week or less	299	60%	396	79%
twice a week	151	30%	68	14%
3 times a week or more	50	10%	36	7%

How often our town people exercise in winter (survey size = 500)

	Usually		This winter	
Snowboarding	127	25%	49	10%
Skiing	49	10%	30	6%
Ball games	25	5%	25	5%

Winter exercises by people who exercise twice a week or more

Normal winter numbers

Usually, about 40% of people in our town exercise twice a week or more. 25% snowboard, 10% go skiing, and 5% play ball games, like tennis and basketball.

Winter numbers this year

This winter, only 21% are exercising twice a week or more. 10% are snowboarding, and only 6% are skiing. The number of people playing ball games is the same (5%).

Reasons for the change

Winters here are usually cold, but people can still exercise in the snow. This winter, there's a lot of rain, and they can't go snowboarding or skiing. But they can play ball games like tennis and basketball indoors.

3 Look at the Critical thinking skill box. Answer the two questions below about the two charts in the exercise report.

CRITICAL THINKING SKILL
Understanding charts

To understand a chart:

1 **Read the title of the chart**
The title usually has useful information.

2 **Read the headings**
Headings give the numbers and words in a box meaning.

3 **Think about what the information tells us**
Is something changing? Do you know why?

1 The first chart shows *how / how often* people exercise.
2 The second chart shows *how / how often* people exercise.

4 The charts tell us that people are exercising less this winter. What reason does the report give?

a they can't play indoor sports.
b the weather is cold and snowy
c the weather is rainy

5 Look at the Writing skill box. Answer the questions.

WRITING SKILL
Writing a report

People sometimes write reports to explain what a survey tells us. Reports often have these parts.

1 A title: Say what the report is about.
2 A reason: Begin with the reason for the report.
3 The survey results: Talk about the numbers. Are any of them interesting or unusual?

At the end of the report, think about what the information tells us. How can we use the information? Give some ideas.

1 What is the reason for the exercise report?
2 Does the report say how we can use the information?

6 Work in pairs. How can the town get more people to exercise this winter?

They can ask people to do more indoor sports ...

7 Look at the Useful language box. Which words do you use with countable nouns? Which do you use with uncountable nouns?

Useful language Describing change

People are (exercising) more.
People are (skiing) less.
More (people) are (playing basketball).
Fewer (people) are (snowboarding).

8 Complete the sentences with *fewer* or *less*.

1 ______________ children are studying at our school this year.
2 I'm trying to spend ______________ money.
3 This year, there are ______________ restaurants in my city.
4 I'm eating ______________ rice today.

WRITING

9 The chart below contains the results of a high school sports survey. Look at the information and make notes.

1 What change do you see?
2 Is the change big or small? Is it good or bad?

SUMMER SPORTS STUDY	Usually (5-year average)	This summer
Total number of final year students	220	220
Final year students who do sports in summer (%)	38%	62%

10 Make notes. Think of one or two reasons for the change this summer. Use your own ideas.

11 **WRITE** Write a report. Use the tips in the Writing skill box and your notes from Exercises 9 and 10 to help you.

12 **CHECK** Use the checklist. My report ...

☐ has a title and an introduction.
☐ describes interesting or unusual changes.
☐ suggests reasons for the changes.
☐ says how we can use the information.

13 **REVIEW** Work in pairs. Read your partner's report. Does it do the things in the checklist?

Go to page 158 for the Reflect and review.

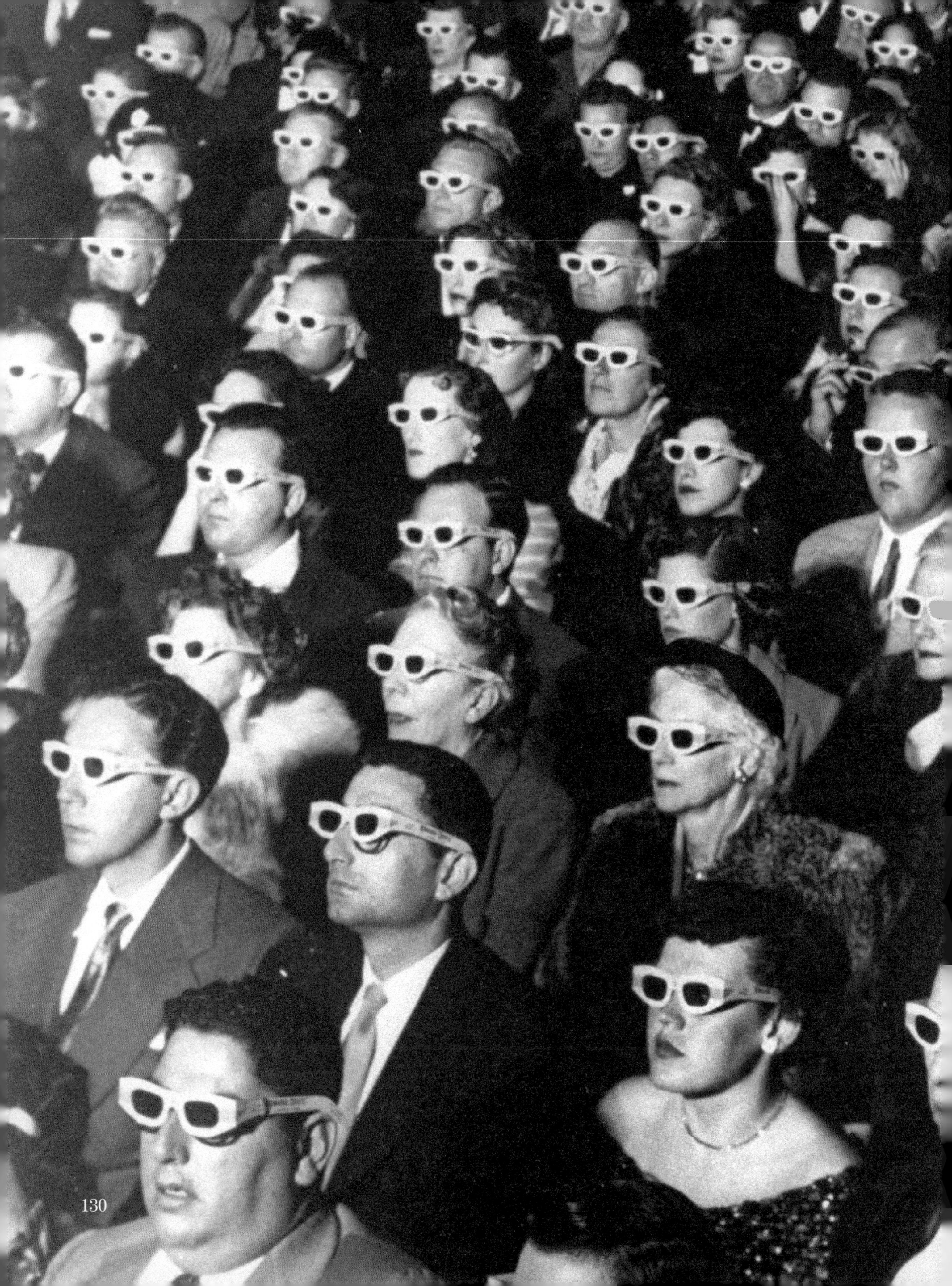

People watching a 3D movie in a cinema.

11

People from the past

GOALS

- Understand time order in an article
- Talk about people and things from the past
- Say when people were born, lived and died
- Understand small and large numbers
- Show interest while listening
- Write a profile about someone from history

1 Work in pairs. Answer the questions.

1 Look at the photo. What do you think is happening?
2 When do you think this was?

WATCH

2 ▶ 11.1 Watch the video. Answer the questions.

NATIONAL GEOGRAPHIC EXPLORERS

LIA NAHOMI KAJIKI

ALEC JACOBSON

1 Who do Lia and Alec talk about?
2 Why were they important to Lia and Alec?

3 Make connections. Work in pairs. Do you have a hero? Why are they important to you?

My grandfather is my hero. He's like a friend and a teacher to me …

11A Life events

LESSON GOALS
- Talk about important life events
- Understand an article about an amazing person
- Understand time order in an article

VOCABULARY

1 Work in pairs. Answer the questions.

1 When were you born?
2 When were your parents born?

2 11.1 Look at the timeline. Then complete the text. Listen and check.

ago	died	for	from	lived	was born

Nelson Mandela [1]______________ in 1918, more than a hundred years [2]______________. He [3]______________ for 95 years, and he [4]______________ in 2013. He was president of South Africa [5]______________ five years, [6]______________ 1994 to 1999.

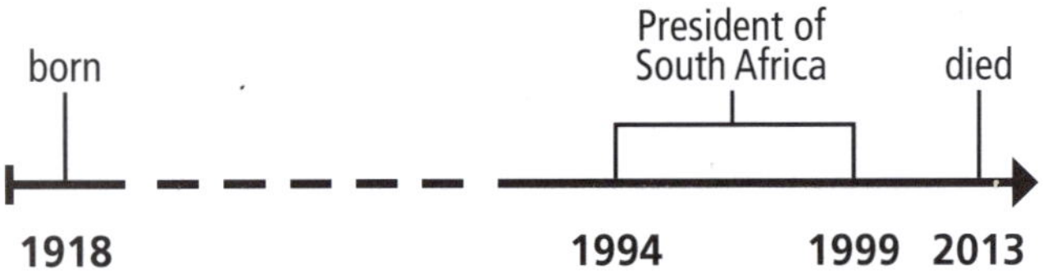

Go to page 165 for the Vocabulary reference.

READING

3 Work in pairs. Look at the photo on page 133. What do you think Hedy Lamarr's job was?

4 Read the article. Answer the questions.

1 When was Hedy Lamarr born?
2 What was Hedy Lamarr's main job?
3 What do people also know her for?
4 What was her invention?
5 When did she die?

5 Look at the Reading skill box. Then look at the events (a–f) below. Write the letters on the timeline.

READING SKILL
Understanding time order

Articles don't always list events in order. To understand the article better ...
- note down events and dates.
- arrange them in order.

Sometimes, it also helps to draw a timeline.

Hedy Lamarr's Life

a Hedy Lamarr was born.
b She died.
c She was in the film *Samson and Delilah*.
d She was in the film *Boom Town*.
e She started a film company.
f She invented a way to send messages.

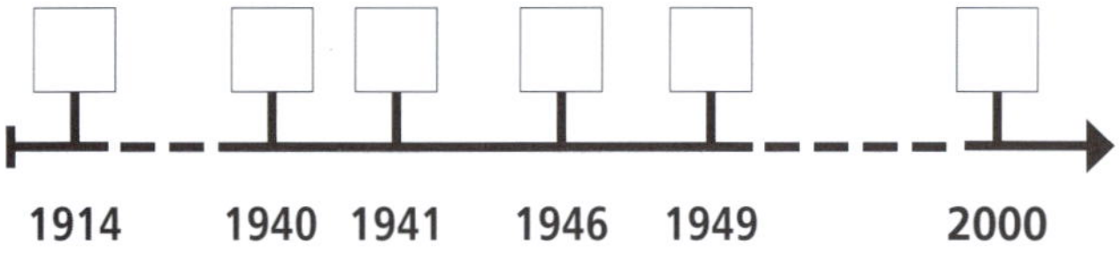

SPEAKING

6 Would you like to be famous? Choose three things you would like to be or think of your own ideas.

- a film star
- a great scientist
- someone who helps people
- someone who helps animals
- a sportsperson
- a business person
- an artist

7 Work in pairs. Discuss the three things you chose in Exercise 6. Explain why you would like to be those things.

I'd like to be a scientist so I can help people.

I'd like to be a sportsperson. I like golf, and I'd like to play golf all the time!

EXPLORE MORE!

Hedy Lamarr was a famous actor and a scientist. Find out about other people like her. Search online using the words 'famous people with two jobs'.

One woman, two lives

Hedy Lamarr was born in 1914 in Vienna, Austria. From the 1930s to the 1950s, she was in about thirty films and was a big Hollywood film star. But Hedy also lived a second life …

Life number one

For many years, Hedy's face was famous all over the world. She was a star in many famous films, like *Boom Town* in 1940 and *Samson and Delilah* in 1949. She was also a filmmaker, and from 1946 to 1949, she was the head of her own film company. To most people, Hedy Lamarr was a big name in the world of film.

Life number two

Many people did not know that Hedy was also an inventor. In her book *Bombshell*, she says, 'Inventions are easy for me to do. I don't have to work on ideas, they come naturally.' Her biggest invention was in 1941. It was a way to send messages through the air. Today, Hedy's invention makes WiFi, Bluetooth and smartphones possible.

Hedy Lamarr died in the year 2000. She lived a long and interesting life. Hedy was an actor, but she was also a business woman and a scientist. She was a star in more ways than one.

11B Who was the artist?

LESSON GOALS

- Understand people talking about artists they like
- Use the past simple form of *be*
- Practise the strong and weak forms of *was* and *were*

LISTENING AND GRAMMAR

1 Work in pairs. Ask and answer the questions.

1 Can you draw or paint? Are you good at it?
2 Do you know anyone who's good at drawing or painting?

I can draw, but I'm not very good.

My friend Mika is great at art. He studies in an art school.

2 Work in pairs. Look at the photos of the two artists below.

1 Do you know who the artists are and where they're from?
2 Can you name other famous artists from your country and around the world?

Leonardo da Vinci was a famous artist. He was from Italy.

Frida Kahlo was a famous painter from Mexico.

Pablo Picasso

Natalia Goncharova

3 Look at the two photos of the artists above. Then look at the self-portraits on the right.

1 Do the artists look the same in their paintings?
2 Which painting do you like more? Why?

I think Goncharova looks the same in her painting.

I think the Picasso painting is more interesting.

4 11.2 Listen to people talking about the two painters. Complete the table.

artist	Picasso	Goncharova
country		
year born		
year died		
year of painting		

5 Read the Grammar box. Answer the questions.

1 Which word is the past form of *is* and *am*?
2 Which word is the past form of *are*?

GRAMMAR Past simple *be*

The word *be* has two past forms: *was* and *were*.
Use *I/he/she/it* + *was*:
He was *from Spain.*
She was *a famous Russian painter.*
Use *we/you/they* + *were*:
They were *famous painters.*
Use *not* to make negative sentences:
He wasn't *from Paris.*
They weren't *French.*

Go to page 175 for the Grammar reference.

6 Complete the sentences. Use *was* or *were*.

1 Picasso ______________ a famous painter.
2 My sister and I ______________ born in Germany.
3 I ______________ a student in this school.
4 His book ______________ really famous.
5 We ______________ really happy to see Kyle.
6 You ______________ very quiet today.
7 They ______________ late for the meeting.
8 The film ______________ about a scientist.
9 It ______________ a story about three friends.
10 The chairs ______________ in the wrong room.

7 Put the words in order to make sentences.

1 was / he / from / not / France
2 and I / were / school / Ronda / not / friends / in
3 bag / phone / in / wasn't / Ava's / her
4 not / Desmond's / born / were / parents / in / the US

PRONUNCIATION

8 11.3 Look at the Clear voice box and listen to the examples. Notice the difference between the weak and strong forms of *was* and *were*.

CLEAR VOICE
Understanding *was* and *were*

Was and *were* have strong and weak forms. People often use the weak forms when the words are at the start or in the middle of a sentence.
Andy ***was*** *late for the party.* ***Was*** *he in class?*
They ***were*** *not at school.* ***Were*** *they at home?*
People often use the strong forms when the words are at the end of a sentence.
Yes, he ***was****.*
Yes, they ***were****.*

9 11.4 Listen. What form of *was* do you hear? Write strong form (S) or weak form (W).

1 **Was** she a famous painter?
2 Yes, she **was**.
3 Yes. She **was** very famous!

SPEAKING

10 Make notes about two famous people you know. Use the internet to help you.

1 Who were they?
2 When were they born?
3 Where were they from?
4 Why were they famous?

11 Work in groups. Tell your partners true and false statements about your people in Exercise 10. Your partners guess which statements are false.

A: Vincent Van Gogh was a famous artist from Germany.
B: Wait. That's not true!

EXPLORE MORE!

Are there any good artists in your town, city or country? Search for 'amazing artists from ... '. Look for photos of paintings you like.

11C Important events

LESSON GOALS

- Learn past time expression
- Understand people talking about events from the past
- Understand small and large numbers

The Leica 1 was an important camera in the history of photography.

VOCABULARY

1 Discuss in groups. Where were you yesterday?

2 11.5 Work in pairs. Write the letters on the timeline. Then listen and check.

a the last century
b last week
c last night
d the 19th century
e the year 2000
f last year

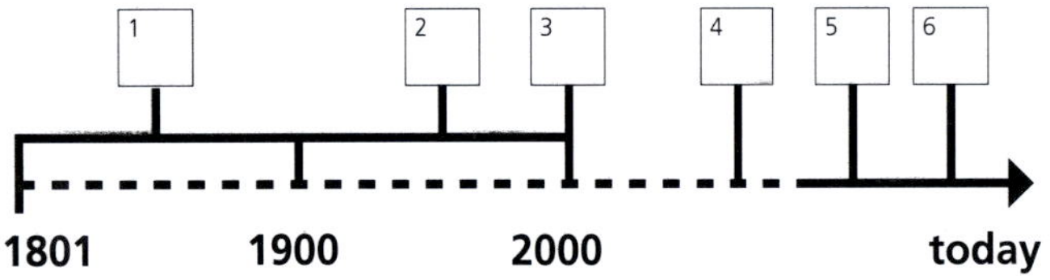

3 Work in pairs. Think of ...

1 a fun day from last year.
2 an important person from the last century.

Go to page 165 for the Vocabulary reference.

LISTENING

4 Work in pairs. Discuss the questions.

1 What important events from the past do you know about?
2 When were they?
3 Why were they important?

NATIONAL GEOGRAPHIC EXPLORERS

5 11.6 Listen to Alec Jacobson and Lia Nahomi Kajiki talking about historical events. Are the sentences true (T) or false (F)?

1 Alec is talking about a famous photograph.
2 Alec's favourite event was in 1925.
3 The Leica 1 was big and heavy.
4 Lia is talking about an old film.
5 Lia's favourite event was in 1895.
6 The film was called *The Lumière Brothers*.

6 Look at the Listening skill box. Then answer the questions.

LISTENING SKILL
Understanding small and large numbers

Sometimes, people want to show that a number is important, interesting or unusual. Here are three ways to do this.

1 Use very large numbers: pay attention to words like *thousands, millions* or *billions*.
2 Explain that a number is small: listen for words like *only* or *just*.
3 Explain that a number is large: listen for words like *more than* or *over*.

1 What words tell you that a number is small?
2 What words tell you that a number is large?

7 11.6 Listen again and write the words you hear. Then work in pairs. Why do Alec and Lia use these words?

1 The Leica 1 was ____________ 125 grams.
2 The film was ____________ a minute long.
3 Today, ____________ of people watch films at cinemas.

8 Read the Grammar box. Does the subject go before or after *was* and *were* in questions?

GRAMMAR Questions with *was / were*

Questions with *was / were* have the same form as questions with *is / are*:
(question word +) *be* + subject
Is *it very popular?* ➔ ***Was*** *it very popular?*
What ***is*** *the movie about?* ➔ *What* ***was*** *the movie about?*
Use *was* with *I, he, she* and *it*.
Where ***was it****?*
Use *were* with *you, we* and *they*.
Who ***were they****?*

Go to page 175 for the Grammar reference.

9 Complete the questions with *was* or *were*.

1 *Was / Were* she a dancer?
2 *Was / Were* they from the same town?
3 Who *was / were* she with yesterday?
4 Who *was / were* those people on TV?
5 Where *was / were* she from?
6 When *was / were* you a student there?

10 Complete the conversation. Write *was* or *were*.

A: Jen, do you remember the Football World Cup in South Africa? When [1]____________ it?
B: Hmm. I think it [2]____________ in 2010. Yes, that's right.
A: Which teams [3]____________ in the finals?
B: Spain and the Netherlands.
A: Ah yes. I remember. It [4]____________ an interesting match ...
B: How old [5]____________ you back then?
A: In 2010? I [6]____________ only 15 years old. But I remember the match ...

SPEAKING

11 Think of a famous event in the last five years. Complete the table for yourself. Use the topics below to help you.

- An event in your country
- An important world event
- A sports event

12 Work in pairs. Ask questions and complete the table for your partner. Guess your partner's event.

A: Was it an event in this country?
B: Yes, it was.
A: Was it a sports event?

	My event	My partner's event
Event		
Type of event		
When		
Where		
Why was it important?		

11D Showing interest

LESSON GOALS
- Learn how to show interest
- Respond to good and bad news
- Tell an interesting story

SPEAKING

1 Work in pairs. Discuss the questions.

1 Do you or your friends sometimes tell stories in English or your first language?

2 Do you or your friends do or say things to let the speaker know you're interested in the story?

Sometimes, I ask questions.

I nod my head and look at the speaker.

I put away my mobile phone!

MY VOICE ▶

2 ▶ 11.2 Watch the video. Answer the questions.

1 Why does the speaker think his story isn't interesting?

2 What are two ways to show interest when listening?

3 Can you think of other ways to show interest?

I laugh when my friends say something funny.

If the story is happy, I try to show that I'm happy too.

3 Look at the Communication skill box. Discuss in pairs. Do people make the same polite sounds in your first language?

COMMUNICATION SKILL
Showing interest

It's good to show the speaker that you are interested in their story. Here are some ways:

Make polite sounds:

Uh-huh

Mm

Oh

Ask questions:

Where was that?

Was it good?

In my language, people often say mm, but they don't say uh-huh.

4 Look at the Useful language box. Discuss questions 1–3 in pairs.

Useful language Expressions for showing interest

Really?
I see.
Interesting.
Wow!
Amazing!
No way!
Oh no!
That's terrible.

1 Which expressions can you say when you hear good news?

2 Which expressions can you say when you hear bad news?

3 Which expressions are for information that isn't good or bad?

5 Read the sentences below. Which do you think is the better response?

1 I was three hours late and I was in the wrong shirt. It was awful.
  a Really?
  b Oh no!

2 The food was amazing. And it was really cheap too!
  a Wow!
  b That's terrible!

3 She wasn't at home. She was at the party – with Sam!
  a No way!
  b That's interesting.

4 She was really sad. Her test results were in, and they weren't great.
  a That's terrible.
  b Amazing!

5 The café was alright. Their food wasn't great, but they were open all night.
  a No way!
  b Interesting.

PRONUNCIATION

6 🎧 11.7 Look at the Clear voice box. Listen and notice how the tone changes when responding to good and bad news.

CLEAR VOICE
Responding to good and bad news

When people respond to something good or interesting, they often use a high voice.

Wow! *That's amazing!*

When they respond to bad news or to something sad, they usually use a low voice.

Oh no! *That's awful.*

7 Work in pairs. Practise the conversations in Exercise 5. When responding, use a high voice for good news and a low voice for bad news.

SPEAKING

8 **OWN IT!** Look at the four boxes (A–D). Choose a topic to tell a story about. Make notes.

A An interesting day in your life

B A bad day at work or school

C A fun birthday

D An interesting story about someone you know

- When did the events happen?
- Where was it?
- How does the story begin?
- What happened?
- How did you feel?

9 Work in pairs. Tell each other stories.

Student A: Tell your partner your story. Use your notes from Exercise 8.

Student B: Show interest. Use polite sounds and ask questions to find out more.

My story is about a fun birthday. It was in 2017. I was in college with my friends. We were …

11E Important people and their lives

LESSON GOALS
- Learn how to write someone's profile
- Explain why someone is special
- Write a profile of someone from history

SPEAKING

1 Work in pairs. Think of some important people from history. Why are they important?

sport	
the arts	
science	
other	

READING FOR WRITING

2 Read the profile. Write the headings in the correct places.

a An amazing book b An interesting life

3 Find the words in the article. Circle the answers.

1 A novel is …
  a a book that tells a story.
  b a person who writes a book.
2 A sailor is …
  a a person who works on a ship or boat.
  b a person who writes books and stories.
3 A hero is …
  a a famous person with a lot of money
  b a brave person who helps people

Miguel de Cervantes

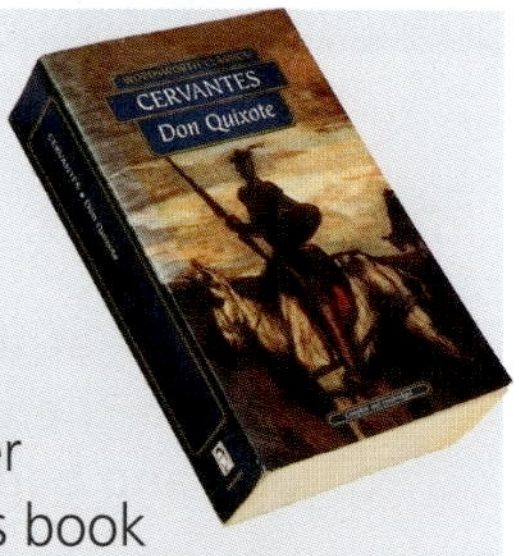

Miguel de Cervantes was a great writer and an important person in history. His book *Don Quixote* (from 1615) is famous all over the world. Many people say it is the first European **novel**.

1 ______________________

Cervantes was born in 1547 in a city near Madrid, Spain. He lived with his parents and his six brothers and sisters. They were very poor. Later in his life, Cervantes was a **sailor** on a ship. He also lived in Italy for a few years. Cervantes died in Spain in 1616. He was 69 years old.

2 ______________________

The book *Don Quixote* is about two people. Don Quixote is not an important person, but he thinks he is. He wants to be a **hero** and help people. He asks someone to help him and the two go on many crazy adventures together. The book is clever and funny, and it's still very popular today.

Marie Curie was the first person to win two Nobel Prizes.

4 Look at the Writing skill box. Then read the profile again.

1 Why is Miguel de Cervantes special?
2 What life events are in the profile?

WRITING SKILL
Writing a person's profile

A good profile explains why a person is interesting or special. To write a simple profile, include the following.

An introduction:

Get the reader interested. Write two or three sentences about the person and why they're important.

Important life events:

Where was the person from? When were they born? Where did they live? And when did they die?

Why the person is special:

Explain why the person is important. If you can, write about their personality too.

5 Look at the Critical thinking skill box. Which questions does Miguel de Cervantes's profile answer?

CRITICAL THINKING SKILL
Explaining why someone is special

You can't just say someone is special. You have to give reasons.

- Were they good at something?
- Were they the first to do something?
- What do people think of them now?

The profile says he was the first to …

The profile says that today, his book is …

6 Look at the Useful language box. Use the expressions to talk about the people in your table in Exercise 1.

Useful language Talking about important people

He was a great …
He was the best …
She was the first person to …
She was (very funny and kind) …
His (book) was the first (European novel) …
Many people still (read his book) today.

WRITING TASK

7 Think of an important person from history. Look at the Writing skill box and write notes about them.

Marie Curie:
- scientist from Poland
- born in 1867
- first person to win two Nobel Prizes
- died in 1934

8 **WRITE** Write the person's profile. Use your notes and Miguel de Cervantes's profile as a model.

9 **CHECK** Use the checklist. My profile …

☐ includes Important life events.
☐ explains Why the person is special.
☐ describes how people remember the person.

10 **REVIEW** Work in pairs. Read your partner's profile. Is there anything else you want to know about the person?

Go to page 159 for the Reflect and review.

EXPLORE MORE!

Find out about famous people in history from different countries. Search using the words 'famous historical people + [country]'.

Iris Apfel is famous in the world of fashion.

12

My story

GOALS

- Understand voices and audiences in an article
- Talk about things people did in the past
- Discuss life stages and emotions
- Understand funny stories
- Use English in the real world
- Write about your life

1 Work in pairs. Discuss the questions.

1 Look at the photo. What is the woman famous for?

2 Does she look like an interesting person?

WATCH

2 ▶ 12.1 Watch the video. Answer the questions.

NATIONAL GEOGRAPHIC EXPLORERS

AFROZ SHAH

MARIA FADIMAN

1 What question did Afroz ask when he was young?

2 Why did Maria go to the rainforest?

3 How did these experiences change their lives?

3 Make connections. Work in pairs. Do you have a special experience of your own? How did it change you?

When I was thirteen, I was on holiday in Sri Lanka with my …

12A My life story

LESSON GOALS

- Talk about important life stages
- Read about an interesting life
- Understand voices and audiences in an article

VOCABULARY

1 Work in pairs. Look at the timeline.

1 Are you a child, a teenager or an adult?
2 At what age are people no longer young? At what age are they old?
3 Do you think the answers to question 2 are the same everywhere?

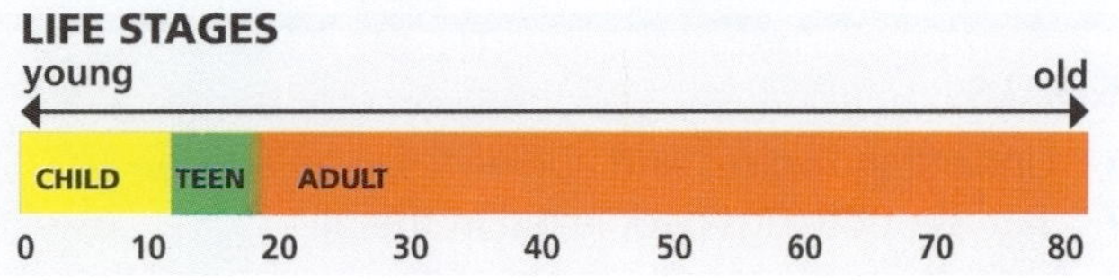

2 12.1 Work in pairs. Listen and repeat the life events. Tick (✓) the things you want to do.

a go to university
b get a job
c get married
d start a business
e finish university
f buy a house
g have children
h live in another country

3 Work in pairs. Look at the life events above.

1 At what age do people usually do these things?
2 In what order do people usually do these things in your country?

Go to page 165 for the Vocabulary reference.

READING

NATIONAL GEOGRAPHIC EXPLORER

4 Read Afroz Shah's life story. Answer the questions.

1 Where does Afroz live now?
2 Where did Afroz grow up?
3 What does Afroz study?

5 Read again. Are the sentences true (T) or false (F)?

1 Afroz works as a photographer.
2 Afroz's mother was a teacher.
3 Afroz's secondary school was in India.
4 Afroz felt many earthquakes when he was young.

6 Look at the Reading skill box. Then look at the article. Find examples of the following:

1 an interviewer asking someone questions
2 a person answering an interviewer's question
3 the writer speaking to the reader

READING SKILL
Understanding voices and audiences

Some articles have several 'voices'. Think about about who is speaking and who they're speaking to.

	Speaker	Speaking to
What was your life like ... ?	interviewer	explorer
Afroz Shah is a National Geographic Explorer.	writer	reader

PRONUNCIATION

7 12.2 Look at the Clear voice box. Listen and repeat.

CLEAR VOICE
Saying syllables with two vowel sounds

Some words have diphthongs. These are two vowel sounds together.

1 /ɪə/ *y**ear*** *h**ere***
2 /ɔɪ/ *b**oy*** *destr**oy***
3 /aʊ/ *n**ow*** *ab**out***

8 12.3 Which vowel sounds are in these words? Write 1, 2 or 3. Listen, check and repeat.

a n**ear** c br**ow**n e t**ow**n
b b**oi**l d cl**ear** f t**oi**let

SPEAKING

9 Work in pairs. Ask and answer these questions from the article. Are your life experiences similar or different?

1 What was your life like when you were a child?
2 Where did you study?

A: When I was a child, I was always with my friends.
B: Me too. I think our lives were similar …

MY LIFE STORY

Afroz Shah is a National Geographic Explorer. He lives in Brunei, where he works as a professor. We ask him some questions about his life.

What was your life like when you were a child?

I was born in a small village in Kashmir, India. The Himalayan mountains were all around me – I was always amazed by them! I lived with my mum, my dad, my two brothers and my sister. My mum worked as a teacher and my dad was a builder. Our village was great – it was like a big family. We didn't have much, but everyone in the village loved us and cared for us.

Where did you study?

My primary and secondary schools were in Jammu and Kashmir, India. I later went to university in Aligarh, India, and I graduated with a Master's degree in Earth sciences. After that, I studied in Australia and got a doctoral degree in geology.

Tell us about your work.

As you know, I study earthquakes. There were many earthquakes in Kashmir when I was young. Most weren't strong, but in the year 2005, a big earthquake destroyed many homes, and people's lives too. Today, I know a lot more about earthquakes and why they happen. Yes, some are dangerous, but they're also an important part of life on Earth.

Afroz in Australia.

Afroz studying a rock.

Afroz was born in the Anantnag District of Jammu & Kashmir, India.

12B Changing the world

LESSON GOALS
- Understand an article about how a footballer helped people
- Learn to use the past simple form of verbs
- Talk about things you did in the past

READING AND GRAMMAR

1 **Discuss in pairs. Can young people change the world? How?**

Yes, they can. There are many things they can do ...

2 **Look at the photo and scan the article. Answer the questions.**

1 Who is the article about?
2 What is his job?
3 What is he also famous for?

3 **Answer the questions. Put the events in order (1–6).**

a Marcus Rashford was born. *1*
b Rashford got his idea to help people.
c Rashford hurt his back.
d Sometimes, Rashford's family didn't have money for food.
e Rashford helped get millions of meals to poor children.
f Rashford joined Manchester United Football Club.

4 **Read the Grammar box. Do you use the past simple form of verbs in negative sentences?**

GRAMMAR Past simple (regular verbs)

Past simple verbs show that something happened in the past.
*He **lived** with his family.*
To make the past simple form of a verb:
1 add *d* to the infinitive
*live → liv**ed***
2 add *ed* to the infinitive
*play → play**ed***
3 repeat the last letter and add *ed*
*stop → stopp**ed***
To make negative sentences, use *did not* (*didn't*) + infinitive:
*They **didn't** have money for food.*

Go to page 176 for the Grammar reference.

5 **Complete the past simple sentences. Use the correct form of the verbs in brackets.**

1 Petra ______________ (score) a lot of home runs last year.
2 My friends ______________ (play) basketball yesterday.
3 We ______________ (not watch) the news last night.
4 My sister and I ______________ (not like) the TV show.
5 She ______________ (ask) him to do something, but he ______________ (not help).
6 I ______________ (visit) her in the summer, and ______________ (stay) at her home for three weeks.

6 **Read the Grammar box. Do you use regular and irregular past tense verbs the same way?**

GRAMMAR Past simple (irregular verbs)

Some past tense forms are irregular. We don't add *d* or *ed*. We change the verb in different ways.
*hurt → **hurt***
*He **hurt** his back.*
*have → **had***
*He **had** a big idea.*
For negative sentences, irregular verbs are like regular verbs. They don't change form.
~~*I didn't knew that.*~~
*I didn't **know** that.*

Go to page 176 for the Grammar reference.

7 **Read the sentences. What are the present tense forms of the bold words?**

1 I didn't want to be late, so I **ran** to school.
2 Nadia **felt** tired because she went to bed late.
3 I **got** home at five o'clock.
4 He **became** a teacher last year.
5 We **had** no time to shower after the match.
6 I **did** my homework in the morning.

EXPLORE MORE!

What other things did Marcus Rashford do to help people? What awards did he get?
Is he still helping people today? Search online for 'Marcus Rashford + Charity'.

MARCUS RASHFORD: CHANGING THE WORLD

To people around the world, Marcus Rashford is a football hero. But to many children in the UK, he is a hero for a different reason.

Growing up

Rashford was born in 1997. He lived with his family in Manchester, England. Life for his family was hard. His mother had three jobs, and sometimes they didn't have money for food. Things changed when Rashford joined Manchester United Football Club. He played his first game for them when he was 18, and soon after, he played his first game for England.

A big idea

In 2020, Rashford hurt his back and had to rest. That was when he had a big idea.There were still many families in the UK that didn't have enough food. Rashford knew what that was like, so he decided to do something. He asked the government and the people of Manchester for help. In a few months, he collected more than £20 million and helped get millions of meals to families in the UK.

8 Complete the sentences. Write the past form of the verbs. Use the *Irregular verbs* list to help you (page 178).

give go have say see sleep take

1 I ______________ Ruth at the cinema yesterday.
2 I ______________ to the park last week.
3 She ______________ lunch with Maya today.
4 Eric ______________ he woke up late.
5 Mala ______________ us her email address.
6 He ______________ the wrong bus to school.
7 Sanya ______________ for nine hours last night.

SPEAKING

9 Make notes. What did you do at the different times below? Write two things for each time. Use the *Irregular verbs* list to help you (page 178).

1 yesterday
2 last week
3 last month
4 last year

10 Work in groups. Talk about the things you did in Exercise 9.

I studied for a test yesterday.

I went to my friend's house last week.

12C A funny thing happened to me

LESSON GOALS

- Understand a funny story
- Ask questions about what people did
- Practise word stress in questions
- Learn about different feelings

SPEAKING

1 Work in pairs. Ask and answer the questions.

1 Do you know anyone who is funny?
2 Do you like telling funny stories in English or in your first language?

LISTENING

NATIONAL GEOGRAPHIC EXPLORER

2 12.4 Listen to Maria Fadiman tell a story. Answer the questions.

1 Jorge and Raul were from *Brazil / Ecuador*.
2 They were walking *in a river / up a mountain*.
3 The journey was *easy / difficult* for Maria.
4 Jorge said Maria walked like a *cat / chicken*.
5 Maria fell because she was *excited / sad*.

3 12.4 Look at the Listening skill box. Then listen again and answer the questions.

LISTENING SKILL
Understanding funny stories

Funny stories often have punchlines. The listener thinks a story ends one way, but the punchline explains how it really ends. People usually make the punchline sound important. They:

- say it at the end of the story
- pause before they say it
- say it louder

1 What is Maria's punchline?
2 What does Maria say just before the punchline?

4 Work in pairs. Do you think Jorge told the truth when he said *'No, no, that's good! Chickens are great at walking!'*?

EXPLORE MORE!

Jokes are questions with funny answers, or funny stories that often aren't real. Search for 'simple jokes' and learn a few.

5 12.5 Listen to the story. Answer the questions.

1 What is the punchline of the story?
2 Why is the story funny or interesting?

'It was very late, and I was super quiet – I didn't want my parents to hear me. I went into my bedroom and climbed into bed. But there was someone there. I jumped out of bed and turned on the lights. It was my mum ... I was in the wrong room!'

GRAMMAR

6 Read the Grammar box. Are the sentences true (T) or false (F)?

GRAMMAR Past simple questions

To make a question, use:
(question word +) *did* + subject + infinitive
Did she fall *into the water?*
(Yes, he did. / No, he didn't.)
Why did she fall *into the water?*

Go to page 177 for the Grammar reference

1 The subject goes between *did* and the verb.
2 You use the past simple form of verbs in questions.

7 Complete the questions with *did* and verbs from the box. Then ask and answer the questions in pairs.

go have live play speak

When you were a child:

1 ______________ you ______________ a best friend?
2 What language ______________ you ______________ at home?
3 What town or city ______________ you ______________ in?
4 How ______________ you ______________ to school?
5 What sports ______________ you ______________?

A: Did you have a best friend?
B: Yes. Her name was Monica ...

PRONUNCIATION

8 12.6 Look at the Clear voice box. Listen and repeat.

CLEAR VOICE
Stressing words in questions

In questions, the subject is usually not stressed.
In *yes/no* questions, stress the verb.
Did you ***like*** *it?*
In *wh-* and *how* questions, stress the question word and the verb.
Where *did you* ***live?***

VOCABULARY

9 12.7 Listen and repeat the words. When do you have these feelings? Which are good feelings?

happy excited
tired surprised
sad angry
bored afraid

10 Complete the sentences. Use the word from Exercise 9 you think works best.

1 Who was that? What was that noise? I was so ______________.
2 I worked fourteen hours yesterday. I was really ______________.
3 I didn't know about the party. I was so ______________!
4 There was nothing to do. I was really ______________.

Go to page 165 for the Vocabulary reference.

SPEAKING

11 Make notes. Think of a story about you or someone you know.

- When and where did it happen?
- How does the story begin?
- What happened then?
- How did the people in the story feel?
- How does the story end?

12 Work in pairs. Share your story. Ask your partner questions about their story.

My story happened last year. I was at home with my sister. I was bored, so I asked her to ...

12D Using English in the real world

LESSON GOALS

- Understand how to use English in the real world
- Learn phrases to explain a word or idea
- Talk about a difficult topic

SPEAKING

1 Work in pairs. Discuss the questions.

1 Is speaking English inside the classroom easy for you?
2 Is speaking English outside the classroom easy for you?
3 What do you find the most difficult about speaking in English?

MY VOICE

2 ▶ 12.2 Watch the video. Circle the answers.

1 People usually ______ you when you make a few mistakes.
   a understand   b don't understand
2 When you don't know a word or idea, ...
   a change the topic.   b explain it.
3 Try to ______ when speaking English.
   a relax and smile   b talk quickly
4 The video tells us to speak ______.
   a better English   b English often

3 Look at the Communication skill box. Which tip do you think is the most important? Why?

COMMUNICATION SKILL
Using English in the real world

To improve your English, use it with other people. Here are some tips.
1 Don't worry about mistakes.
2 When you don't know a word ...
- think of another similar word or words.
- explain the word or idea you are trying to say.

3 Relax!

4 Look at the Useful language box. Then work in pairs. What words do you think the phrases in the box describe?

Useful language phrases to explain a word
It's like a (boat) but (very big).
How do you say it? (Finished college)?
It's a kind of (animal from Australia).
You use it to (make bread).

jet ski

muffin

5 Look at the four photos and their labels. Then complete the sentences below. Choose an object for each sentence and write about it. Don't use the name of the object.

1 It's like a ... , but ...
2 It's a ... how do you say it?
3 You use it to ...
4 It's a kind of ...

6 Work in pairs. Read your sentences from Exercise 5 to your partner. Guess the item your partner is describing in each sentence.

A: It's like a ... , but it's ...

B: Is it a jet ski?

SPEAKING

7 Choose a topic below to describe to your partner in Exercise 8. Make notes.

- A film I really like
- A book I read
- The world two hundred years ago
- How animals can help people

The world two hundred years ago:

- no cars or planes *- no internet*
- people rode horses *- fewer people*

8 **OWN IT!** Work in pairs. Discuss your topics in Exercise 7. Use the Useful language to help you explain difficult words or ideas. And remember: don't worry about mistakes!

A: Two hundred years ago, the world was different. There weren't any cars or planes.

B: How did people travel?

A: They rode horses and other animals like ... how do you say it? It's like a ...

9 Work in pairs. Look at the checklist. Tick (✓) the items your partner did well. Then talk about your checklists.

My partner ...

- ☐ smiled and looked relaxed.
- ☐ was friendly.
- ☐ was not worried about mistakes.
- ☐ looked at me when they spoke.
- ☐ explained words they didn't know.
- ☐ explained difficult ideas well.

A: Great job! You were very relaxed.

B: You were great too. You explained difficult words and ideas well, like ...

EXPLORE MORE!

Where do people speak English? Which countries have the most English speakers? Do any of the countries surprise you? Search online for 'Countries with the most English speakers'.

12E This is me

LESSON GOALS

- Learn how to include interesting information
- Learn expressions for talking about the past
- Write your life story

SPEAKING

1 Work in pairs. Discuss the questions.

1 What are some words that describe your personality?

2 What are some words that describe your personality when you were a young child?

I think I'm a quiet person. When I was a child, I was always very excited ...

READING FOR WRITING

2 Read Adriana's life story. Answer the questions.

1 How was life different when Adriana was a child?

2 What were the evenings in her town like?

3 Why did Adriana's life in the US get better?

3 Read again. Are the sentences true (T) or false (F)?

1 Adriana is from Morocco.

2 Life was fun when she was a child.

3 Her first guitar was expensive.

4 She got married last year.

5 She now has three children.

MY LIFE STORY

I'm Adriana. I'm from Mexico. I'm 34 years old and I play music.

When I was a child, I lived in a small town far from the city. Things were different back then. There weren't any tall buildings or shopping centres in town, and most of us didn't have mobile phones. But life was fun! We played football and other games in the park every day. I remember we always stopped at 6 p.m. There weren't any street lights, and the evenings were very dark!

When I was a teenager, my family moved to the US. It was a bad time for me because I didn't have friends. But then I got a guitar, and my life changed. It was a cheap guitar. It didn't sound good or look nice, but I loved it! I practised every day, started a band and made a lot of great new friends.

In 2015, I married my husband, Ricardo. We now have two beautiful children and a black cat named Sabrina. I'm very happy with my life.

4 Look at the Writing skill box. What interesting information does Adriana give the reader?

WRITING SKILL
Including interesting information

When you write, include interesting information. For each main idea, note down one or two interesting points:

Main idea:

When I was a child, I lived in a small town.

Interesting points

Things were different back then. There weren't any tall buildings or shopping centres in town, and most of us didn't have mobile phones.

Use adjectives to say how things looked or felt:

There weren't any street lights, and the evenings were very ***dark****!*

5 Look at the Useful language box. Then complete the conversation. Practise it in pairs.

Useful language Expressions to talk about the past

When I was young / a child / at school,
Back then,
Things were different
Life was different
I remember (we always stopped at 6 p.m.)

A: When I 1______________ at school, life was 2______________.

B: Yes, it was. I 3______________ the long walks to school. There weren't any trains!

A: That's right. 4______________ were really different!

B: Were you happy back 5______________?

A: Yes, I was. Life was great 6______________ I was a child!

6 Look at the Critical thinking skill box. Then work in pairs. Think about when you were a young child. What would a reader want to know?

CRITICAL THINKING SKILL
Guessing what the reader wants

When you write, imagine you are the reader. You don't know the story. Ask these questions:

- What does the reader need to know?
- How can the story be more interesting?

WRITING TASK

7 Think about your life story and make notes. Write four main ideas. For each main idea, write one or two interesting points.

Main idea 1: ______________________________

Main idea 2: ______________________________

Main idea 3: ______________________________

Main idea 4: ______________________________

8 Look at your notes in Exercise 7. Think of adjectives you can use to describe how things looked or felt. Add them to your notes.

9 **WRITE** Write your life story. Use your notes to help you, and Adriana's life story as a model. Try to make your story interesting.

10 **CHECK** Use the checklist. My story ...

- ☐ includes three or four main ideas.
- ☐ includes interesting points.
- ☐ describes how things looked or felt.
- ☐ uses the past simple correctly.

11 **REVIEW** Work in pairs. Read your partner's life story. Do they do all the things in the checklist? Tell them what you think is interesting about their stories. Be positive!

Go to page 159 for the Reflect and review.

Reflect and review

1 Hello! *Pages 10–21*

1 **Look at the goals from Unit 1. How confident do you feel about them? Write the letters (a–f) on the line.**

a Scan for names and places
b Talk about yourself and other people
c Learn about countries, nationalities and numbers
d Listen to long numbers
e Introduce yourself
f Write your information on an employee pass

1 – very confident
2 – confident
3 – OK
4 – not so confident
5 – not confident at all

2 **Work in pairs. Complete the sentences.**

1 Three examples of countries are ...
2 Three examples of nationalities are ...
3 To introduce myself, I can say ...

3 **Choose two ways to practise the Unit 1 goals. Add one more idea. Then share your ideas with a partner.**

- Read about countries and nationalities
- Read about people
- Introduce myself to people
- Talk to other students in class
- Practise asking for phone numbers
- Practise reading social media profiles
- Read the unit again
- Watch videos in English

My idea ______________________________

2 My home *Pages 22–33*

1 **Look at the goals from Unit 2. Write ✓ for the ones you're confident about. Write ✗ for the ones you're not confident about.**

- Guess the meanings of words
- Talk about groups of people
- Learn about places at home and in town
- Get ready for listening tasks
- Ask people where things are
- Write a friendly email

2 **Work in pairs. Discuss the questions.**

1 What is your favourite room in the house?
2 What's your favourite place in town?
3 What are four words you can use to describe where things are?

3 **Complete the sentences (1–3) with these ideas or your own ideas.**

ask more questions
breathe and relax
check that I understand
keep things quiet
look at photos and pictures
point and ask
read the text again, slowly

1 To guess the meaning of new words, I can ...
2 To get ready for a listening task, I can ...
3 When I ask where things are, I can ...

3 My stuff *Pages 34–45*

1 **Look at the goals from Unit 3. How confident do you feel about them? Order them from 1 (very confident) to 6 (not confident at all).**

Understand commas and the word *and*
Learn how to talk about your things
Describe things by their colours
Listen for important words
Ask questions to help you understand
Write a social media post about a special item

2 **Think about the Unit 3 goals. Complete the sentences with your own ideas.**

1 I find it difficult to ______________.
2 I enjoyed ______________.
3 ______________ is something I can improve.

3 **Think about the Unit 3 goals. Choose two things to improve. Write your ideas of how to improve them.**

I want to improve ...

understanding commas and the word *and*.
talking about my things.
describing things by their colours.
listening for important words.
asking questions to help me understand.
writing about special items.

To improve these things, I can:

1 ________________________________
2 ________________________________

4 Habits *Pages 46–57*

1 **Look at the goals from Unit 4. How confident do you feel about them? Write the letters (a–f) in the table.**

a Scan an article for useful information
b Talk about people's habits
c Say the time and the days of the week
d Listen for tone
e Make plans
f Write a work email

😀	😐

2 **Work in pairs. Discuss the questions.**

1 Which goals from the unit can you do well?
2 Which goals can you improve on?
3 What five expressions can you remember from the unit?

3 **Write three ways to improve one of the goals from Exercise 2, question 2. Use these phrases or your own ideas.**

read more news articles
ask people about their habits
talk about my schedule
listen to actors on TV to hear their tone
do more grammar exercises
read the unit again
practise writing emails in English
keep a diary of expressions

Three things I can do to improve my goal are ...

- ________________________________
- ________________________________
- ________________________________

Reflect and review

5 Inside or outside? Pages 58–69

1 **Look at the goals from Unit 5. Tick (✓) the three you feel most confident about.**

- Get ready to read an article
- Talk about activities people like doing
- Talk about the months and seasons
- Know what information to listen for
- Invite people to do things
- Write a bucket list

2 **Work in pairs. Complete the sentences.**

1 Four fun activities are ...
2 Four question words are ...
3 Three ways of ordering a list are ...

3 **Complete the sentences with these ideas or your own ideas.**

choose an activity we both like
find a time we are both free
read the questions
read the question words
listen for key words
think about a good place for both of us
think about the topic and what I know
think of words I know about the topic

1 Before I read an article, I can ...
2 Before I do a listening task, I can ...
3 When doing a listening task, I can ...
4 When I invite someone to do an activity with me, I can ...

6 Food around the world Pages 70–81

1 **Look at the goals from Unit 6. Work in pairs. Use these words and phrases to say how you feel about each goal. You can use the words and phrases more than once.**

improve very confident more practice
important happy OK

- Skim a text for general information
- Talk about countable and uncountable things
- Learn about different food items and dishes
- Listen and write notes
- Order food at a restaurant
- Write a simple restaurant review

2 **Complete the sentences with your own ideas. Then compare with a partner.**

1 Three countable things are ...
2 Three uncountable things are ...
3 Some phrases for ordering food at a restaurant are ...

3 **Think about the goals in Exercise 1. Choose two things to improve. How can you improve them? Discuss with a partner.**

I want to improve …

- skimming a text for general information
- talking about countable and uncountable things
- understanding different food items and dishes
- listening and writing notes
- ordering food at a restaurant
- writing restaurant reviews

7 Family and friends *Pages 82–93*

1 **Look at the goals from Unit 7. How confident do you feel about them? Write the letters (a–f) in the table.**

a Understand the purpose of a text
b Ask questions with the present simple
c Talk about people in your family
d Listen to descriptions of people
e Show appreciation
f Write a text message asking for help

I feel confident	I need more practice

2 **Complete the sentences with your own ideas.**

1 The members of my family are ...
2 Examples of some open and closed present simple questions are ...
3 I can describe my best friend as ...

3 **Choose two Unit 7 goals to practise more, and two ways to practise them. Discuss with a partner.**

Read different texts and think about what the author wants
Ask people about their daily lives
Ask people about their families
Make a family tree
Practise listening more
Practise describing people
Say 'thank you' more often
Write more text messages

8 Things we can do *Pages 94–105*

1 **Look at the goals from Unit 8. Tick (✓) the three you feel most confident about.**

Understand pronouns
Talk about things people can do
Learn common adjectives
Listen for general information
Ask others for help
Write a job application

2 **Work in pairs. Discuss the questions.**

1 What are some things you can do?
2 What are some interesting things animals can do?
3 What are some phrases you can use to ask for or offer help?

3 **Think about the goals you didn't tick in Exercise 1. Choose two ways you can practise these goals. Add two more ideas. Then share your ideas with a partner.**

Read more stories about people
Talk to my friends about their abilities
Practise describing things
Listen for big ideas, not just details
Try asking friends for help more often
Read different job ads
Think about what skills I have
Think about the skills companies want

My ideas:

___

___

Reflect and review

9 Travel Pages 106–117

1 Look at the goals from Unit 9. How confident do you feel about them? Order them from 1 (very confident) to 6 (not confident at all).

- Understand words in brackets
- Use *there is* and *there are*
- Talk about transport and the weather
- Listen to advertisements
- Speak on the phone
- Write a postcard

2 Work in pairs. Discuss the questions.

1 What do you think you did well in the unit?
2 Which of the goals can you improve on?
3 What five vocabulary items can you remember from the unit?

3 Think about the goal you gave number 6 in Exercise 1. Choose the best way to practise this goal. Then share your ideas with a partner.

1 I can practise ...
- reading.
- writing.
- speaking.
- listening.

2 I can ...
- read more travel articles.
- watch the weather news on TV.
- watch travel shows online.
- talk to friends about places I want to visit.
- write a letter about my own town or city.

10 Staying healthy Pages 118–129

1 Look at the goals from Unit 10. Work in pairs. Tell your partner if you agree or disagree with each statement below and why.

After studying Unit 10, I can ...

1 understand headings and parts of an article.
2 describe things that are happening now.
3 name different parts of the body.
4 listen for specific information.
5 ask for and give directions.
6 write a simple report.

2 Complete the sentences with your own ideas.

1 To identify parts of an article, I can ...
2 Some parts of the body are ...
3 Some phrases for asking for directions are ...

3 Complete the sentences with these ideas or your own ideas.

read magazine articles
ask others for directions more often
talk more with people about daily life
listen to interviews
practise my intonation
practise reading the titles and headings of articles
read more tables
pay better attention when people speak

1 To practise my reading skills, I can ...
2 To practise my listening skills, I can ...
3 To practise my speaking skills, I can ...

11 People from the past *Pages 130–141*

1 Look at the goals from Unit 11. Tick (✓) the goals you feel confident about. Underline the goals you want to practise more.

Understand time order in an article
Talk about people and things from the past
Say when people were born, lived and died
Understand small and large numbers
Show interest while listening
Write a profile about someone from history

2 Complete the sentences with your own ideas.

1 To understand the order of events in an article, I can ...
2 Some words for discussing when a past event happened are ...
3 One way to show interest in a story is to ...

3 Choose one of the goals from Exercise 1 to improve. Tick (✓) one thing you can do to improve it. Add one more idea of your own.

Read articles about the lives of famous people.
Practise making timelines.
Discuss the lives of people I admire.
Talk about my own personal history.
Share an important event from my past with others.
Watch history programmes on TV.
Use phrases and sounds to show interest.
Read profiles of people that lived in the past.
Practise writing profiles of people I admire.

My idea ______________________

12 My story *Pages 142–153*

1 Look at the goals from Unit 12. Work in pairs. Use these words and phrases to say how you feel about each goal. You can use the words and phrases more than once.

happy   important   improve
more practice   OK   very confident

- Understand voices and audiences in an article
- Talk about things people did in the past
- Discuss life stages and emotions
- Understand funny stories
- Use English in the real world
- Write about my life

2 Work in pairs. Discuss the questions.

1 What do you think you did well in the unit?
2 What do you think is the most useful thing you learned? Why?
3 Which goals do you want to improve on? Why?

3 Think about the Unit 12 goals. Choose two things to improve. Write your ideas of how to improve them.

I want to be better at ...

understanding voices and audiences in an article.
talking about things people did in the past.
discussing life stages and emotions.
understanding funny stories
using English in the real world.
writing about my life.

To improve these things, I can ...

____

____

____

Vocabulary reference

UNIT 1

Countries and nationalities

Argentina /ˌɑːdʒən'tiːnə/ *He's from Argentina.*
Brazil /brə'zɪl/ *Brazil is very beautiful.*
Brazilian /brə'zɪliən/ *Brazilian food is great!*
British /'brɪtɪʃ/ *My teacher is British.*
China /'tʃaɪnə/ *Many people live in China.*
France /frɑːns/ *Maya's home is in France.*
Germany /'dʒɜːməni/ *Germany is famous for cars.*
German /'dʒɜːmən/ *He's German.*
Japan /dʒə'pæn/ *Tokyo is in Japan.*
Moroccan /mə'rɒkən/ *She's Moroccan.*
Omani /əʊ'mɑːni/ *She's not Omani.*
Peruvian /pə'ruːviən/ *That dish is Peruvian.*
the United Kingdom /ðə juˌnaɪtɪd 'kɪŋdəm/ *She's a teacher from the United Kingdom.*
the United States /ðə juːˌnaɪtɪd steɪts/ *The United States is big.*
Turkish /'tɜː.kɪʃ/ *My friend is Turkish.*
Vietnamese /ˌvjetnə'miːz/ *I like Vietnamese food.*

Numbers (0–10)

zero /'zɪərəʊ/ *The number 0 is zero.*
one /wʌn/ *Max has one pencil.*
two /tuː/ *Ichiro is two years old.*
three /θriː/ *Three cups are on the table.*
four /fɔː/ *Rosa has four classes today.*
five /faɪv/ *I go home at five o'clock.*
six /sɪks/ *Alan's family has six people.*
seven /'sevən/ *The class has seven students.*
eight /eɪt/ *I have eight pens in my bag.*
nine /naɪn/ *The garden has nine trees.*
ten /ten/ *This test has ten questions.*

1 Look at the countries. Complete the table.

Country	Number of letters	Nationality
Argentina	*nine*	*Argentinian*
Germany		
Japan		
Oman		
Turkey		
The UK		

2 Work in pairs. Answer the questions.
1 Which country would you like to visit? Why?
2 Do you know anyone from these countries?

UNIT 2

Rooms in a house

bathroom (n) /'bɑːθruːm/ *Where is the bathroom?*
bed (n) /bed/ *The cat is under the bed.*
bedroom (n) /'bedruːm/ *This flat has two bedrooms.*
dining room (n) /'daɪnɪŋ ruːm/ *This is a small dining room.*
dining table (n) /'daɪnɪŋ 'teɪbəl/ *It's on the dining table.*
fridge (n) /frɪdʒ/ *The oranges are in the fridge.*
kitchen (n) /'kɪtʃɪn/ *Jenny cooks in the kitchen.*
living room (n) /'lɪvɪŋ ruːm/ *The living room has four chairs.*
shower (n) /'ʃaʊə(r)/ *This house has two showers.*
sofa (n) /'səʊfə/ *The children are on the sofa.*
toilet (n) /'tɔɪlət/ *The toilet is in the bathroom.*
TV (n) /tiː'viː/ *The TV is in the living room.*

Places in town

bus station (n) /bʌs 'steɪʃən/ *He's at the bus station.*
cinema (n) /'sɪnɪmə/ *The cinema has a new film.*
city (n) /'sɪti/ *New York is a large city.*
library (n) /'laɪbrəri/ *This book is from the library.*
museum (n) /mjuː'zɪəm/ *A museum has old things.*
park (n) /pɑːk/ *You can see many birds at the park.*
restaurant (n) /'restrɒnt/ *This restaurant is great!*
school (n) /skuːl/ *How do you like school?*
shopping centre (n) /'ʃɒpɪŋ 'sentə(r)/ *This city has many shopping centres.*
supermarket (n) /'suːpəmɑːkɪt/ *I shop at the supermarket.*
town (n) /taʊn/ *Jen comes from a small town.*
train station (n) /treɪn 'steɪʃən/ *This is a new train station.*
village (n) /'vɪlɪdʒ/ *Nicole lives in a small village.*

1 Match the descriptions with the words.

1 where you see films — a bedroom
2 what you sit on — b TV
3 a place with books — c town
4 where you sleep — d cinema
5 what you watch — e sofa
6 a small city — f library

2 Work in pairs. Discuss these questions.
1 What is in your house?
2 What room in your house are you in the most?
3 Which places above are in your city or town?

UNIT 3

Travel items

bag (n) /bæg/ *How many pens are in your bag?*
bank card (n) /bæŋk kɑːd/ *This is my bank card.*
book (n) /bʊk/ *That book is from China.*
camera (n) /ˈkæmərə/ *This is Ren's camera.*
dress (n) /dres/ *Maria's dress is on the bed.*
keys (n) /kiːz/ *Are these your keys?*
notepad (n) /ˈnəʊtpæd/ *Please bring your notepad.*
passport (n) /ˈpɑːspɔːt/ *I always carry my passport.*
phone (n) /fəʊn/ *Where's my phone?*
toothbrush (n) /ˈtuːθbrʌʃ/ *My toothbrush is in the bag.*
T-shirt (n) /ˈtiːʃɜːt/ *Kim's T-shirt is nice.*
water bottle (n) /ˈwɔːtə ˈbɒtəl/ *Is that your water bottle?*

Colours

black (adj) /blæk/ *Ali drives a black car.*
blue (adj) /bluː/ *Terry is in a blue shirt.*
green (adj) /griːn/ *The grass is green.*
orange (adj) /ˈɒrɪndʒ/ *The toy is orange.*
pink (adj) /pɪŋk/ *Dani's favourite colour is pink.*
purple (adj) /ˈpɜːpəl/ *My phone is in the purple bag.*
red (adj) /red/ *Those flowers are red.*
white (adj) /waɪt/ *Is this Min-seo's white guitar?*
yellow (adj) /ˈjeləʊ/ *He lives in a yellow house.*

1 Write the correct item to match each description.

1 You take photos with it. ______________
2 You carry your things in it. ______________
3 You call people with it. ______________
4 You use this to get money. ______________
5 You read stories in this. ______________
6 You use this to open the door. ______________
7 You can write things in this. ______________

2 Complete the sentences by writing the colour. The first letter is given.

1 Zhong is in a w______________ T-shirt.
2 Are the flowers y______________?
3 Karl's favourite colour is o______________.
4 Patty has two r______________ dresses.
5 Yuki's bag is g______________.

3 Work in pairs. Discuss these questions.

1 What do you take with you on trips?
2 What do you have with you now?
3 What is your favourite colour? Why?

UNIT 4

Numbers (11–100)

eleven /ɪˈlevən/ *This house has eleven rooms.*
twelve /twelv/ *A year has twelve months.*
thirteen /θɜːˈtiːn/ *He has thirteen pens.*
fourteen /fɔːˈtiːn/ *Hadid is fourteen years old.*
fifteen /fɪfˈtiːn/ *The bus leaves in fifteen minutes.*
sixteen /sɪksˈtiːn/ *The class has sixteen students.*
seventeen /sevənˈtiːn/ *I have seventeen books.*
eighteen /eɪˈtiːn/ *Bus eighteen goes to the park.*
nineteen /naɪnˈtiːn/ *School ends in nineteen days.*
twenty /ˈtwenti/ *This box has twenty water bottles.*
thirty /ˈθɜːti/ *My house is thirty kilometres away.*
forty /ˈfɔːti/ *The class has forty people in it.*
fifty /ˈfɪfti/ *Ben's report is fifty pages long.*
sixty /ˈsɪksti/ *This zoo has more than sixty animals.*
seventy /ˈsevənti/ *Gina has seventy online friends.*
eighty /ˈeɪti/ *Elsa's village has only eighty houses.*
ninety /ˈnaɪnti/ *The film is ninety minutes long.*
one hundred /wʌn ˈhʌndrəd/ *The test has one hundred questions.*

Days of the week

Sunday /ˈsʌndeɪ/ *I don't work on Sunday.*
Monday /ˈmʌndeɪ/ *Luca begins work on Monday.*
Tuesday /ˈtjuːzdeɪ/ *Is today Tuesday?*
Wednesday /ˈwenzdeɪ/ *Wednesday is a busy day.*
Thursday /ˈθɜːzdeɪ/ *I have a test on Thursday.*
Friday /ˈfraɪdeɪ/ *Are you free on Friday?*
Saturday /ˈsætədeɪ/ *Ian plays football on Saturday.*

1 Write out the numbers.

1 12 ______________
2 19 ______________
3 43 ______________
4 58 ______________

2 Complete the sentences by writing the day. Some letters are given.

1 On M______________, Aliya goes to school.
2 There will be a test this Th______________.
3 Lin's birthday is on Sa______________.
4 Let's have lunch together on W______________.

3 Work in pairs. Discuss these questions.

1 How old is your best friend?
2 What day do you like best? Why?
3 On which days are you busy?

Vocabulary reference

UNIT 5

Common activities

call a friend /kɔːl ə frend/ *She needs to call a friend.*
chat online /tʃæt ɒn'laɪn/ *Fran loves chatting online.*
draw a picture /drɔː ə 'pɪktʃə(r)/ *Malik likes drawing pictures in the park.*
listen to music /'lɪsən tə 'mjuːzɪk/ *Tim listens to music on the way to school.*
play video games /pleɪ 'vɪdɪəʊ geɪmz/ *I play video games online with my friends.*
read a book /riːd ə bʊk/ *I like to read a book before bed.*
sing a song /sɪŋ ə sɒŋ/ *He wants to sing a song with my band.*
watch TV /wɒtʃ tiː'viː/ *Karl always watches TV after dinner.*

Months

January /'dʒænjuəri/ *The year begins in January.*
February /'februəri/ *February is a cold month.*
March /mɑːtʃ/ *March is the start of spring.*
April /'eɪprəl/ *It often rains in April.*
May /meɪ/ *In May, there are many new flowers.*
June /dʒuːn/ *Summer begins in June.*
July /dʒʊ'laɪ/ *In July, we go to the beach a lot.*
August /ɔː'gəst/ *Jeff's birthday is in August.*
September /sep'tembə(r)/ *School starts in September.*
October /ɒk'təʊbə(r)/ *The weather is cool in October.*
November /nəʊ'vembə(r)/ *School ends in November.*
December /dɪ'sembə(r)/ *Winter starts in December.*

Seasons

spring (n) /sprɪŋ/ *The flowers are beautiful in spring.*
summer (n) /'sʌmə/ *Summer here is very hot.*
autumn (n) /'ɔːtəm/ *Autumn is called 'fall' in the US.*
winter (n) /'wɪntə/ *Winters here are very cold.*

1 Complete the sentences with the correct verb.

1 Do you want to ______________ TV?
2 Malia always ______________ online with me.
3 They ______________ video games on Saturday.
4 Sometimes, I like to ______________ a friend.
5 I want to ______________ a picture of my cat.
6 I usually ______________ to music at night.

2 Work in pairs. Discuss these questions.

1 Which do you like: winter or summer? Why?
2 What is your favourite month? Why?
3 Do you like four seasons or one long warm season?

UNIT 6

Food

bread (n) /bred/ *Sean often has bread for breakfast.*
cheese (n) /tʃiːz/ *Rei loves to eat cheese.*
coffee (n) /'kɒfi/ *I drink two cups of coffee a day.*
eggs (n) /egz/ *How many eggs do we need?*
fish (n) /fɪʃ/ *There are many fish in the sea.*
fruit (n) /fruːt/ *Bananas and oranges are types of fruit.*
meat (n) /miːt/ *Some people do not eat meat.*
milk (n) /mɪlk/ *Cheese is made from milk.*
noodles (n) /'nuːdəlz/ *Tessa wants noodles for dinner.*
rice (n) /raɪs/ *Rice is popular in many countries.*
tea (n) /tiː/ *Would you like a cup of tea?*
vegetables (n) /'vedʒtəbəlz/ *Please eat your vegetables!*

Places for groceries

corner shop (n) /'kɔːnər ʃɒp/ *I buy milk from the small corner shop.*
market (n) /'mɑːkɪt/ *The market is busy on Sunday.*
supermarket (n) /'suːpəmɑːkɪt/ *Are you going to the supermarket?*

1 Complete the sentences with these words.

coffee fruit market noodles meat vegetables

1 Oranges are a kind of ______________.
2 ______________ are a popular food from China.
3 Mateo likes drinking ______________ in the park.
4 I like potatoes and other ______________.
5 Sally shops at the ______________ on Sundays.
6 ______________ comes from animals.

2 Choose the correct option to complete the sentences.

1 I eat *bread* / *tea* for breakfast.
2 *Eggs* / *Vegetables* come from birds.
3 Steve loves *cheese* / *tea* on his pizza.
4 *Bread* / *Fish* are animals from the sea.
5 Jon drinks a glass of *cheese* / *milk* every day.

3 Work in pairs. Discuss these questions.

1 What do you like eating for lunch?
2 What sweet foods and spicy dishes do you like?
3 What is a popular drink in your country?

UNIT 7

Family members

brother (n) /'brʌðə/ *Leo is my brother.*
children (n) /'tʃɪldrən/ *Carla has three children.*
daughter (n) /'dɔːtə/ *Their daughter is Fatma.*
father (n) /'fɑːðə/ *Her father is 60 years old.*
grandfather (n) /'grændfɑːðə(r)/ *His grandfather is old.*
grandmother (n) /'grændmʌðə(r)/ *Yasuke lives with his grandmother.*
husband (n) /'hʌzbənd/ *Mai's husband is a scientist.*
mother (n) /mʌðə/ *Adam's mother lives in London.*
parent (n) /'peərənt/ *His parents are from Indonesia.*
sister (n) /'sɪstə/ *Max has three sisters.*
son (n) /sʌn/ *Hasan's son is in grade three.*
wife (n) /waɪf/ *David's wife is from China.*

Appearance and personality

blonde (adj) /blɒnd/ *She has blonde hair.*
clever (adj) /'klevə(r)/ *He's a clever boy.*
dark (adj) /dɑːk/ *Jim's hair is dark.*
funny (adj) /'fʌni/ *Nora is really funny.*
interesting (adj) /'ɪntrəstɪŋ/ *Josh is an interesting writer.*
long (adj) /lɒŋ/ *She has long, dark hair.*
nice (adj) /naɪs/ *She's a really nice person.*
quiet (adj) /'kwaɪət/ *He's quiet when he's in a group.*
short (adj) /ʃɔːt/ *Leah is really short.*
tall (adj) /tɔːl/ *Bill is very tall.*

1 Match these words to the sentences.

1 Her father's father. a father
2 The boy that is their child. b grandfather
3 His mother's husband. c son
4 Her grandmother's daughter. d mother

2 Choose the correct option to complete the sentences.

1 Cheryl has *blonde / tall* hair.
2 Ahmed is good at maths. He's *clever / friendly*.
3 He tells good stories. He's *dark / interesting*.
4 She makes people laugh. She's *funny / long*.
5 Peter has *dark / friendly* hair.

3 Work in pairs. Discuss these questions.

1 Who is in your family?
2 How would you describe yourself?
3 What kind of person is your best friend?

UNIT 8

Common abilities

bake a cake /beɪk ə keɪk/ *I can't bake a cake.*
climb a mountain /klaɪm ə 'maʊntɪn/ *Climbing a mountain is hard work.*
cook a meal /kʊk ə mɪəl/ *Let's cook a meal for lunch.*
drive a car /draɪv ə kɑː/ *Do you know how to drive a car?*
paint a picture /peɪnt ə 'pɪktʃər/ *My son wants to paint a picture of me.*
play a musical instrument /pleɪ ə 'mjuːzɪkəl 'ɪn.strə.mənt/ *Can you play a musical instrument?*
ride a bike /raɪd ə baɪk/ *Mara's son doesn't know how to ride a bike.*
speak a language /spiːk ə 'læŋgwɪdʒ/ *I want to learn to speak a new language.*

Adjectives for animals

beautiful (adj) /'bjuːtɪfəl/ *That bird is beautiful.*
fast (adj) /fɑːst/ *The bird flies very fast.*
heavy (adj) /'hevi/ *That tortoise is big and heavy.*
large (adj) /lɑːdʒ/ *The elephant is very large.*
light (adj) /laɪt/ *That bag is light and easy to carry.*
slow (adj) /sləʊ/ *Tortoises are very slow.*
small (adj) /smɔːl/ *A mouse is a small animal.*
strong (adj) /strɒŋ/ *Bears can be very strong.*

1 Complete the sentences with the correct verb.

1 Fatma likes to ______________ pictures.
2 Audrey wants to ______________ some bread.
3 Ken ______________ one new mountain every year.
4 Laura ______________ her bike to school.
5 Rami knows how to ______________ the piano.

2 Chose the correct option to complete the sentences.

1 That painting is really *beautiful / light*!
2 His house is *large / slow* with many rooms.
3 This train is very *slow / strong*. It will take us hours to get to London!
4 Elephants are *fast / strong*. They can carry many things.
5 Birds can fly because they're *light / slow*.

3 Work in pairs. Discuss these questions.

1 Which of the activities above can you do?
2 Which of the activities above do you enjoy?
3 What's your favourite animal? Describe it.

Vocabulary reference

UNIT 9

Different ways to travel

car (n) /kɑː/ *Bill drives his car to work every day.*
bike (n) /baɪk/ *Maria rides her bike to school.*
boat (n) /bəʊt/ *They like travelling by boat.*
bus (n) /bʌs/ *Riding a bus is cheap.*
drive (v) /draɪv/ *Alexey drives a taxi at night.*
fly (v) /flaɪ/ *I fly to France on Monday.*
motorbike (n) /ˈməʊtəbaɪk/ *Leah rides her motorbike to work.*
plane (n) /pleɪn/ *The plane leaves at 9 a.m.*
ride (v) /raɪd/ *Rami loves to ride his motorbike.*
sail (v) /seɪl/ *He sails his boat around the world.*
take (v) /teɪk/ *Do you want to take a bus to town?*
taxi (n) /ˈtæksi/ *He wants to call a taxi.*
train (n) /treɪn/ *This train is really fast.*
travel by (v) /ˈtrævəl baɪ/ *Jane loves to travel by bus.*

The weather

rain (n) /ˈreɪn/ *She doesn't like the rain.*
snow (n) /ˈsnəʊ/ *I like playing in the snow.*
sun (n) /ˈsʌn/ *The sun is really hot today!*
wind (n) /ˈwɪnd/ *The wind outside is very strong.*

1 Complete the sentences. Choose the correct option.

1 He likes *driving / sailing* boats.
2 Deena knows how to fly a *plane / taxi*.
3 They drive their *bikes / cars* to work
4 Josh wants to take a *boat / bus* across Europe.
5 Andrew *drives / takes* the train to work.
6 Mel doesn't ride her *car / motorbike* on rainy days.

2 Complete the sentences. Use these words.

rain snow sun wind

1 There's a lot of ______________. I can go skiing!
2 This ______________ is great for sailing.
3 Is that ______________ outside? Bring your umbrella!
4 The ______________ is out. Let's go to the beach!

3 Work in pairs. Discuss these questions.

1 What kind of transport do you take to school or work?
2 What kind of transport do you take on long trips? Why?
3 What weather do you not like? Why?

UNIT 10

Body parts

arm (n) /ɑːm/ *We have two arms.*
ear (n) /ɪə/ *We use our ears to listen.*
eye (n) /aɪ/ *Monika has beautiful, brown eyes.*
foot (n) /fʊt/ *We walk with our feet.*
hair (n) /heə(r)/ *She has short, blonde hair.*
hand (n) /hænd/ *What's that in your hand?*
head (n) /hed/ *Maya has her head on her desk.*
leg (n) /leg/ *Carla's legs are tired from exercising.*
mouth (n) /maʊθ/ *We use our mouths to eat with.*
nose (n) /nəʊz/ *We use our noses to smell.*

Exercise and training

exercise (v) /ˈeksəsaɪz/ *He exercises to stay healthy.*
learn (v) /lɜːn/ *Melania wants to learn a new sport.*
practise (v) /ˈpræktɪs/ *The team practises every Sunday.*
prepare for (v) /prɪˈpɛː fɔː/ *Joachim is preparing for the football match on Saturday.*

1 Match the descriptions with the words.

1 You put your shoes on these.	a head
2 You cut this when it grows long.	b eyes
3 You need this to talk with.	c ears
4 You see with these.	d hair
5 You can wear a hat on this.	e feet
6 You use these for hearing.	f mouth

2 Complete the sentences. Use the correct form of the verbs.

exercise learn practise prepare

1 We need to ______________ for the test.
2 She wants to ______________ how to swim.
3 Alex ______________ a lot. He runs and does yoga.
4 She loves playing the ukulele. She ______________ all the time.

3 Work in pairs. Discuss these questions.

1 What part of your body is most useful? Why?
2 Do you know someone who exercises or does a lot of sports? What do they do?
3 What sport or activity would you like to learn? Why?

UNIT 11

Life events

ago (adv) /ə'ɡəʊ/ *I was there three years ago.*

died (v) /daɪd/ *She died when she was 93 years old.*

for (prep) /fɔːr/ *He was in Italy for seven years.*

from (prep) /frɒm/ *The class is from 2 p.m. to 4 p.m.*

lived (v) /lɪvd/ *Adam lived in Germany for three years.*

was born (v) /wəz bɔːn/ *He was born in Tokyo.*

Past time expressions

century (n) /'sentʃəri/ *A century is 100 years.*

last century (n) /lɑːst 'sentʃəri/ *There were many wars in the last century.*

last night /lɑːst naɪt/ *I was with Jenny last night.*

last week /lɑːst wiːk/ *Were you in class last week?*

last year /lɑːst jɪə(r)/ *His son was born last year.*

the year 2000 /ðə jɪə tuː 'θaʊzənd/ *The year 2000 was more than 20 years ago.*

the 19th century /ðə ˌnaɪn'tiːnθ 'sentʃəri/ *There were no planes in the 19th century.*

yesterday /'jestədeɪ/ *The shop was closed yesterday.*

1 Put the sentences in the correct order (1–5).

a Einstein lived in Switzerland from 1895 to 1914.
b Einstein was born in Germany more than a century ago, in 1879.
c Einstein returned to Germany in 1914.
d Einstein died in the year 1955.
e Einstein lived in the US for 22 years, from 1933 to 1955.

2 Complete the sentences with these words.

century last night week year

1 The last ______________ was 1901 to 2000.
2 What did I do yesterday? I watched a film ______________ with Paul.
3 Last ______________, winter was really cold and summer was really hot.
4 There was only one class last ______________, on Tuesday.

3 Work in pairs. Use the words above. Discuss ...

1 the life of someone you know.
2 what you did last week.
3 important events in the last century.

UNIT 12

Life stages

buy a house /baɪ ə haʊs/ *We bought a house last year.*

finish university /'fɪnɪʃ juːnɪ'vɜːsɪti/ *Ayako finished university in 2012.*

get a job /get ə dʒɒb/ *He got a job as a teacher.*

get married /get 'mærɪd/ *They got married in April.*

go to university /ɡəʊ tə juːnɪ'vɜːsɪti/ *Ron went to university in Australia.*

have children /hav 'tʃɪldrən/ *Farah and Mansour want to have three children.*

live in another country /lɪv ɪn ə'nʌðə 'kʌntri/ *He lived in another country from 2001 to 2003.*

start a business /stɑːt ə 'bɪznəs/ *Many people hope to start a business of their own.*

Feelings

afraid (adj) /ə'freɪd/ *Tim is afraid of spiders.*

angry (adj) /'æŋgri/ *Marla got angry at the shop owner.*

bored (adj) /bɔːd/ *I'm always bored when I'm at home.*

excited (adj) /ɪk'saɪtɪd/ *They're very excited about the match.*

happy (adj) /'hæpi/ *Trina looks very happy.*

sad (adj) /sæd/ *He cries when he watches sad films.*

surprised (adj) /sə'praɪzd/ *He was surprised by the gift.*

tired (adj) /taɪəd/ *Matteo looked tired after the run.*

1 Complete the sentences with the correct verb.

1 Javier would like to ______________ a business with Sam.
2 Hank hopes to ______________ a house soon.
3 They want to ______________ married in June.
4 After he ______________ university, he wants to ______________ a job.

2 Read the sentences. Write the correct emotions.

afraid bored happy sad tired

1 He didn't sleep last night. He's ______________.
2 She doesn't like this film. She's ______________.
3 Mia's grandmother died. She's ______________.
4 Leo doesn't like high places. He's ______________.
5 Leia won the maths contest. She's ______________.

3 Work in pairs. Use the words above. Discuss ...

1 your life when you were a child.
2 things that make you angry.
3 events that made you happy.

Grammar reference

UNIT 1

1B Present simple *be* (singular positive)

Positive	Short form
I **am**	I**'m**
You **are**	You**'re**
He/She/It **is**	He**'s**/She**'s**/It**'s**

- Use singular noun + *be* to talk about a person or a thing.
  My teacher *is British.*
  Paolo is *from Peru.*
  Berlin is *in Germany.*
- You can also use singular subject pronoun + *be*. The singular subject pronouns are: *I, you, he, she, it*.
  I am *Ming.* (name)
  You are *Vietnamese.* (nationality)
  She is *a teacher.* (job)
  He is *from Peru.* (where a person is from)
  It is *in Germany.* (where something is)
- When people talk, they usually use short forms:
  *I**'m** from Japan.*
  *You**'re** at school.*
  *She**'s** Jennifer.*

1 Complete the sentences with the correct form of *be*.

1 She ________________ Australian.
2 The book ________________ from China.
3 Omar's phone number ________________ 578-2768.
4 I ________________ from Bolivia.
5 The address ________________ 1646 Oak Lane.
6 It ________________ on the chair.

1B Present simple *be* (singular negative)

Negative	Short form
I **am not**	**I'm not**
You **are not**	You **aren't**
He/She/It **is not**	He/She/It **isn't**

- To make *be* negative, use *be* + *not*.
  *I **am not** Charles.*
  *You **are not** from France.*
  *It **is not** on the table.*
- You can also use short forms of *be*.
  *I**'m not** a teacher.*
  *You **aren't** from Rome.*
  *He **isn't** Turkish.*
  Use *I'm not.* NOT ~~*I amn't*~~.
- You can also use the short form *'re not* for *are not* and *'s not* for *is not*.
  *You**'re not** in Morocco.*
  *She**'s not** in class.*
  *It**'s not** 489-3377.*

2 Choose the correct option to complete the sentences.

1 Her name *aren't / isn't* Camila.
2 *I'm not / I isn't* an actor.
3 Mr Zhen *am not / isn't* from China.
4 You *aren't / isn't* Omani.
5 Her address *aren't / isn't* 7830 East Road.

1C Yes/No questions with *be* (singular)

Yes/No questions with *be* (singular)
Am I in the right class? **Are you** a footballer? **Is he/she/it** American?

- In your question, change the order of the subject and verb.
  I am *an actor.* → ***Am I*** *an actor?*
  You are *from Greece.* → ***Are you*** *from Greece?*
  He is *Diego.* → ***Is he*** *Diego?*
- To say *Yes*, use *Yes*, + subject + *be*.
  *A: **Are you** the teacher?* *B: Yes, **I am**.*
  *A: **Is Bing** from Beijing?* *B: Yes, **she is**.*
  *A: **Is the book** on the table?* *B: Yes, **it is.***
- Don't use short forms in *yes* answers. For example ...
  Use *Yes, I am. / Yes, you are. / Yes, he is.*
  NOT ~~*Yes, I'm. / Yes, you're. / Yes, he's.*~~
- To say *No*, use *No*, + subject + *be* + *not*.
  *A: **Is he** Moroccan?* *B: No, **he isn't**.*
  *A: **Are you** from Mexico?* *B: No, **I'm not**.*
- You can also answer just *Yes* or *No*.

3 Use the correct options to complete the conversations.

1 A: Hi, I'm Kalil. ¹*Are / Is* this my class?
  B: Yes, it ²*are / is*. I'm your teacher, Ted.
2 A: ³*Am / Are* you from New York?
  B: No, ⁴*I'm / you're* not.
3 A: ⁵*Are / Is* your phone number 673-9920?
  B: No, ⁶*I'm not / it isn't*.

UNIT 2

2B Present simple *be* (plural, positive and negative)

Positive	Short form	Negative	Short form
We **are**	We**'re**	We **are not**	We **aren't**
You **are**	You**'re**	You **are not**	You **aren't**
They **are**	They**'re**	They **are not**	They **aren't**

- Use plural noun + *be* to talk about more than one person or thing.
  *The students **are** in the living room.*
  *Jan and Bill **are** Italian.*
- You can also use plural subject pronoun + *be*. The three plural subject pronouns are *we, you* and *they*.
  *We **are** on the sofa.*
  *You **are** at school.*
  *They **are** in the fridge.*
- *We* is for more than one person.
- *You* is for one person or more than one person.
- *They* is for more than one person or thing.
- To make a negative, use *be* + *not*.
  *We **are not** at the dining table.*
  *You **are not** in the kitchen.*
  *They **are not** from Argentina.*
- People usually use short forms when they talk.
  *We**'re** students.*
  *They **aren't** cheap.*
- They also use the short form *'re not* for *are not*.
  *They**'re not** in the living room.*

1 **Complete the sentences with the positive (+) or negative (–) form of *be*.**

1 We ________________ from Oman. (–)
2 They ________________ Peruvian singers. (+)
3 The books ________________ under the chair. (+)
4 We ________________ next to the house. (+)
5 You ________________ Egyptian. (–)

2B *Yes/No* questions with *be* (plural)

***Yes/No* questions with *be* (plural)**

Are you in Tokyo?
Are we in the right class?
Are they in the kitchen?

- For questions, change the order of the subject and verb.
  ***We are** late. → **Are we** late?*
  ***You are** from Athens. → **Are you** from Athens?*
  ***They are** American. → **Are they** American?*
- A *yes* answer is *Yes,* + subject + *be*.
  *A: **Are we** in the right chairs?* *B: Yes, **you are**.*
  *A: **Are you** Vietnamese?* *B: Yes, **we are**.*
  *A: **Are they** next to the bed?* *B: Yes, **they are**.*
- Don't use short forms in *yes* answers.
  Use *Yes, we are. / Yes, you are. / Yes, they are.*
  NOT ~~Yes, we're. / Yes, you're. / Yes, they're.~~
- A *no* answer is *No,* + subject + *be* + *not*.
  *A: **Are we** on Pine Street?* *B: No, **you aren't**.*
  *A: **Are you** Pete and Bill?* *B: No, **we aren't**.*
  *A: **Are they** portable?* *B: No, **they aren't**.*
- You can also answer just *Yes* or *No*.

2 **Complete the conversations. Circle the answers.**

1 A: Hey, Wen. Are you and Jen in the dining room?
B: Yes, [1]*you are / we are*.
2 A: I need some books for class. [2]*Are they / Are we* cheap?
B: No, [3]*they aren't / we aren't*.

2C *Who, what, where*

Who, what, where

Where am I?
Who are you?
What is it?

- Use question word + *be* + subject to form questions.
  ***Who are** they?*
  ***What are** your friends' names?*
  ***Where is** the TV?*
- People usually use short forms with *is*.
  ***Who's** the boy next to you?*
  ***What's** your address?*
  ***Where's** Zahra?*

Remember!
Who people *What* things *Where* places

3 **Write the correct *wh-* question word and *be*.**

1 Excuse me. ________________ the bus station?
2 Adel, ________________ your English teacher?
3 ________________ the names of those two women?
4 ________________ the pens? I can't find them.
5 ________________ that thing in your hand?

Grammar reference

UNIT 3

3B *this, that, these, those*

This/That is my train ticket.	
This/That water bottle is green.	
These/Those are Hugo's keys.	
These/Those notepads are cheap.	

- Use *this* or *these* to talk about people or things near us. Use *this* + singular noun and *these* + plural noun.
  ***This** is a small table.*
  ***These** are my friends.*
- Use *that* or *those* to talk about people or things that are not near us. Use *that* + singular noun and *those* + plural noun.
  ***That**'s Klaus's car.*
  ***Those** are his bank cards.*
- You can begin a sentence with *this/that/these/*those + noun.
  ***That song** is my favourite.*
- You can begin a sentence with *this/that/these/those* + *be*.
  ***That is** my favourite song.*
- You can also put *this/that/these/those* before a noun anywhere in a sentence.
  *I want **these books**.*
- The short form of *that is* is *that's*.
  ***That is** my car. → **That's** my car.*
  This is and *these/those are* have no short forms.

1 Complete the sentences with *this*, *that*, *these* or *those*.

1 ______________ red flowers outside are beautiful.
2 ______________ is Gina's phone over on that table.
3 ______________ dolls here are my favourite!
4 Who's ______________ person over there?

3C Possessive adjectives and *'s*

Possessive adjectives

Subject pronouns	Possessive adjectives
I	my
you	your
he/she/it	his/her/its
we	our
you	your
they	their

- You can use possessive adjectives before a noun to show who something belongs to.
  *That's **my** guitar.* (I own the guitar.)
  *Are those **her** keys?* (Does she own the keys?)
- You can also use possessive adjectives to talk about people.
  ***His** parents are old.*
- Use *its* for objects, animals or places.
- *Its* and *It's* are different. *Its* is for possession and *it's* is the short form of *it is*.

2 Complete the sentences. Circle the answers.

1 *Its / It's* not *I / my* black laptop.
2 *It / They* are not *he / his* bank cards.
3 Is *you / your* car the black one?
4 Am *I / my* in *her / she* chair?
5 *Their / They* are *their / they* friends.

Possessive *'s*

- Use a *'s* to show that a thing belongs to someone or something.
  *They are Rosa**'s** dolls.* (The dolls belong to Rosa.)
- Use *'s* after a singular noun or a plural noun without *-s*.
  *These are my father**'s** bags.*
  *The children**'s** bus is here.*
- For plural nouns with *s*, place the apostrophe after the *s*.
  *This is the students**'** favourite song.*

3 Put the apostrophe in the correct place.

1 This is Bens old clock.
2 The teachers lunch hour is from 12 to 1. They often eat at this restaurant.
3 The womens football team plays on Monday.
4 Hanss sister is beautiful.
5 All the students desks are white.

UNIT 4

4B Present simple

Subject	Positive	Negative
I	study	don't study
You	read	don't read
He/She/It	works	doesn't work
We	play	don't play
You	exercise	don't exercise
They	sleep	don't sleep

- You can use the present simple to talk about things that happen regularly.
  *I **exercise** in the morning.*
- You can also use it to talk about things that are usually true.
  *Most Americans **speak** English.*
- For *he*, *she* or *it*, add *-s* to most verbs:
  *He **sleeps** in the afternoon.*

- For verbs that end in *-y*, change the *y* to *i* and add *-es*.
  *She **studies** every night.*
- If a verb ends in *-s, -x, -ch* or *-sh*, add *-es* to the verb.
  *He **teaches** me the guitar.*
- Some verbs like *do*, *go* and *have* are irregular.
  *Sabirah **does** yoga on Sundays.*
  *He **goes** shopping at the weekend.*
  *Donato **has** many good friends.*
- To form the negative with *I, you, we* or *they*, use *do not* (*don't*) + infinitive.
  *They **don't have** class today.*
- To form the negative with *he, she* or *it*, use *does not* (*doesn't*) + infinitive.
  *She **doesn't want** coffee.*

1 **Put the words in order to make present simple sentences.**

1 brushes / in the morning / Emma / her teeth
2 every night / Tahir / eight hours / sleeps
3 in the library / and Tomoko / study / Rie
4 I / at 5:30 / work / finish
5 play / on Saturday / We / football
6 a lot / rains / in spring / It

4B Present simple questions and answers

Yes/No questions and answers

Do / Does	Subject	Infinitive
Do	I/you	work late?
Does	he/she/it	wake up at 5?
Do	we/you/they	carry a passport?

- Use *Do* or *Does* + subject + infinitive to make *yes/no* questions in the present simple.
  ***Do you take** the train to work?*
  ***Does she eat** lunch in the park?*
- Use *do* for *I, you, we* and they.
  ***Do you** think your class is fun?*
- Use *does* for *he, she* or *it*.
  ***Does he** play video games on Sunday?*
- A *yes* answer is *Yes,* + subject + *do/does*.
  A: Do they live in the city? *B: Yes, they do.*
  A: Does Mila study at home? *B: Yes, she does.*
- A *no* answer is *No,* + subject + *don't/doesn't*.
  A: Do they work in London? *B: No, they don't.*
  A: Does Mani study here? *B: No, he doesn't.*
- You can also answer just *Yes* or *No*.

Wh- and *how* questions

Question word	do / does	Subject	Infinitive
Where	do	I	eat?
What	do	you	study?
Why	does	he/she/it	like work?
Who	do	we	see?
When	do	you	wake up?
How	do	they	exercise?

- For *I, you, we* and *they*, use question word + *do* + subject + infinitive.
  ***Why do you like** this song?*
- For *he, she* or *it*, use question word + *does* + subject + infinitive.
  ***Where does he live**?*

2 **Complete the conversations. Circle the answers.**

1 A: [1]*Do / Does* Charlene take the bus to school?
B: Yes, she [2]*do / does*.
2 A: Who [3]*do / does* you study with?
B: I study with Andrea.
3 A: [4]*Do / Does* Karl and Eve play video games?
B: No, they [5]*doesn't / don't*.
4 A: Where [6]*do / does* Francisco live?
B: He lives in the city.

4C Adverbs of frequency

↑ always (100%)
usually
sometimes
↓ never (0%)

- Use adverbs of frequency with the present simple to say how often something happens.
  *She **usually** goes to bed at 9 p.m.*
  *He **never** exercises.*
- The adverb goes before most verbs.
  *Liz **sometimes goes** to the cinema.*
- But the adverb goes after *be*.
  *Class **is usually** in the morning.*
- You can start a sentence with *sometimes* or *usually*. Use a comma.
  ***Usually,** I wake up early.*
  ***Sometimes,** I wake up late.*
- For something that usually happens on a certain day, add an *-s* to the name of the day.
  *I go to yoga class on **Tuesdays**.*

Grammar reference

3 **Rewrite the sentences using the adverbs of frequency.**

1 I call my mother on Saturday night. (sometimes)
2 Mika gets home before 6 p.m. (never)
3 Stef and Paul have lunch here. (always)
4 We are free on Friday night. (usually)
5 Theo studies in the library. (never)
6 She is busy on Tuesday. (sometimes)

UNIT 5

5B *Love, like* and *don't like* + *-ing* form

Subject	*love/like*	Activity
I	love	reading.
You	like	chatting online.
He/She/It	likes	drawing.
We	love	camping.
They	like	swimming.

- When people like an activity, use subject + *love/like* + *-ing* form.
  *I **like running**.*
  *Sven **loves cycling**.*
- When people don't like an activity, use subject + *don't/doesn't* + *like* + *-ing* form.
  *We **don't like** doing yoga.*
  *She **doesn't** like watching TV.*
- For most verbs, just add *-ing*.
  *read ➔ read**ing**, watch ➔ watch**ing***
- For verbs ending in *-e*, remove the e and add *-ing*.
  *cycle ➔ cycl**ing**, ride ➔ rid**ing***
- For many short verbs ending in vowel + consonant, repeat the consonant and add *-ing*.
  *chat ➔ chat**ting**, run ➔ run**ning***
  This is not true of all verbs ending in vowel + consonant.
  *play ➔ play**ing**, listen ➔ listen**ing***

Remember!
For *he*, *she* or *it*, add *-s* to *love* and *like*.
***He likes** playing video games.*

1 **Complete the sentences. Use the *-ing* form of the verbs.**

chat do listen run swim watch

1 I like ______________ in the sea.
2 Sasha loves ______________ yoga.
3 Jeff likes ______________ to music
4 Omar likes ______________ in the park.
5 He doesn't like ______________ online.
6 They don't like ______________ old films.

questions with *love / like* + *-ing* form

Do/Does	Subject	*love/like*	Activity
Do	I	like	reading?
Do	you	love	climbing?
Does	he/she/it	love	running?
Do	we	like	working?
Do	they	like	studying?

- Use *do/does* + subject + *love/like* + verb+*ing* to make questions.
  ***Do they like** swimming?*
  ***Does she love** playing football?*
- A *yes* answer is *Yes*, + subject + *do/does*.
  A: Does Jackie like studying? *B: Yes, she does.*
- A *no* answer is *No*, + subject + *don't/doesn't*.
  A: Do you like camping? *B: No, I don't.*
- You can also answer just *Yes* or *No*.

2 **Complete the conversations. Circle the answers.**

1 A: [1]*Do / Does* you like staying at home?
B: No, I [2]*doesn't / don't*. I like going outside.
2 A: [3]*Do / Does* they like going to school?
B: Yes, they [4]*do / does*. They love it!
3 A: [5]*Do / Does* he love running?
B: No, he [6]*don't / doesn't*. He loves cycling.

5C Prepositions of time

I play football	at the weekend.
	in autumn.
	on Saturday.

- *At*, *in* or *on* go before a time word.
  ***at** night, **in** 1953, **on** Monday*
- *At/in/on* + time word usually comes at the end of a sentence.
  *Tom finishes work **at 5 p.m.***
- *At/in/on* + time word can also come at the beginning of a sentence. Use a comma.
  ***On Mondays,** Jeffrey plays tennis.*
- Use *at* before *the weekend, night* and the time.
- Use *in* for the month, the year, the season and *morning/afternoon/evening*.
- Use *on* for days and dates.

3 Complete the sentences with the correct preposition.

1 Ming likes camping ______________ spring.
2 Jay gets up ______________ 6 a.m.
3 We go to class ______________ Mondays.
4 I work ______________ night.
5 They study ______________ the evening.
6 I often exercise ______________ the weekend.

UNIT 6

6B Countable and uncountable nouns

- Most nouns are countable.
  a/one apple, two apples, three apples, ...
- The verb changes when the noun is singular or plural.
  *The **apple is** in the fridge.*
  *The **apples are** in the fridge.*
- Some nouns are uncountable. For example:
  bread, cheese, fish, fruit, meat
  coffee, milk, tea, oil
  rice, ice cream, sugar
- Uncountable nouns are always singular.
  ***This** bread **is** delicious!*
  ***This** ice cream **tastes** terrible!*

1 Read the sentences. Are the bold words countable or uncountable? Write C or U.

1 I think **garlic** is delicious. _____
2 This **soup** tastes funny. _____
3 These **potatoes** are great. _____
4 Is olive **oil** good for your health? _____
5 Are those **onions** sweet? _____
6 Those **tomatoes** are from Bulgaria. _____
7 **Peanuts** have a lot of oil in them. _____
8 Japanese **food** is delicious! _____

2 These sentences all have mistakes. Correct them.

1 He likes sugars in his coffee.
2 She eats cheeses with almost every meal.
3 Do you want breads with your soup?
4 We need a garlic and an onion.
5 I'd like more salts in my food, please.
6 I drink two cups of coffees every morning.

6C *How much* and *how many* questions

- For countable nouns, use *How many* + plural noun.
  ***How many biscuits** would you like?*
- For uncountable nouns, use *How much* + singular noun.
  ***How much tea** would you like?*
- Answer *how many* questions with a number.
  *A: **How many** bananas do you want?*
  *B: I want **one banana** / **two bananas**.*
- Answer *How much* questions with *some, a little* or *a lot (of).*
  *A: **How much** milk do you want in your tea?*
  *B: I want **a little** / **some** / **a lot of** milk.*

3 Complete the sentences. Circle the answers.

1 How *many* / *much* salt do you want?
2 I'd like *one* / *some* bread.
3 How *many* / *much* tomatoes are in the fridge?
4 I want *a lot of* / *one* rice.
5 How *many* / *much* sugar do you eat?
6 How *many* / *much* eggs do you have?

UNIT 7

7B Present simple questions (*yes/no* questions)

Questions with *be*

Be	Subject	Complement
Am	I	late to class?
Are	you	married?
Is	he/she/it	tall?

- To make questions, change the order of the subject and *be*.
  ***They are** Anna and Dmitri's children.*
  ***Are they** Anna and Dmitri's children?*
- Answer with *Yes/No*, + subject + *be* (+ *not*).
  Yes, they are. / No, they aren't.

Questions with *do*

Do / Does	Subject	Infinitive
Do	I	need this medicine?
Do	you	travel together?
Does	he/she/it	live here?

- To make questions, add *Do/Does* and keep the word order the same. Don't change the form of the verb.
  ***They play games** together.*
  ***Do they play games** together?*
- Answer with *Yes/No*, + subject + *do/does* (+ *not*).
  Yes, they do. / No, they don't.

Grammar reference

1 **Change the following sentences into *yes/no* questions.**

1 He is from Australia.
Is he from Australia?
2 They eat together.
3 Lina helps her grandmother.
4 The class is at 9 a.m.
5 Silvia is Alan's daughter.
6 Kamala and Eva travel together.

7B Present simple questions (open questions)

- *Wh-* and *how* questions are open. You can't answer them with *yes* or *no*.

Wh-* and *how* questions with *be

Question word	*be*	Subject
What	is	your name?
Where	are	we?
How	are	you?

- To make questions, use question word + *be* + subject.
Who is *your mother?*
My mother is Hanna.
What are *their names?*
Their names are Nadia and Ivan.

Wh-* questions with *do

Question word	*do / does*	Subject	Infinitive
Who	do	you	play games with?
When	do	they	eat together?
Why	does	she	like chatting online?

- To make questions, use question word + *do/does* + subject + infinitive.
Who do *you celebrate special events with?*
I celebrate special events with my family.
Where does *he go on holiday?*
He goes to Spain on holiday.

Remember!

Who	people	*Where*	places	*Why*	reason
What	things	*When*	time	*How*	manner

2 **Put the words in order. Make questions.**

1 are / from? / where / you
2 his father's / is / name? / what
3 study / does / English? / why / she
4 home? / when / go / they / do
5 how / weather? / the / is
6 does / where / lunch? / eat / Martin

7C Adjectives

- Use adjectives to describe nouns.
He's very ***friendly****.*
She has ***blonde*** *hair.*
- To describe the subject of a sentence, use subject + *be* + adjective.
Her eyes are ***green****.*
She is ***interesting****.*
- To describe other nouns in a sentence, put the adjective before the noun.
She has ***brown eyes****.*
She likes Jenna's ***long hair****.*
- Sometimes, two or more adjectives can go before a noun. Separate the adjectives using commas.
He has ***short****,* ***brown*** *hair.*

3 **Put the words in the correct order.**

1 is / Ali's / hair / short / .
2 short / has / Ali / hair / .
3 eyes / Ivan's / blue / are / .
4 Ivan / eyes / has / blue / .
5 bag / purple / is / Jill's / .
6 purple / a / has / bag / Jill / .

UNIT 8

8B *Can* and *can't*

- Use *can* + infinitive to talk about abilities.
I ***can fly*** *a plane.*
They ***can play*** *basketball.*
- Use *can't* + infinitive to talk about something you aren't good at or don't know how to do. *Can't* is the short form of *cannot*.
She ***can't speak*** *French.*
We ***can't play*** *the guitar.*
- For questions with *can*, use *Can* + subject + infinitive.
Can *they* ***sing****?*
Can *you* ***drive*** *a car?*
- To answer, use *Yes/No*, + subject + *can/can't*.
Yes, I ***can****. / No, I* ***can't****.*
Yes, they ***can****. / No, they* ***can't****.*

1 **Write positive sentences (+), negative sentences (–) or questions (?) using *can / can't*.**

1 Ramesh / play / football (+)
2 Jerry / swim (–)

3 Mayumi / do / difficult maths (?)
4 they / play / the guitar (–)
5 she / sing / very well (+)
6 he / run / a marathon (?)

8C *And, or, but, because*

- Use *and, or, but* and *because* to connect things or ideas.
- *Because* gives the reason or explains why. The reason goes after *because*.
  Fact or idea: Usain Bolt is famous.
  Reason: He can run very fast.
  *Usain Bolt is famous **because** he can run very fast.*
- *And* is for listing two or more things. *And* can also link two or more facts or ideas.
  Tortoises are slow. They live a long time.
  *Tortoises are slow **and** they live a long time.*
- *Or* tells you there is a choice between two or more things.
  *Would you like tea **or** would you like coffee?*
- *But* tells you that two facts or ideas are different. You usually use a comma before *but*.
  *This snake is beautiful, **but** it's dangerous.*
- When joining two sentences with *and* or *or*, people often don't repeat the subject or first few words.
  *Would you like tea **or** coffee?*
  NOT ~~*Would you like tea or would you like coffee?*~~
- For *but*, when you don't repeat the subject or the first few words, don't use a comma.
  *This snake is beautiful **but** dangerous.*
  NOT ~~*This snake is beautiful, but dangerous.*~~

2 **Join the two sentences using *and, or, but* or *because*. Don't repeat words when possible.**

1 Elephants are large. They are strong.
  Elephants are large and strong.
2 He can't drive. He can't see well.
3 Alisha can cook Indian food. She can't cook Italian food.
4 We can speak French. We can speak English.
5 He gets good marks. He studies hard.
6 Do you want to eat at home? Do you want to go to a restaurant?
7 Cheetahs are beautiful. They can run fast.
8 Rick is really good at maths. He has trouble remembering things.

UNIT 9

9B *There is* and *there are*

Statements with *there is* and *there are*

Singular nouns	**There is** a nice restaurant.
	There isn't a nice restaurant.
Plural nouns	**There are** some nice restaurants.
	There aren't any nice restaurants.

- Use *there is/there are* to talk about the things in a place.
  ***There is** an old building.*
  ***There are** some museums.*
- For one thing, use *there is* + *a/an* + singular noun. You can also use the short form, *there's*.
  ***There's a** large mountain.*
- For more than one thing, use *there are* + plural noun. You can use numbers to say how many.
  ***There are two** shopping centres in town.*
- When there is more than one thing but you can't or don't want to say how many, use *there are* + *some/many* + plural noun.
  ***There are some** cheap hotels.*
  ***There are many** wonderful beaches.*
- For negative sentences with countable nouns, use *there aren't any* + plural noun.
  ***There aren't any** taxis tonight.*
- For negative sentences with uncountable nouns, use *there isn't any* + singular noun.
  *There **isn't any ice cream** in the fridge.*
  *There **isn't any bread** at home.*

Remember!
Uncountable nouns are things we can't count, e.g. *bread, cheese, coffee, milk, rice*.

1 **Write positive sentences (+) or negative sentences (–) using *there is* or *there are*.**

1 sugar / at the corner shop (–)
2 bus station / near the library (+)
3 some keys / on the table (+)
4 bank cards / in my wallet (–)
5 a lot of eggs / in the fridge (+)
6 park / in the village (–)

Questions with *there is* and *there are*

Singular nouns	**Is there** a hotel near the beach?
Plural nouns	**Are there any** hotels near the beach?

Grammar reference

- To ask about one thing, change the order of *there* and *is*.
  ***There is** a museum in the city.*
  ***Is there** a museum in the city?*
- To ask about more than one thing, change the order of *there* and *are*, and use *any*.
  ***There are some** trains to Lima.*
  ***Are there any** trains to Lima?*
- To ask about uncountable nouns, use *Is there* + *any*.
  ***Is there any** bread?*

Remember!
Use *some* for positive sentences. Use *any* for negative sentences and questions.

2 Put the words in order to make questions.

1 there / is / in the flat? / a shower
2 are / in the classroom? / there / students / any
3 in the kitchen? / are / any / there / oranges
4 there / is / near the hotel? / a restaurant
5 on the card? / there / a name / is
6 any / are / in the dining room? / chairs / there

9C Object pronouns

Subject pronouns	Object pronouns
I	me
you	you
he/she/it	him/her/it
we	us
you	you
they	them

- *Me, you, him, her, it, us* and *them* are called object pronouns.
- Use object pronouns as the object of verbs.
  *She eats with **him** every day.*
- You can also use object pronouns after a preposition (*for, to, from, with*, etc.).
  *He plays tennis with **her.***

3 Complete the sentences. Choose the correct option.

1 David often helps *her* / *she* with homework.
2 Our teacher sometimes tells *us* / *we* stories.
3 My parents always give *I* / *me* a birthday gift.
4 He eats with *them* / *they* on Saturday nights.
5 I can give *they* / *you* the money tomorrow.
6 We need to buy the tickets from *her* / *she*.
7 She plays video games with *he* / *him* after school.

UNIT 10

10B Present continuous

Present continuous sentences

Subject	*be*	*-ing* verb
I	am	exercising.
You	are	
He/She/It	is	
We/You/They	are	

- Use the present continuous to talk about things happening as you're speaking. To write present continuous sentences, use subject + *be* + *-ing* verb.
  *He**'s running** with his friends.*
- To make negative sentences, use subject + *be* + *not* + *-ing* verb.
  *They**'re not buying** running shoes today.*
- There are several ways to make *-ing* verbs.
  Add *-ing* to the verb:
  eat ➔ eating
  Repeat the last letter and add *-ing:*
  run ➔ running
  Drop the letter *e* at the end and add *-ing:*
  hike ➔ hiking

1 Put the words in order to make sentences.

1 are / to Malta / travelling / they
2 staying / Ali / is / at a hotel
3 at a restaurant / are / Ellie and Nadia / eating
4 am / I / my friend / calling / on the phone
5 the train there / are / we / taking
6 is / a / she / holiday in Japan / planning

***Yes/No* questions and answers**

Be	Subject	*-ing* verb
Am	I	practising?
Are	you	
Is	he/she/it	
Are	we/you/they	

- To ask present continuous questions, change the order of the subject and *be*.
  ***He is** going to the cinema*
  ***Is he** going to the cinema?*

- To answer, use *Yes/No,* + subject + *be* (+ *not*).
  A: Is she studying? *B:* ***Yes, she is.***
  A: Are you taking a break? *B:* ***No, I'm not.***

Wh- and how questions

- Use question word + *be* + subject + *-ing* verb.
  ***What are** you **learning**?*
  How are** they **training?
- To answer, use present continuous sentences.
  A: What is she doing? *B: She's doing yoga.*
  A: Where are they going? *B: They're going home.*

2 **Choose the correct option to complete the conversations.**

1 A: Hi, Tom. Where [1]*are you / you are* going?
B: Oh, hi Sally. [2]*I'm / You're* going to the library. Would you like to come with me?
A: I can't. My friend [3]*are / is* waiting for me.

2 A: [4]*Are you / You are* studying maths?
B: Yes, [5]*I'm / I am*. Why?
A: Can I join you?

3 A: How [6]*is Ivan / Ivan is* going to work?
B: I'm not sure. [7]*He is / Is he* driving?

10C Present continuous vs present simple

- Compare the present simple with the present continuous:
  *I **walk** to school.* (= in general, on most days)
  *I'**m walking** to school.* (= right now)
- Use both tenses together to show the difference between what usually happens and what is happening now.
  *Usually, I never **exercise**. This week, I'm **exercising** every day.*

3 **Complete the sentences with the correct form of the verbs in brackets.**

1 Maria ______________ (prepare) for the exam today.
2 They often ______________ (take) the bus to the shop.
3 Nora usually ______________ (eat) dinner at home, but right now she is ______________ (camp) with some friends.
4 Bastian is at home. He ______________ (watch) TV.
5 We ______________ (practise) until 8 o'clock on Mondays.
6 The family ______________ (go) to the park on Saturdays.

UNIT 11

11B Past simple *be*

Subject	Positive	Negative
I	was	wasn't/was not
You	were	weren't/were not
He/She/It	was	wasn't/was not
We	were	weren't/were not
You	were	weren't/were not
They	were	weren't/were not

- Use the past simple forms of *be* to talk about people, things or events from the past.
  *Thomas Edison **was** a famous inventor.*
  *They **were** in a famous rock band.*
- You can also use past time expressions to describe when in the past you are talking about.
  *They **were** late to class **yesterday**.*
  *I **was** in Fiji **last year**.*
- To make negative sentences, use *was/were* + *not*.
  *Li **wasn't** happy about his test score.*
  *You **weren't** at home last week.*

Remember!
Always use *be* before *born* to talk about a birthday or birthplace, e.g. *I was born in November. / She was born in Italy.*

1 **Write positive sentences (+) or negative sentences (–) using *was/were*.**

1 they / very late / for the party (+)
2 she / at school / on Monday (–)
3 the weather / great / last week (–)
4 Gandhi / born / in the 19th century (+)
5 we / quiet / during the film (+)
6 Marie Curie / from Poland (+)
7 they / excited / about the game (–)
8 I / at the tennis match / on Sunday (+)

11C Questions with *was / were*

***Yes/no* questions**

- To make *yes/no* questions, change the order of *was/were* and the subject. The structure is *was/were* + subject.
  ***He was** born in China. → **Was he** born in China?*
  ***They were** French. → **Were they** French?*

Grammar reference

- To answer, you can just say *Yes* or *No*. You can also use *Yes/No*, + subject + *was/were* (+ *not*).

A: Were you at the party? *B: Yes, **I was**.*
A: Was she a movie star? *B: No, **she wasn't**.*

Wh- and how Questions

- For *wh-* and *how* questions, use question word + *was/were* + subject.

***How was he**?*
***When were they** at the park?*

2 Choose the correct option to complete the conversations.

1 A: [1]*Was / Were* you at the game on Friday?
B: No, I [2]*wasn't / weren't*.
A: Where [3]*was / were* you?
B: I was at home playing video games.

2 A: Why [4]*Amira was / was Amira* late to class?
B: She was in an accident.
A: Oh, no! [5]*She was / Was she* hurt?
B: No, [6]*she wasn't / wasn't she*.

3 A: [7]*Were who / Who were* the stars of that film?
B: No one famous.
A: But [8]*the film was / was the film* any good?
B: Yes, [9]*it's / it was*!

UNIT 12

12B Past simple (regular verbs)

- Use the past simple to talk about things that happened before now.

*We **watched** a film last night.*
*He **lived** in the United States in the 1940s.*

- You can use time expressions with past simple verbs to say when something happened in the past.

*I **finished** university **last year**.*
*She **died in 1968**.*

- For most regular verbs, make the past simple form by adding *-ed* to the infinitive.

*climb ➔ climb**ed***
*start ➔ start**ed***

- If a verb ends in *-e*, add *-d*.

*exercise ➔ exercis**ed***
*practise ➔ practis**ed***

- If a verb ends in a consonant + *-y*, remove the *-y* and add *-ied*.

*study ➔ stud**ied***
*cry ➔ cr**ied***

- For most short verbs ending in consonant + vowel + consonant, repeat the last consonant and add *-ed*.

*chat ➔ chat**ted***
*stop ➔ stop**ped***

- To make a negative sentence, use subject + *didn't* + infinitive.

*She **didn't start** a business.*
*They **didn't have** children.*

1 Complete the sentences with the past simple form of the verbs in brackets.

1 Frank and Linda ______________ (live) in another country for three years.
2 She ______________ (not play) in the match last night.
3 I ______________ (help) a woman with her groceries yesterday.
4 Edison ______________ (invent) his light bulb in 1879.
5 Leo ______________ (not finish) university.
6 Alan and Clara ______________ (not carry) an umbrella.
7 They ______________ (start) the marathon two hours ago.
8 We ______________ (not learn) her name.

12B Past simple (irregular verbs)

- Many verbs are irregular. You don't make the past forms of these words by adding *d* or *-ed*.

buy ➔ bought
do ➔ did
drive ➔ drove
fly ➔ flew
get ➔ got
go ➔ went
have ➔ had
hear ➔ heard
ride ➔ rode
see ➔ saw
take ➔ took

- You can find a list of common irregular verbs on page 178.

2 Complete the sentences with the past simple form of the verbs in brackets.

1 We ______________ (drive) to Denmark last summer for our holiday.
2 They ______________ (do) their homework in the park on Saturday.
3 Bing and Yue ______________ (get) married in March.

4 Olga ________________ (go) to university in Oslo.
5 Trent and I ________________ (buy) a large pizza for lunch.
6 They ________________ (have) three children and five grandchildren.
7 He ________________ (take) a train to Moscow because he didn't like planes.
8 I ________________ (fly) to Beijing last spring. I ________________ (see) many interesting things.

12C Past simple questions

- The past form of *do* is *did*. To make a *yes/no* question, use *did* + subject + infinitive. You can also use time expressions in your questions.
  Did you finish *school?*
  Did they visit *the museum* ***last year****?*
- To answer, you can just say *yes* or *no*. You can also say *Yes/ No*, + subject + *did* (+ *not*).
  A: Did you listen to the song? *B:* ***Yes, I did.***
  A: Did they play baseball? *B:* ***No, they didn't.***
- To make a *wh-* or *how* question, use question word + *did* + subject + infinitive.
  A: ***Who did he chat*** *with last night?*
  B: He chatted with his brother.
  A: ***When did she call*** *you?*
  B: She called me last night.

3 Make past simple questions with the words below.

1 when / Arnold / start / university ?
2 they / prepare for / the exam ?
3 how / you / travel / to Canada ?
4 where / she / live / as a child ?
5 you / study maths / in university ?
6 he / remember / his bank card ?
7 why / Tara / stop practising / with the team ?
8 we / close / the windows / in the kitchen ?

Irregular verbs

INFINITIVE	PAST SIMPLE
be	was / were
become	became
begin	began
bring	brought
build	built
buy	bought
choose	chose
can	could
come	came
do	did
drink	drank
drive	drove
eat	ate
feel	felt
find	found
fly	flew
forget	forgot
get	got
give	gave
go	went
have	had
hold	held
keep	kept
know	knew
leave	left
lose	lost

INFINITIVE	PAST SIMPLE
make	made
meet	met
pay	paid
put	put
read	read
ride	rode
run	ran
say	said
see	saw
sell	sold
send	sent
sing	sang
sit	sat
sleep	slept
speak	spoke
stand (up)	stood
swim	swam
take	took
teach	taught
tell	told
think	thought
understand	understood
wake (up)	woke
wear	wore
win	won
write	wrote

Extra speaking tasks

PAGE 84, 7A, EXERCISE 7

My name is Michael and this is my family. My mum is Jillian and my dad is Luke. I have one sister, Cassandra. My dad's parents live with us. My grandmother is Martha and her husband is William. My mother's sister and brother live next door. Their names are Jean and Hans. My mum's parents live in a different city. Their names are Darlene and Shawn.

PAGE 123, 10B, EXERCISE 10, STUDENT A

Look at the picture. The women's names are missing. Ask questions to find out who the women are.

Is Sandra standing near the door?

Cindy Jojo Lizzie Rina Sandra

Extra speaking tasks

PAGE 36, 3A, EXERCISES 7 AND 8

Imagine you're at these places. What items from page 36 would you take with you? What other items would you take?

PAGE 65, 5C, EXERCISES 11 AND 12

Think of a place you want to visit. Complete the table. Write the seasons and activities you can do in the different months.

Place: ______________________________

Months	Season	Activities
Mar–May		
Jun–Aug		
Sep–Nov		
Dec–Feb		

PAGE 111, 9B, EXERCISE 9

Choose a photo. Don't tell your partner. Answer your partner's questions.

PAGE 115, 9D, EXERCISE 8, STUDENT B

You work at the Riverside Hotel. Use the calendar below and help your partner book a room. The red dates are fully booked.

August

Monday	Tuesday	Wednesday	Thursday	Friday	Saturday	Sunday
1st	2nd	3rd	4th	5th	6th	7th
8th	9th	10th	11th	12th	13th	14th
15th	16th	17th	18th	19th	20th	21st
22nd	23rd	24th	25th	26th	27th	28th
29th	30th	31st	1st	2nd	3rd	4th

** red dates are fully booked.*

PAGE 123, 10B, EXERCISE 10, STUDENT B

Look at the picture. The men's names are missing. Ask questions to find out who the men are.

Is Wes talking to someone?

Jon Nico Sid Akito Wes

Audioscripts

UNIT 1

1.6

Narrator: 1

V= Vaishna, A = Ali

V: Hi, Ali. How are you?

A: Hey, Vaishna. I'm great!

V: Is your phone number 020-238-5810?

A: No, it's not. It's 020-238-9810.

V: Oh, OK. 020-238-9810. Thanks!

Narrator: 2

B = bank teller, L = Mr Lim

B: Mr Lim, is this your bank account number?

L: Let me see. No, it isn't. My bank account number is 024-6911-724-65.

B: Sorry. Say it again, please?

L: 024-6911-724-65.

B: Great. Thanks!

Narrator: 3

R = Ruth, J = John

R: What's your address, John?

J: It's 7-4-8 West Street.

R: I'm sorry. Is it 7-5-8?

J: No. It's 7-4-8. My postal code is 5-6-4, 2-1-9.

R: 5-6-4, 2-1-9. Got it!

1.7

Narrator: 1

W = Wei Ming, N = Nader

W: Hello. I'm Wei Ming. What's your name?

N: Hi. I'm Nader. Nice to meet you, Wei Ming!

W: Nice to meet you too, Nader.

Narrator: 2

R = Raul, A = Ahmed

R: Good morning. Are you Ahmed?

A: Yes, that's right. Are you Raul?

R: Yes, I am. It's nice to meet you!

Narrator: 3

C = Colleen, B = Brian

C: Good afternoon. I'm Colleen, from the UK.

B: Hi. I'm Brian. I'm from the UK too.

C: Nice to meet you, Brian.

UNIT 2

2.2

E = Ella, F = Felix

E: Hello?

F: Hi, Ella. It's Felix. Are you and Josef at home?

E: Hi Felix. Yes, we are. We're in the dining room. We work from home now.

F: Oh, wow. I work from home too! I'm in the living room. Where are your work desks?

E: Um ... We don't have work desks. Our laptops, books and pens ... They're on the dining table.

F: Oh, OK. My work desk is in my living room. All my things are on my desk – my laptop, my books, my pens, pencils ... Anyway ...

2.6

I = Interviewer, J = Jeff, A = Alec

I: Hello, Jeff. Please tell our listeners: Who are you?

J: Hi. I'm Jeff Kerby. I'm a scientist and a photographer. I study plants and animals.

I: You live in Denmark now. But where's your hometown – your childhood home?

J: It's a town called Sparta.

I: Hmm. Where's Sparta?

J: It's in New Jersey, in the United States.

I: I see! And what's in your hometown?

J: It has many things: a library, a park, many lakes and good restaurants.

I: Hello, Alec. Please tell our listeners: Who are you? And where's your hometown?

A: Hi, everyone. I'm Alec Jacobson. I'm a photographer. I live in Canada, but I'm from Williston. It's in Vermont.

I: I see. Where's Vermont?

A: It's in the US.

I: Ah.What's in your hometown?

A: It's a small town. There's a school, a supermarket, and many trees. It's near the forest.

UNIT 3

3.2

Many people collect things. These four people talk about what they collect.

Alsana: My name's Alsana. These are my coins.They're from different countries. These are from Spain, and those are from Thailand. This one is my favourite. It's from Peru. It's very old!

Silvio: I'm Silvio. These are my old mobile phones. I love this one. It's forty years old! It's so big. And look. That one in the box is really small. It's my favourite.

Peter: Hi. I'm Peter. I collect old plastic bottles, and I make things, like this table and those chairs over there in the garden. They're all made from old plastic bottles.

Danica: My name's Danica. These are my old train tickets. My tickets are from my family and friends from around the world. This one is from Russia. It's from a friend.

3.5

N = narrator, E = Ellie, J = Jenny

N: Ellie and Jenny are National Geographic Explorers. We ask them about their favourite colours.

E: Hello! I'm Ellie. My favourite colour is yellow. I like bright colours, like yellow, pink, orange, blue and purple. A lot of my things are these colours.

J: Hi, I'm Jenny. My favourite colour is pink. Many of my clothes are pink, and other things too.

N: Jenny is from the US, and Ellie is from the Philippines. What colours are in their country's flags?

J: The US flag is red, white and blue.

E: The Philippines flag is red, white, blue and yellow.

N: And what are their country's favourite colours?

E: In the Philippines, people like happy colours. I think our favourite colour is red.

J: Our favourite colour? I don't know ... I don't think America has a favourite colour.

UNIT 4

4.5

I = Interviewer, J = Josh, Y = Yasmin

I: How much sleep do we need? Doctors say seven to nine hours. But how long do we really sleep? Josh, please tell us ...

J: I sleep a lot – about nine hours. I go to bed at 1:30. And I wake up at 10:30.

I: What about you, Yasmin?

Y: I sleep for eight hours. I go to bed at 11:30, and I wake up at 7:30.

I: Do your families sleep a lot?

J: My parents finish work late. They start work early. They don't sleep a lot. They go to bed at 12 o'clock, and they wake up at 6 o'clock – that's six hours.

Y: I live with my brother, Tom. He works at night.

I: Interesting. What does he work as?

Y: He's a doctor. He goes to bed at 10 o'clock in the morning, and he wakes up at 5 o'clock in the afternoon. That's seven hours.

4.7

Abbey: My name is Abbey. I study the ocean. I usually work from Mondays to Fridays, in an office. I often work on Saturdays and Sundays too. But sometimes, I work on a boat – out on the sea, near the country Belize. Work on the boat is difficult, but it's fun. I always find new and amazing animals. They're my co-workers, and we work together in a really beautiful place – the ocean!

Jeff: My name is Jeff. I'm a scientist. I work in a lab and I study tiny animals from the ocean. Usually, I work about five days a week – on both weekdays and weekends. In the morning, I often read emails and reports by other scientists. Sometimes, I write reports too. In the afternoon, I usually work in the lab. My days in the lab are never the same. Every day is new and exciting!

UNIT 5

5.2

Jeff: I like doing things outside, and I don't like being at home all day. I love camping. It's quiet and I get to see many animals. I'm lucky – I go camping a lot for my job. I also like camping in my free time. I usually go alone.

I love playing football too. I play football with my friends every week – on Sunday mornings and on Tuesday and Thursday evenings.

Exercise is very important to me. I like playing tennis and running. I love trying new activities, but I don't always enjoy them. I don't like doing yoga, for example. I'm really bad at it!

5.5

Alain: My name's Alain. I'm from Libreville, Gabon. Gabon is hot all year. I don't like going outside in the afternoon, when it's really hot. But in the evenings, it's not so hot. It's cool. I love going to the park. My friends are there. We play football and basketball.

Hannah: I'm Hannah. I live in Winterberg, Germany. My favourite months are December to March. It's winter, and I love snowboarding. Winterberg is a great place for snowboarding and skiing. I love the snow. My brother and I like making snowmen after school and throwing snowballs at each other!

Isidora: I'm Isidora. I live in Santiago. It's in Chile. In winter, it's very cold, and the nights are long. I don't like the long nights. My favourite months are December to March. It's summer, and the weather is warm. I love hiking with my sister. I also love dancing in the evenings with my friends. It's really fun!

5.6

A: Hi, Ling, would you like to go to the cinema?

B: No thanks!

A: Do you want to have lunch?

B: Hmm ...

A: Would you like to go for a walk?

B: That sounds great.

A: Fantastic! Let's meet at the park.

Audioscripts

UNIT 6

6.4

I = interviewer, M = Maria, A = Alexis

I: Maria, tell us. Where do you go to buy food?

M: Sometimes, I go to a supermarket. But usually, I go to a farmer's market. I buy food from the people who grow it.

I: Why do you go to the farmer's market?

M: The food is fresh, not old. And it's clean. Yes, it's more expensive. But good food is important to me. It's healthy, and it tastes amazing.

I: I see. What do you usually buy?

M: I usually buy bread, pasta and nuts from the supermarket. I buy vegetables and fruit from the farmer's market. I really love the apples there.

I: How many apples do you buy?

M: I buy a lot of apples. I usually eat one or two apples a day.

I: Alexis, what about you? Where do you shop?

A: I usually buy my groceries at a local market. The food there is local – it's not from a different country, so it doesn't travel far. Also, there's no plastic packaging. I think that's good for the world.

I: Interesting. What do you usually buy?

A: I like healthy food, and I'm a vegetarian too – I don't eat meat. But I eat eggs. I usually buy these, and vegetables and fruit too. I also buy bread.

I: How much bread do you buy?

A: I'm French, and French people love bread! But I live in Indonesia. It's not easy to find good French bread here, so I don't buy a lot.

UNIT 7

7.2

I = Interviewer, F = Family expert

I: Is your family happy? Today, we ask a family expert: What do happy families do?

F: Well ... Number one is 'talk to each other'.

I: Ahh. What do we talk about?

F: Anything, really. Be open. Say what you think and how you feel about things. Parents need to be easy to talk to. Husbands and wives too.

I: Yes, that's really important. What's number two?

F: Happy families know their family history. Tell children where they come from.

I: Hmm. How do I do that? And why is it important?

F: Children need to know they are part of something big. Who are their grandparents? Where are they from? What are their parents' life stories? These are important questions with important answers.

I: I see! And what's number three?

F: I like this one. Happy families eat together!

I: Oh, that's easy. My family loves to eat!

F: That's great! Meals are a great way for families to come together. Do you usually eat at home?

I: No, we don't. We usually eat out.

F: That's good, but try to eat at home too. Not always, but often – dinner, lunch or breakfast.

7.7

Ellie: I'm Ellie, and my best friend is Mittsu. She has long, dark hair. It's really beautiful! Her eyes are dark brown, and she's about 1.6 metres tall, like me. Mittsu is very clever, and she's really nice. Plus she's a great cook! We're really close. She's like a sister to me.

Lia: I'm Lia, and my best friend is my sister – Miriam. Miriam looks a lot like me. She's about 1.7 metres tall, with short, dark hair and brown eyes. Miriam and I like the same things, like doing yoga, birdwatching, and travelling. She's really interesting and clever.

7.8

A = Alvin, C = Cindy

Narrator: Conversation 1

A: Hi, Cindy. Here's my report. One day early!

C: Is it all there? All the pages?

A: Um ... yes. And all the photos and charts too.

C: OK. Leave it on my desk.

J = Juan, P = Pei Ling

Narrator: Conversation 2

J: Hi, Pei Ling. Here's my report. One day early!

P: Wow, that's amazing, Juan. Thanks! Is it all there?

J: Yes, it is. And all the photos and charts too.

P: Really? Thanks so much, Juan. And great work!

UNIT 8

8.2

Naofumi Ogasawara is a teacher. He's very good with numbers and he can do difficult maths in his head – without a pen, paper or computer. He's very quick.

Rebecca Sharrock can remember every day of her life. She remembers her dreams from long ago, and she remembers her first birthday. She can't forget the things she sees or feels.

Krishnan Kumar is very good at yoga. He can do many difficult yoga poses, and he can stay there for a long time. He can stand on his head for more than three hours.

Courtney Dauwalter is an amazing runner. She can run many kilometres. Some of her races are about eighty kilometres long. Some races are one hundred and sixty kilometres long. And some are more than three hundred kilometres long.

8.6

Anusha: I love hummingbirds because they're beautiful. They live in North and South America. There are about three hundred and thirty types of hummingbirds, and they are many different colours.

Hummingbirds aren't big. Large hummingbirds are about seven to thirteen centimetres long, but small ones are only four centimetres long – about the size of your little finger! They aren't heavy, either. Large hummingbirds weigh about twenty grams, and small hummingbirds weigh just two grams.

Hummingbirds are tiny, but they're really fast – they can fly about forty kilometres an hour! They can also hover, or stay in the same place when they fly. And they can fly backwards. Other birds can't fly backwards. Hummingbirds get their food from plants. They drink the nectar, or sugar water, from flowers.

UNIT 9

9.2

Jenny: Sometimes, I travel for fun, not for work. I really love visiting Iceland. There are many things to see! There are beautiful beaches with black sand, and hot water pools for resting in when you're tired. At night, you can see the northern lights. These are beautiful, colourful lights in the sky. You can only see them at night, when there isn't a big moon and there aren't any clouds. Iceland's capital city Reykjavik is great. There are lots of museums, and there's a hot pool in the middle of the city. There are many nice restaurants, and lots of friendly people!

9.4

Narrator: 1

Want to go somewhere nice and warm? Come to Jamaica. Everyone loves it! The weather is perfect, and there are so many things to do! Relax at our wonderful hotel. It's right next to the beach, far from the noise of the city. Or have fun in the sun. Swim in the sea or join us on a lovely boat ride. The wind is always strong – perfect for sailing! Interested in Jamaican food? Our chef Luisa is a wonderful cook. Join one of our classes and learn to cook delicious Jamaican dishes with her. Finally, enjoy some reggae music with us. We have an amazing band, so don't forget your dancing shoes!

Narrator: 2

Do you love the snow? Visit Finland in December! Learn to snowboard with our friendly snowboarding teachers. Or go on a dog sled adventure with our team of amazing dogs. Get to know them, and let them take you on an exciting journey! Don't worry about the weather. Visit our saunas. These hot rooms are the perfect place to rest on a cold winter day. Finally, end your day the Finnish way. Swim in a cold lake and feel alive! We want to hear from you. Email us to find out more.

UNIT 10

10.3

I = Interviewer, A, B and C = Customers

I: I'm here at a sports shop and I'm interviewing people to find out what they're buying.

Narrator: 1

I: Hello there. What are you buying today?

A: I'm buying running shoes. I'm training for a marathon.

I: A marathon? Wow. That's a really long run – 42 kilometres!

A: Yeah. It's a long distance, so I'm looking for something light ...

Narrator: 2

I: Excuse me. Hi. What are you looking for today?

B: I'm learning how to play tennis, so I'm buying a new tennis racquet. This is my coach, Liz. She's helping me choose.

I: I see! So, how are your lessons?

B: They're good. I'm learning a lot, but I need a better racquet! Right now, I'm using a very old and heavy racquet ...

Narrator: 3

I: Excuse me. Are you buying these new football boots?

C: No, I'm not. I'm just looking at them. I'm getting this new football shirt.

I: Ah. That's a nice shirt! Do you play football often?

C: Um ... No, I don't play football. But I love the shirt!

10.7

Rubén: Hi, I'm Rubén. I'm a photographer. My health is very important to me, so I usually exercise often. But I also travel a lot for my work. It's not always easy to go out and exercise, so I often exercise in my hotel room! Right now, I'm using an app to help me. It teaches me exercises I can do anywhere. I can get all the exercise I need in just twenty minutes – which is great when I'm travelling a lot.

Nora: Hello, I'm Nora. I usually exercise four times a week. Sometimes, I go to the gym to lift some light weights. And sometimes, I go to the track for a run. But I also get a lot of exercise at work too! I'm an archaeologist – I look for really old things people leave in the ground. I'm always running around and climbing up and down ladders all day. It's hard work, but it's great exercise.

Audioscripts

UNIT 11

11.2

Narrator: 1
My favourite painter is Pablo Picasso. Picasso was from Spain, but he lived a lot of his life in France. He was born in 1881, and he died in 1973. Many people remember Picasso for inventing Cubism – a style of painting that uses different shapes. But I like some of his older paintings too. One of my favourite Picasso paintings is a self-portrait – a painting of himself, from 1907.

Narrator: 2
My favourite painter is Natalia Goncharova. She was a famous artist from Russia. She was born there in 1881, but she lived in France from 1921 to 1962, when she died. People remember Goncharova for her paintings that used light in interesting ways. But my favourite Goncharova painting is her self-portrait from the year 1907.

11.6

I = Interviewer, A = Alec, L = Lia

I: So Alec, tell us … What's your favourite event from history?
A: My favourite event was the invention of the Leica 1 – a 35-millimetre camera.
I: Interesting! When was that? And who was the inventor?
A: It was in 1925. The inventor was Oscar Barnack.
I: Were cameras huge back then?
A: Yes, they were. But the Leica 1 was tiny. It weighed just 125 grams!
I: And why is this event important to you?
A: The Leica 1 was a very important camera. Photographers were suddenly free to take their cameras anywhere. This was the start of photojournalism – my job! I use photographs to tell the stories of people and places from around the world.

I: Lia, what's your favourite event from history?
L: My favourite event was a film by the Lumière brothers: *Workers Leaving the Lumière Factory.*
I: When was it? And who were the Lumière brothers?
L: It was in 1895. The Lumière brothers were inventors from France.
I: What was the film about? And why was it special?
L: It was a short film – only a minute long. And it was really simple: just people leaving a factory. But it was big! I think it was the first film on a large screen.
I: Like cinemas today! Was it very popular?
L: Yes, it was. It was the first great film, I think. Today, millions of people watch films at cinemas around the world. I can't imagine a world without films!

UNIT 12

12.4

Maria: So, a funny thing happened to me. I was in the rainforest in Ecuador with two local people, Jorge and Raul. We had to walk along a small river, in the water. It was difficult for me, but not for Jorge and Raul. They made it look easy! They knew where all the right stones were.

I wanted to look good in front of them. I didn't want them to know it was difficult for me. But Jorge looked at me and told Raul, 'You know, she walks like a chicken.' 'Like a chicken?' I asked. I felt a little sad. Jorge said, 'No, no, that's good! Chickens are great at walking!'

I felt great, and I lifted my arms to celebrate. Suddenly … *whoosh*! I slipped and fell into the water. Jorge and Raul laughed so much! They helped me up, and I felt terrible. But later, I laughed too.

Acknowledgements

The Voices publishing team would like to thank all of the explorers for their time and participation on this course – and for their amazing stories and photos.

The team would also like to thank the following teachers, who provided detailed and invaluable feedback on this course.

Asia

SS. Abdurrosyid, University of Muhammadiyah Tangerang, Banten; Hằng Ánh, Hanoi University of Science Technology, Hanoi; Yoko Atsumi, Seirei Christopher University, Hamamatsu; Dr. Nida Boonma, Assumption University, Bangkok; Portia Chang, SEE Education, New Taipei City; Brian Cullen, Nagoya Institute of Technology, Nagoya; David Daniel, Houhai English, Beijing; Professor Doan, Hanoi University, Hanoi; Kim Huong Duong, HCMC University of Technology, Ho Chi Minh; Natalie Ann Gregory, University of Kota Kinabalu, Sabah; Shawn Greynolds, AUA Language Centre, Bangkok; Thi Minh Ly Hoang, University of Economics – Technology for Industries, Hanoi; Mike Honywood, Shinshu University, Nagano; Jessie Huang, National Central University, Taoyuan City; Edward Jones, Nagoya International School, Nagoya; Ajarn Kiangkai, Sirnakarintrawirote University, Bangkok; Zhou Lei, New Oriental Education & Technology Group, Beijing; Louis Liu, METEN, Guangzhou; Jeng-Jia (Caroline) Luo Tunghai University, Taichung City; Thi Ly Luong, Huflit University, Ho Chi Minh City; Michael McCollister, Feng Chia University, Taichung; Robert McLaughlin, Tokoha University, Shizuoka; Hal Miller, Houhai English, Beijing; Jason Moser, Kanto Gakuin University, Yokohama; Hudson Murrell, Baiko Gakuin University, Shimonoseki; Takayuki Nagamine, Nagoya University of Foreign Studies, Nagoya; Sanuch Natalang, Thammasart University, Bangkok; Nguyen Bá Học, Hanoi University of Public Health, Hanoi; Nguyen Cong Tri, Ho Chi Minh City University of Technology, Ho Chi Minh; Nguyen Ngoc Vu, Hoa Sen University, Ho Chi Minh City; Professor Nguyen, Hanoi University, Hanoi; Dr Nguyen, Hao Sen University, Ho Chi Minh City; Nguyễn Quang Vịnh, Hanoi University, Hanoi; Wilaichitra Nilsawaddi, Phranakhon Rajabhat University, Bangkok; Suchada Nimmanit, Rangsit University, Bangkok; Ms. Cao Thien Ai Nuong, Hoa Sen University, Ho Chi Minh City; Donald Patterson, Seirei Christopher University, Shizuoka; Douglas Perkins, Musashino University Junior and Senior High School, Tokyo; Phan The Hung, Van Lang University, Ho Chi Minh City; Fathimah Razman, Northern University, Sintok, Kedah; Bruce Riseley, Holmesglen (Language Centre of University Of Muhammadiyah Tangerang for General English), Jakarta; Anthony Robins, Aichi University of Education, Aichi; Greg Rouault, Hiroshima Shudo University, Hiroshima; Dr Sawaluk, Sirnakarintrawirote University, Bangkok; Dr Supattra, Rangsit University, Lak Hok; Dr Thananchai, Dhurakijbundit University, Bangkok; Thao Le Phuong, Open University, Ho Chi Minh; Thap Doanh Thuong, Thu Dau Mot University, Thu Dau Mot; Kinsella Valies, University of Shizuoka, Shizuoka; Gerrit Van der Westhuizen, Houhai English, Beijing; Dr Viraijitta, Rajjabhat Pranakorn University, Bangkok; Dr Viraijittra, Phranakhon Rajabhat University, Bangkok; Vo Dinh Phuoc, University of Economics, Ho Chi Minh City; Dr Nussara Wajsom, Assumption University, Bangkok; Scott A.Walters, Woosong University, Daejon; Yungkai Weng, PingoSpace & Elite Learning, Beijing; Ray Wu, Wall Street English, Hong Kong.

Europe, Middle East and Africa (EMEA)

Saju Abraham, Sohar University, Sohar; Huda Murad Al Balushi, International Maritime College , Sohar; Salah Al Hanshi, Modern College of Business and Science, Muscat; Victor Alarcón, EOI Badalona, Barcelona; Yana Alaveranova, International House, Kiev; Alexandra Alexandrova, Almaty; Blanca Alvarez, EOI San Sebastian de los Reyes, Madrid; Emma Antolin, EOI San Sebastian de los Reyes, Madrid; Manuela Ayna, Liceo Primo Levi, Bollate, Milan; Elizabeth Beck, British Council, Milan; Charlotte Bentham, Adveti, Sharjah; Carol Butters, Edinburgh College, Edinburgh; Patrizia Cassin, International House, Milan; Elisabet Comelles, EIM - Universitat de Barcelona, Barcelona; Sara De Angeles, Istituto Superiore Giorgi, Milan; Carla Dell'Acqua, Liceo Primo Levi, Bollate, Milan; John Dench, BEET Language Centre, Bournemouth; Angela di Staso, Liceo Banfi, Vimercate, Milan; Sarah Donno, Edinburgh College, Edinburgh, UK; Eugenia Dume, EOI San Sebastian de los Reyes, Madrid; Rory Fergus Duncan; BKC-IH Moscow, Moscow; Ms Evelyn Kandalaft El Moualem, AMIDEAST, Beirut; Raul Pope Farguell, BKC-IH Moscow, Moscow; Chris Farrell, CES, Dublin; Dr Aleksandra, Filipowicz, Warsaw University of Technology, Warsaw; Diana Golovan, Linguist LLC, Kiev, Ukraine; Jaap Gouman, Pieter Zandt, Kampen; Maryam Kamal, British Council, Doha; Galina Kaptug, Moonlight, Minsk; Ms Rebecca Nabil Keedi, College des Peres Antonines, Hadath; Dr. Michael King, Community College of Qatar, Doha; Gabriela Kleckova, University of West Bohemia, Pilsen; Mrs Marija Klečkovska, Pope John Paul II gymnasium, Vilnius; Kate Knight, International Language School, Milan; Natalia Kolina, Moscow; David Koster, P.A.R.K., Brno; Suzanne Littlewood, Zayed University, Dubai; Natalia Lopez, EOI Terrassa, Barcelona; Maria Lopez-Abeijon, EOI Las Rozas, Madrid; Pauline Loriggio, International House London, London; Gabriella Luise, International Language School Milan, Milan; Klara Malowiecka, Lang Ltc, Warsaw; Fernando Martin, EOI Valdemoro, Madrid; Robert Martinez, La Cunza, Gipuzkoa; Mario Martinez, EOI Las Rozas, Madrid; Marina Melnichuk, Financial University, Moscow; Martina Menova, PĚVÁČEK vzdělávací centrum, Prague; Marlene Merkt, Kantonsschule Zurich Nord, Zurich; Iva Meštrović, Učilište Jantar, Zagreb; Silvia Milian, EOI El Prat, Barcelona; Jack Montelatici, British School Milan, Milan; Muntsa Moral, Centre de Formació de Persones Adultes Pere Calders,

Acknowledgements

Barcelona; Julian Oakley, Wimbledon School of English, London; Virginia Pardo, EOI Badalona, Barcelona;

William Phillips, Aga Khan Educational Service; Joe Planas, Centre de Formació de Persones Adultes Pere Calders, Barcelona; Carmen Prieto, EOI Carabanchel, Madrid; Sonya Punch, International House, Milan; Magdalena Rasmus, Cavendish School, Bournemouth; Laura Rodríguez, EOI El Prat, Barcelona; Victoria Samaniego, EOI Pozuelo, Madrid; Beatriz Sanchez, EOI San Sebastian de los Reyes, Madrid; Gigi Saurer, Migros-Genossenschafts-Bund, Zurich; Jonathan Smilow, BKC-IH, Moscow; Prem Sourek, Anderson House, Bergamo; Svitlana Surgai, British Council, Kyiv; Peter Szabo, Libra Books, Budapest; Richard Twigg, International House, Milan; Evgeny Usachev, Moscow International Academy, Moscow; Eric van Luijt, Tilburg University Language Centre, Tilburg; Tanya Varchuk, Fluent English School, Ukraine; Yulia Vershinina, YES Center, Moscow; Małgorzata Witczak, Warsaw University of Technology, Warsaw; Susanna Wright, Stafford House London, London; Chin-Yunn Yang, Padagogische Maturitaetsschule Kreuzlingen, Kreuzlingen; Maria Zarudnaya, Plekhanov Russian University of Economics, Moscow; Michelle Zelenay, KV Winterthur, Winterthur.

Latin America

Jorge Aguilar, Universidad Autónoma de Sinaloa, Culiacán; Carlos Bernardo Anaya, UNIVA Zamora, Zamora; Sergio Balam, Academia Municipal de Inglés, Mérida; Josélia Batista, CCL Centro de Línguas, Fortaleza; Aida Borja, ITESM GDL, Guadalajara; Diego Bruekers Deschamp, Ingles Express, Belo Horizonte; Alejandra Cabrera, Universidad Politécnica de Yucatán, Mérida; Luis Cabrera Rocha, ENNAULT – UNAM, Mexico City; Bruna Caltabiano, Caltabiano Idiomas, Sao Paulo; Hortensia Camacho, FES Iztacala – UNAM, Mexico City; Gustavo Cruz Torres, Instituto Cultural México – Norteamericano, Guadalajara; Maria Jose D'Alessandro Nogueira, FCM Foundation School, Belo Horizonte; Gabriela da Cunha Barbosa Saldanha, FCM Foundation School, Belo Horizonte; Maria Da Graça Gallina Flack, Challenge School, Porto Alegre; Pedro Venicio da Silva Guerra, U-Talk Idiomas, São Bernardo do Campo; Julice Daijo, JD Language Consultant, Rua Oscar Freire; Olívia de Cássia Scorsafava, U-Talk Idiomas, São Bernardo do Campo; Marcia Del Corona, UNISINOS, Porto Alegre; Carlos Alberto Díaz Najera, Colegio Salesiano Anáhuac Revolución, Guadalajara; Antônio César Ferraz Gomes, 4 Flags, São Bernardo do Campo; Brenda Pérez Ferrer, Universidad Politécnica de Querétaro, Querétaro; Sheila Flores, Cetys Universidad, Mexicali; Ángela Gamboa, Universidad Metropolitana, Mérida; Alejandro Garcia, Colegio Ciencias y Letras, Tepic; Carlos Gomora, CILC, Toluca; Kamila Gonçalves, Challenge School, Porto Alegre; Herivelton Gonçalves, Prime English, Vitória; Idalia Gonzales, Británico, Lima; Marisol Gutiérrez Olaiz, LAMAR Universidad, Guadalajara; Arturo Hernandez, ITESM GDL, Guadalajara; Gabriel Cortés Hernandez, BP- Intitute, Morelia; Daniel Vázquez Hernández, Preparatoria 2, Mérida; Erica Jiménez, Centro Escolar, Tepeyac; Leticia Juárez, FES Acatlán – UNAM, Mexico City; Teresa Martínez, Universidad Iberoamericana, Tijuana; Elsa María del Carmen Mejía Franco, CELE Mex, Toluca; José Alejandro Mejía Tello, CELE Mex, Toluca; Óscar León Mendoza Jimenéz, Angloamericano Idiomas, Mexico City; Karla Mera Ubando, Instituto Cultural, Mexico City; Elena Mioto, UNIVA, Guadalajara; Ana Carolina Moreira Paulino, SENAC, Porto Alegre; Paula Mota, 4 Flags, São Bernardo do Campo; Adila Beatriz Naud de Moura, UNISINOS, Porto Alegre; Monica Navarro Morales, Instituto Cultural, Mexico City; Wilma F Neves, Caltabiano Idiomas, Sao Paulo; Marcelo Noronha, Caltabiano Idiomas, Sao Paulo; Enrique Ossio, ITESM Morelia, Morelia; Filipe Pereira Bezerra, U-Talk Idiomas, Sao Bernardo do Campo; Florencia Pesce, Centro Universitario de Idiomas, Buenos Aires, Argentina; Kamila Pimenta, CCBEU, São Bernardo do Campo; Leopoldo Pinzón Escobar, Universidad Santo Tomás, Bogotá; Mary Ruth Popov Hibas, Ingles Express, Belo Horizonte; Alejandra Prado Barrera, UVM, Mexico City; Letícia Puccinelli Redondo, U-Talk Idiomas, São Bernardo do Campo; Leni Puppin, Centro de Línguas de UFES, Vitória; Maria Fernanda Quijano, Universidad Tec Milenio, Culiacan; Jorge Quintal, Colegio Rogers, Mérida; Sabrina Ramos Gomes, FCM Foundation School, Belo Horizonte; Mariana Roberto Billia, 4 Flags, São Bernardo do Campo; Monalisa Sala de Sá 4 Flags, São Bernardo do Campo; Yamel Sánchez Vízcarra, CELE Mex, Toluca; Vagner Serafim, CCBEU, São Bernardo do Campo; Claudia Serna, UNISER, Mexicali; Alejandro Serna, CCL, Morelia; Simone Teruko Nakamura, U-Talk Idiomas, São Bernardo do Campo; Desirée Carla Troyack, FCM Foundation School, Belo Horizonte; Sandra Vargas Boecher Prates, Centro de Línguas da UFES, Vitória; Carlos Villareal, Facultad de Ingenierías Universidad Autónoma de Querétaro, Querétaro; Rosa Zarco Mondragón, Instituto Cultural, Mexico City.

US and Canada

Rachel Bricker, Arizona State University, Tempe; Jonathan Bronson, Approach International Student Center, Boston; Elaine Brookfield, EC Boston, Boston; Linda Hasenfus, Approach International Language Center, Boston; Andrew Haynes, ELS Boston, Boston; Cheryl House, ILSC, Toronto; Rachel Kadish, FLS International, Boston; Mackenzie Kerby, ELS Language Centers, Boston; Rob McCourt FLS Boston; Haviva Parnes, EC English Language Centres, Boston; Shayla Reid, Approach International Student Center, Boston.

Credits

Illustration: All illustrations are owned by © Cengage.

Cover: ©Juan Arredondo; **3** sorincolac/iStock/Getty Images; **4** (tl1) Design Pics Inc/Alamy Stock Photo, (tl2) Mikal Ludlow/Alamy Stock Photo, (cl1) Hai Bo, courtesy Pace Gallery, (cl2) Anadolu Agency/Getty Images, (bl1) Courtesy of Ida Josefin Eriksson, (bl2) knape/E+/Getty Images; **6** (tl1) Yuri Kozyrev/Noor/Redux Pictures, (tl2) © Mike Coots, (cl1) sorincolac/iStock/Getty Images, (cl2) © Kagoshima Prefecture Visitors Bureau-K.P.V.B, (bl1) J R Eyerman/The Life Picture Collection/Shutterstock.com, (bl2) Chester Higgins Jr./The New York Times/Redux Pictures; **8** (tl1) Courtesy of Abigail Engleman, (tl2) Courtesy of Afroz Ahmad Shah, (tr1) © Alexis Chappuis, (tr2) Courtesy of Anusha Shankar, (cl) © Alec Jacobson, (cr1) Courtesy of Llenel de Castro, (cr2) © Isaí Madriz; **8-9** Robert Harding Picture Library/National Geographic Image Collection; **9** (tl1) Courtesy of Jeffrey Kerby, (tl2) Jeffrey Marlow, (tr1) Courtesy of Maria Fadiman, (tr2) © Nora Shawki, (cl1) Courtesy of Jennifer Adler, (cl2) © Caio Felipe Santos da Silva; (cr) Courtesy of Ruben Salgado; **10-11** Design Pics Inc/ Alamy Stock Photo; **11** (cr1) Courtesy of Abigail Engleman, (cr2) © Isaí Madriz; **13** (tc) © Isaí Madriz, (c) Andrei Minsk/Shutterstock.com, (bc) Courtesy of Abigail Engleman; **14** (bl1) aliaksei kruhlenia/Shutterstock.com, (bl2) Cosmic_Design/Shutterstock.com, (bl3) AAVAA/Shutterstock.com; **15** (tl) Baptiste Fernandez/ Icon Sport/Getty Images, (tc) San Francisco Chronicle/Hearst Newspapers/Getty Images, (tr) Kyodo News/Getty Images; **16** (cl1) Markusunger/iStock/Getty Images, (cl2) ineskoleva/E+/Getty Images, (cl3) Science Photo Library/Alamy Stock Photo, (bl1) DJ Srki/Shutterstock.com, (bl2) Juanmonino/E+/Getty Images; **17** Confidence Nzewi/Alamy Stock Photo; **18** Sudowoodo/ Shutterstock.com; **19** (tr) chee gin tan/E+/Getty Images, (cr) Maskot/Cavan Images, (br) PhotoAlto/James Hardy/Getty Images; **20** (tl) Rafael Elias/Moment/Getty Images, (tr) Solskin/DigitalVision/ Getty Images, (br) adamkaz/E+/Getty Images; **21** FG Trade/E+/ Getty Images; **22-23** Mikal Ludlow/Alamy Stock Photo; **23** (cr1) © Alec Jacobson, (cr2) Courtesy of Jeffrey Kerby; **24** (tl) Zahrotul Fuadah/Shutterstock.com, (cl) tharrison/DigitalVision Vectors/Getty Images, (bl1) Janis Abolins/Shutterstock.com, (bl2) DoridoDesign/ Shutterstock.com, (bl3) kajiwori/Shutterstock.com, (bl4) 13ree.design/Shutterstock.com, (bl5) Best Vector Elements/Shutterstock.com, (bl6) Janis Abolins/Shutterstock.com; **25** (tl1) Junjun123/ Shutterstock.com, (tl2) sasa graphic/Shutterstock.com, (tl3) ShallArt/Shutterstock.com, (tr1) IhorZigor/Shutterstock.com, (tr2) cavidali/Shutterstock.com, (c) © Jeff Minton; **27** (tc) fotostorm/ iStock/Getty Images, (bc) Tartila/Shutterstock.com; **28** (tl) -izabell-/ Depositphotos.com, (tc1) hallojulie/iStock/Getty Images, (tc2) Taken by Lee Williams/Moment/Getty Images, (tr) sammy/Alamy Stock Photo, (cr1) Piano107/Dreamstime.com, (cr2) Valentin Armian/Dreamstime.com, (c) Radu Bercan/Shutterstock.com, (br1) Stavros Markopoulos/Moment/Getty Images, (br2) Aardvark/ Alamy Stock Photo, (bc1) Richard Thornton/Shutterstock.com, (bc2) Steve Vidler/Alamy Stock Photo; **29** Tony Cenicola/The New York Times/Redux Pictures; **30** LisaValder/iStock/Getty Images; **31** © Geraldine Sy/Good Illustration/Cengage; **32** Oleksandra Korobova/Moment/Getty Images; **34-35** Hai Bo, courtesy Pace Gallery; **35** (cl) Courtesy of Llenel de Castro, (cr) Courtesy of Jennifer Adler; **36** (cl1) Zoonar GmbH/Alamy Stock Photo, (cl2) gerasimov_foto_174/Shutterstock.com, (cl3) David Hare/Alamy Stock Photo, (cr1) Billion Photos/Shutterstock.com, (cr2) cobalt88/ Shutterstock.com, (cr3) Natkamol Panomnantakit/Alamy Stock Photo, (bl1) David Lee/Alamy Stock Photo, (bl3) chris brignell/ Alamy Stock Photo, (bl3) GaryAlvis/E+/Getty Images, (br1) Africa Studio/Shutterstock.com, (br2) mawielobob/iStock/Getty Images, (br3) studiocasper/E+/Getty Images; **37** (tr) © Llenel de Castro, (t) 4LUCK/Shutterstock.com, (bl) © Ian Segebarth; **38** Marilyn Nieves/ Moment/Getty Images; **39** (cl) © Javier Joaquin, (cr1) Paul Quezada-Neiman/Alamy Stock Photo, (cr2)(cr3) © NovelCreations on Etsy, (br) morningarage/iStock/Getty Images, **40** (tl1) jgroup/ iStock/Getty Images, (tl2) Pongnathee Kluaythong/EyeEm/Getty Images, (tl3) Dziggyfoto/iStock/Getty Images, (cl1) seregam/iStock/ Getty Images, (cl2) StudioSmart/Shutterstock.com, (cl3) ZargonDesign/E+/Getty Images, (cl4) Olga Kovalenko/ Shutterstock.com, (cl5) TPopova/iStock/Getty Images, (cl6) Ng Sok Lian/EyeEm/Getty Images; **41** John W Banagan/The Image Bank/ Getty Images; **42** © Javier Joaquin/Beehive Illustration; **43** Gorodenkoff/Shutterstock.com; **44** (bl) Vecc Schiafino/Alamy Stock Photo, (bc) Emily Marie Wilson/Shutterstock.com, (br) PhotographerIncognito/Shutterstock.com; **45** (cl1) Vector Tradition/Shutterstock.com, (cl2) Belidongs/Shutterstock.com, (bl) Anke Wittkowski/EyeEm/Getty Images; **46-47** Anadolu Agency/ Getty Images; **47** (cr1) Courtesy of Abigail Engleman, (cr2) © Jeffrey Marlow; **48** Aleksandr Bryliaev/Shutterstock.com; **49** (tc) Carolyn Drake/Magnum Photos New York, (bc1) Janis Abolins/ Shutterstock.com, (bc2) YouLandAIcon/Shutterstock.com, (bc3) sakmeniko/Shutterstock.com, (bc4) AF studio/Shutterstock.com, (bc5) Andrii Arkhipov/Shutterstock.com; **50** Francesco Ridolfi/ Cavan Images; **52** (bl) Courtesy of Abbey Englemann, (br) © Jeffrey Marlow; **54** Inti St Clair/Getty Images; **56** (tl1) Jacky Co/ Shutterstock.com, (tl2) Drk_Smith/Shutterstock.com, (tl3) BluesMan3000/Shutterstock.com, (tl4) A-spring/Shutterstock.com, (tl5) Alice-vector/Shutterstock.com; **58-59** Courtesy of Ida Josefin Eriksson; **59** (cr1) Courtesy of Jeffrey Kerby, (cr2) Courtesy of Abigail Engleman; **60** (cr1) Rashad Ashur/Shutterstock.com, (cr2) Mr Aesthetics/Shutterstock.com, (cr3) 13ree.design/ Shutterstock.com, (cr4) Kumpeh_Studio/Shutterstock.com, (cr5) Creative icon styles/Shutterstock.com, (cr6) Jane Kelly/ Shutterstock.com, (cr7) TotemArt/Shutterstock.com, (cr8) fad82/ Shutterstock.com; **61** (tl) Alejandra de la Fuente/Moment/Getty Images, (tr) LeoPatrizi/E+/Getty Images, (bl) monkeybusinessimages/iStock/Getty Images, (br) Westend61/ Getty Images; **62** (bl1) David Trood/DigitalVision/Getty Images, (bl2) Oscar Wong/Moment/Getty Images, (bl3) Carlos Mora/ Alamy Stock Photo, (bl4) JGI/Tom Grill/Getty Images, (bc1) GibsonPictures/E+/Getty Images, (bc2) Thomas Barwick/ DigitalVision/Getty Images, (br1) Robin Skjoldborg/DigitalVision/ Getty Images, (br2) Mike Harrington/Stone/Getty Images, (br3) Ulrike Schmitt-Hartmann/DigitalVision/Getty Images, (br4) Johner Images/Getty Images; **63** © Frederik Larsen; **64** Rvector/ Shutterstock.com; **65** (tc) Peter Hermes Furian/Shutterstock.com, (cl) Jacky Parker Photography/Moment/Getty Images. (c1) levente bodo/Moment/Getty Images, (c2) Kasper Nymann/EyeEm/Getty Images, (cr) Dan Reynolds Photography/Moment/Getty Images; **66** Tom Werner/DigitalVision/Getty Images; **67** gbbstock/

Credits

Shutterstock.com; **68, 69** Courtesy of Abigail Engleman; **70-71** knape/E+/Getty Images; **71** (cr1) Courtesy of Maria Fadiman, (cr2) © Alexis Chappuis; **72** (cl1) Tharakorn Arunothai/ EyeEm/Getty Images, (cl2) Filmfoto/Dreamstime.com, (cl3) Mada Jimmy/Dreamstime.com, (cl4) Chatham172/Shutterstock.com, (c1) Tarasyuk Igor/Shutterstock.com, (c2) Tetiana Vitsenko/Alamy Stock Photo, (c3) lee avison/Alamy Stock Photo, (c4) s-cphoto/E+/ Getty Images, (cr1) semenovp/iStock/Getty Images, (cr2) Kakarlapudi Venkata Sivanaga Raju/Dreamstime.com, (cr3) Ryzhkov Photography/Shutterstock.com, (cr4) ATU Images/The Image Bank/Getty Images; **73** (tr) EDP Photography/Shutterstock. com, (cr) Alexander Mychko/Alamy Stock Photo, (br) Simon Reddy/Alamy Stock Photo; **74** (tl1) gresei/Shutterstock.com, (tl2) M. Unal Ozmen/Shutterstock.com, (tl3) StockFood/Getty Images, (tl4) Oleksandr Perepelytsia/Alamy Stock Photo, (br) Westend61/ Getty Images; **75** Felipex/iStock/Getty Images; **76** (bl) Andrew Catta/Alamy Stock Photo, (bc) ferrantraite/iStock/Getty Images, (br) JamesJames Quine/Alamy Stock Photo; **77** Lizardflms/ Shutterstock.com; **78** andresr/E+/Getty Images; **79** Pan-Pavel/ iStock/Getty Images; **80** bonchan/Shutterstock.com; **81** rudisill/E+/ Getty Images; **82-83** Yuri Kozyrev/Noor/Redux Pictures; **83** (cr1) Courtesy of Llenel de Castro, (cr2) © Caio Felipe Santos da Silva; **84** (cl1) Lucy Lambriex/Stone/Getty Images, (cl2) CasarsaGuru/E+/ Getty Images, (cr1) Ronnie Kaufman/The Image Bank/Getty Images, (cr2) JohnnyGreig/E+/Getty Images, (bl1) pondsaksit/ iStock/Getty Images, (bl2) The Good Brigade/DigitalVision/Getty Images, (bc1) EyeWolf/Moment/Getty Images, (bc2) stockfour/ iStock/Getty Images, (bc3) Igor Alecsander/E+/Getty Images, (br1) SolStock/E+/Getty Images, (br2) adamkaz/E+/Getty Images; **85** (tc) © John Stanmeyer, (bc) DrAndY/Shutterstock.com; **86** (tl1) (tl2) (tc1) (tc2) Leremy/Shutterstock.com, (tc3) Martial Red/ Shutterstock.com; (tc4) Kelsey Smith Photography/Cavan Images; **88** (tl) Simon Winnall/Getty Images, (cr) Courtesy of Llenel de, (br) Courtesy of Lia Nahomi-Kajiki; **89** Rawpixel.com/Shutterstock. com; **90** Christian Bertrand/Shutterstock.com; **91** (c) Reza Estakhrian/The Image Bank/Getty Images, (bc1) Westend61/Getty Images, (bc2) rez-art/iStock/Getty Images; **92** (tc) Flueeler Urs/ Alamy Stock Photo, (c) Yelizaveta Tomashevska/Dreamstime.com, (bc1) Artofphoto/Dreamstime.com, (bc2) Yelizaveta Tomashevska/ Dreamstime.com; **94-95** © Mike Coots; 95 Courtesy of Anusha Shankar; **97** (tc) Westend61/Getty Images, (cr) recep-bg/E+/Getty Images; **98** Jean-Pierre Clatot/AFP/Getty Images; **99** © Geraldine Sy/Good Illustration; 100 (t) Donald M. Jones/Minden Pictures, (cl) Anup Shah/Nature Picture Library, (c1) Aleksey Stemmer/ Shutterstock.com. (c2) Eric Baccega/Nature Picture Library, (cr) Westend61/Getty Images; **102** (bl) svetikd/E+/Getty Images, (br) Roger Kisby/Cavan Images; **103** (bl) Antonio Hugo/Alamy Stock Photo, (br) martin-dm/E+/Getty Images; **104** (cl) stock_SK/ Shutterstock.com, (bl) Photobank gallery/Shutterstock.com; **106-107** sorincolac/iStock/Getty Images; **107** Courtesy of Jennifer Adler; **108** IhorZigor/Shutterstock.com; **109** (t) Photononstop Images/Emilie Chaix/Media Bakery, (b) Manuel Medir/Getty Images News/Getty Images; **110** (t) © Jennifer Adler, (cl) Huhulin/ Dreamstime.com, (c1) fad82/Shutterstock.com, (c2) Kppwc/ Shutterstock.com, (cr) Digital Bazaar/Shutterstock.com, (bl) popicon/Shutterstock.com; **111** Krit Jantana/Moment/Getty Images; **112** (tr1) Tatiana Popova/Shutterstock.com, (tr2) ed2806/ Shutterstock.com, (cr1) Colorlife/Shutterstock.com, (cr2) Dzha33/ Shutterstock.com, (cr3) Serhii Tsyhanok/Shutterstock.com, (bl) Westend61/Getty Images, (br) Martin Silva Cosentino/ Shutterstock.com; **114** Inti St Clair/Getty Images; **115** (c) Xenia Artwork/Shutterstock.com; (bc) iPhotoDesign/Shutterstock.com; **116** (tr) Mark Meredith/Moment/Getty Images, (cl1) Johner Images/Getty Images, (cl2) (cr) perysty/iStock/Getty Images; **118-119** © Kagoshima Prefecture Visitors Bureau-K.P.V.B; **119** (cl) Courtesy of Ruben Salgado, (cr) © Nora Shawki; **120** (tl) PhotoAlto/Frederic Cirou/Getty Images, (bl) Drazen_/E+/Getty Images; **121** Astafjeva/Shutterstock.com; **122** (tc) Peter Cade/ Stone/Getty Images, (bl) Dean Drobot/Shutterstock.com, (bl) Eak. Temwanich/Shutterstock.com, (br) Vasyl Shulga/Shutterstock.com; **123** NoSystem images/E+/Getty Images; **124** (bl) © Nora Shawki, © Ruben Salgado Escudero; **126** Alex Ramsay/Alamy Stock Photo; **128** Design Pics/Danita Delimont Stock Photography; **130-131** J R Eyerman/The Life Picture Collection/Shutterstock.com; **131** (cl) © Caio Felipe Santos da Silva, © Alec Jacobson; **132** Wolfgang Moucha/Alamy Stock Photo; **133** Donaldson Collection/Michael Ochs Archives/Getty Images; **134** (tr) Self Portrait, 1907 (oil on canvas)/Picasso, Pablo (1881-1973)/Agenzia Fotografica Luisa Ricciarini/Narodni Muzeum, Prague, Czech Republic/Bridgeman Images, (bl1) GL Archive/Alamy Stock Photo, (bl2) Historic Images/ Alamy Stock Photo, (br) History and Art Collection/Alamy Stock Photo; **136** Danygor/Dreamstime.com; **139** Thomas Barwick/ Stone/Getty Images; **140** (cr) CBW/Alamy Stock Photo, (bl) Old Books Images/Alamy Stock Photo; **141** Popperfoto/Getty Images; **142-143** Chester Higgins Jr./The New York Times/Redux Pictures; **143** (cl) Courtesy of Afroz Ahmad Shah, (cr) Courtesy of Maria Fadiman; **145** (t) (c) Courtesy of Afroz Ahmad Shah, (b) KS-Art/ Shutterstock.com; **147** dpa picture alliance/Alamy Stock Photo; **148** MoMo Productions/DigitalVision/Getty Images; **149** cougarsan/Shutterstock.com; **150** (bl) Hemis/Alamy Stock Photo, (br) Sara Lynn Paige/Moment/Getty Images; **151** (bl) Manisa Allik/EyeEm/Getty Images, (br) Hill Street Studios/Stone/ Getty Images; **152** Alejandra de la Fuente/Moment/Getty Images; **154** (tl) Design Pics Inc/Alamy Stock Photo, (tr) Mikal Ludlow/ Alamy Stock Photo; **155** (tl) Hai Bo, courtesy Pace Gallery, (tr) Anadolu Agency/Getty Images; **156** (tl) Courtesy of Ida Josefin Eriksson, (tr) knape/E+/Getty Images; **157** (tl) Yuri Kozyrev/NoorR/ Redux Pictures, (tr) © Mike Coots; **158** (tl) sorincolac/iStock/Getty Images, (tr) © Kagoshima Prefecture Visitors Bureau-K.P.V.B; **159** (tl) J R Eyerman/The Life Picture Collection/Shutterstock.com, (tr) Chester Higgins Jr./The New York Times/Redux Pictures; **179** (tc) Klaus Vedfelt/DigitalVision/Getty Images; Javier Joaquin; **180** (tl1) paul mansfield photography/Moment Open/Getty Images (tl2) Pachanatt Ounpitipong/Moment/Getty Images, (bl1) Ruben Sanchez @lostintv/Moment/Getty Images, (bl2) somchaisom/iStock/Getty Images, (bc1) DoctorEgg/Moment/Getty Images, (bc2) Suttipong Sutiratanachai/Moment/Getty Images, (bc3) Nick Brundle Photography/Moment/Getty Images, (br) Mo Wu/Shutterstock.com; **181** (tc1) Xenia Artwork/Shutterstock.com, (tc2) iPhotoDesign/Shutterstock.com, Javier Joaquin;

Page Source: CAROLYN DRAKE. (April 2019). This man spends 8 hours every day commuting. He's not alone. Retrieved from https://www.nationalgeographic.com/magazine/article/pictures-show-eight-hour-super-commute-from-san-francisco

0797612135 8 - Eden